the **eco-travel**
guide

alastair fuad-luke

the **eco-travel guide**

with over 800 color illustrations

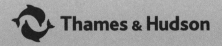
Thames & Hudson

Dedication

To my children, Alexander and Francesca, and their children's children; and to the visionaries in the travel and tourism industry who strive for a better future.

Acknowledgments

I would like to extend my gratitude to all the individuals, owners and managers of the eco-destinations featured in the book – for their vision and energy, and for investing time in answering my questionnaire and supplying information, photographs and illustrations.

Special thanks to the following for the provision of photographs: Craig Zendel, Guido Cozzi, Jonas Sandholm, Chumbe Island Coral Park; Edson Endrigo, Cristalino Jungle Lodge; Åsa Frick and Staffan Widstrand, Larsbo Gård; Dick Sweeney and Mike Gebicki, Paperbark Camp; Simon Heyes at Senderos; the Worldmapper project at the University of Sheffield, UK, with the University of Michigan, USA; Paul Fearn, Youth Hostels Association, UK; Nicola McCrae, Scottish Youth Hostels Association, UK; and Bird Island, Can Marti, Cardamom House, Chan Chich Lodge, Kasbah du Toubkal, Ponta dos Ganchos, Posadas Amazonas Lodge Peru, Soneva Fushi & Six Senses Spa, The Second Paradise Retreat, The Summer House, Tongabezi Lodge and Villas Ecotucan.

I express my gratitude to the designers and manufacturers who contributed to the section on eco-products, especially Gregor Arndt and Christian Rokosch, Supernova Design/ Waldmeister.

I give sincere thanks to Lucas Dietrich and Cat Glover at Thames & Hudson for their unflagging support and steadfast personal contributions throughout the project. As copy editor, Ingrid Cranfield provided rigorous and energetic attention to my text, for which I'm very grateful; and thanks to Grade Design for a wonderful and colourful layout.

Lastly, I am indebted to Dina, my wife, who helped collate data while providing constant sustenance through the long gestation period for the book.

First published in 2008 in paperback in the United States of America by Thames & Hudson Inc., 500 Fifth Avenue, New York, New York 10110

thamesandhudsonusa.com

Library of Congress Catalog Card Number 2008901218

ISBN 978-0-500-28766-8

Printed and bound in Hong Kong by Paramount Printing Company Limited

Designed and layout by Grade Design Consultants, London

Contents

Eco-travel

The concept of 'eco-travel' succinctly manages to combine two of the key challenges of the 21st century. The first challenge is deeply embedded in our contemporary way of living, socializing and doing business, which involves considerable amounts of travel. The second challenge is that all human travel inevitably impacts on the totality of our environment and on nature, including human socio-ecosystems. This is the age of hypermobility': human societies resemble more a 'mobilization' than 'civilization'. Everybody and everything (goods, raw materials) is moving in the global economy, at a pace and in a quantity unprecedented in human history.

'Eco-' signifies 'ecological', a way of acting that tries to reduce adverse impacts on all living creatures and ecosystems (including other humans and their socio-economic systems). *Eco-travel* takes into account socio-cultural and economic impacts to encourage **sustainability**. It embraces *eco-tourism*, but also goes beyond it. To accept the concept of eco-travel is to recognize this multi-dimensionality.

There is no 'one fix' solution for eco-travel because 'eco-' recognizes the unique biology, geology, hydrology and *genius loci*, the real local distinctiveness of each place and its peoples. An eco-traveller has a heightened sense of awareness of the potential and real consequences of his or her actions, but actively seeks ways of travelling better by contributing more to the places visited and by treading with a lighter ecological footprint.

How much do we travel today?

The phenomenon of **globalization** has contributed to increased travel for the purposes of business, socializing, leisure and pleasure (Part 1, 'The Idea of Travel', p. 10). The geographical and virtual range of human networks has spread beyond the village or town or city, beyond identifiable cultural or biological regions (**bio-regions**) and national boundaries. This has fundamentally affected how and where we travel to work, socialize and find relaxation or adventure. Of course, not everyone has experienced this radical shift. Indigenous cultures and societies deeply rooted in place, in specific socio-cultural systems or caught in poverty, may still confine their travelling within well-defined boundaries. Just 10%, or 665 million, of the world's 6.6 billion population form the elite club of globetrotters called tourists. Predictions are that by 2050 there will be 1.6 billion tourists. By default, this privileged group of people carries specific responsibilities for our planet's health.

Travel for work

Over the last 25 years, and especially the last decade, people are travelling more often, for longer distances and are spending more time travelling for work. Travel for work has changed markedly with the advent of low-cost airlines and high-speed trains. Daily commuting between countries in Europe, for the purpose of work, is a reality. Despite improvements in public transport efficiency in Europe, even more time is spent travelling by car. The average Briton travels 10,900 kilometres (6,815 miles) per annum, 80% by car, just within the UK, representing an increase of 5% from 1991 to 2001.[2] Reliance on the car is seen in all facets of life. Many parents in the UK drive their children an average distance of 2.4 kilometres to school, causing congestion, pollution and a higher incidence of asthma for the children who still do walk or cycle.

Travel for leisure and pleasure

The World Tourism Organization notes that the top 15 tourism-spending nations (excluding transport) account for 65.3% of the world market share.[3] The top five countries were the USA (13%), Germany (10.6%), the UK (7.8%), Japan (7.2%) and France (4.1%), accounting for 42.7% of all tourism spending. Between 1985 and 1999, international tourist arrivals worldwide doubled from 326 million to 657 million and receipts grew from US$116 billion to US$455 billion. Tourism is a mega-business.

In the UK, the upward trend in international tourism expenditure seems to be matched by an increased frequency of flying. In just one decade, 1990–2000, the total distance flown by British travellers doubled from 125 billion kilometres to 260 billion kilometres (78 billion miles to 162 billion miles).[4] Is this trend sustainable or do we need to search for alternative experiences?

The evolving idea of eco-travel

The idea of eco-travel evolves in the context of the challenge of **sustainable development**. Eco-travel embraces a wide lexicon of terms in contemporary debate, including numerous definitions of and synonyms for **eco-tourism** (Part 4, 'Resources', Glossary, p. 326): Ron Mader discusses **responsible tourism**, **ethical tourism** or **travel**, conscientious tourism, adventure travel, alternative tourism, agro-tourism, civic tourism, geo-tourism, heritage tourism, independent travel, pro-poor tourism, reality tours, sustainable tourism, volunteer tourism (service learning), rural tourism, urban ecotourism; also, more recently, responsible travel, contrarian travel, urban ecotourism and mutually beneficial tourism.[5] Mowforth and Munt list the many descriptors for new forms of tourism that combine personal, ecological and socio-cultural objectives: Academic, Adventure, Agro-, Alternative, Anthro-, Appropriate, Archaeo-, Contact, Cottage, Culture, Eco-, Ecological, Environmentally friendly, Ethnic, Green, Nature, Risk, Safari, Scientific, Soft, Sustainable, Trekking, Truck, Wilderness and Wildlife.[6] These terms contrast with the general perception of a budget, mass-tourism holiday and suggest a kind of tourism that is about the individual and the host community or place.

Why travel?

Although travel for work seems to be necessary to earn a living in the global economy, our choices for socializing, leisure and pleasure are more flexible. Ultimately, every traveller must ask, 'why travel?' As Alain de Botton notes: 'We are inundated with advice on where to travel to; we hear little of why and how we should go – though the art of travel seems naturally to sustain a number of questions neither so simple nor so trivial and whose study might in modest ways contribute to an understanding of what the Greek philosophers beautifully term *eudaimonia* or human flourishing.'[7]

The *Eco-Travel Handbook* seeks to help raise the reader's awareness and enable him or her to make appropriate choices and decisions. The reality of contemporary travel and tourism is set against emerging eco-innovations for everyday, business, tourist, slow and, even, virtual travel (Part 1, 'The idea of travel'). Part 2, 'Eco-destinations', celebrates the owners and managers of 200 accommodation destinations worldwide in 61 countries that welcome and encourage eco-travellers. Objects and artifacts that assist the eco-traveller are also illustrated, ranging from mobility to personal and specialized products (Part 3, 'Eco-products'). Lastly there is a 'Resources' section (Part 4) offering detailed information and tips for the everyday and specialist eco-traveller.

1 Hypermobility is a term coined by Professor S. Vertovec, Oxford University, to describe the phenomenon induced by low-cost or budget airlines that permits people to travel for leisure, business or new career and lifestyle developments.

2 Cited in L. Hickman (2005) *A Good Life*. London: Transworld Publishers, pp. 142, 144.

3 World Tourism Organization (2001) Tourism Highlights, cited in M. Mowforth and I. Munt (2003) *Tourism and Sustainabilty: Development and new tourism in the Third World*. Third edition. London and New York: Routledge, pp. 16–17.

4 Cited in L. Hickman (2005) *A Good Life*. London: Transworld Publishers, pp. 142, 144.

5 See R. Mader 'Exploring ecotourism', www.planeta.com, accessed 4 January 2007.

6 M. Mowforth and I. Munt (2003) *Tourism and Sustainability: Development and new tourism in the Third World*. Third edition. London and New York: Routledge, p. 93.

7 A. de Botton (2002) *The Art of Travel*. London: Penguin, p. 9.

The idea of travel

Every day there are billions of people on the move, travelling for work, to meet family and friends, for pleasure or, sadly, to avoid oppressive regimes, famine and war. This book focuses on travel for pleasure and work. How can we contribute to reducing the negative impacts of travel on the environment? How is it possible to maximize the benefits we travellers bring to individuals and to communities of which we are transient members? These questions highlight some of the most challenging issues relating to commuting and tourism, including the use of energy and water resources; the generation of waste and pollution; the destruction of habitats, ecosystems and communities; the exploitation of labour; and the economic role of travel today.

A world on the move

The real impacts of travel on the environment, societies, cultures and economies are not evenly distributed around the globe. People from the wealthier nations or from pockets of wealth in the poorer nations account for a higher than average number of journeys by car and by air and consequently have a higher environmental impact than others. Some countries are more visited than others.

An edifying book called *The Atlas of the Real World* [1] is of great help in understanding the complexity of travel today. *The Atlas*, which has been created by three of the team behind the Worldmapper[2] project and gathered from a number of sources including the United Nations, consists of 366 maps each representing 200 territories. The maps are equal-area cartograms, which re-size each territory according to the variable – the quantity of data – being mapped[3], and should be compared and interpreted with a 'baseline' land-area map.

Modes of travel

Air travel

The 'North' clearly accounts for significantly more departures, flights and passengers than the 'South', the most frequent flyers originating from the USA, western Europe (especially the UK and Germany), Japan and Republic of Korea (South Korea). According to the World Tourism Organization (WTO), these countries also tend to have the biggest tourism spend (see pp. 8, 13), although the Worldmapper data does not distinguish between business, tourism and other flights.

Travel by rail

Railways are a popular form of transport in Europe, North Africa, India, China, South Korea and Japan. Rail networks are well developed in Europe, India and Japan, but underdeveloped in the southern hemisphere apart from Australia and New Zealand. Although North America has a good rail network, travellers generally prefer flying to rail travel.

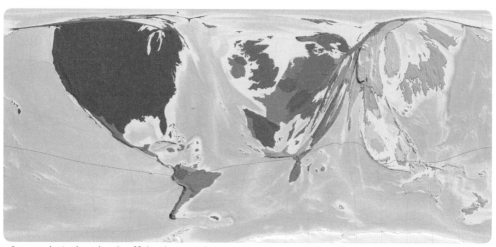

1. Cartogram showing the total number of flights taken in 2000 by passengers on aircraft registered in each territory. Total number of air passengers worldwide in 2000 was 1.6 billion (thousand million).

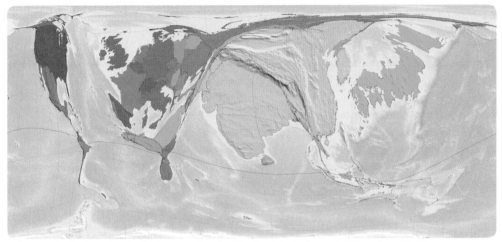

2. Cartogram showing the total number of rail passenger kilometres taken in each territory in 2003. In that year, the world total distance was 2.2 trillion (million million) kilometres.

Between 2004 and 2007 air passenger numbers worldwide increased 8% per year. The UK's Office for National Statistics has reported that trips abroad from the UK trebled from 1981 to 2005 to 66.4 million, air travel accounting for 81% of the trips. Most sources predict that global air travel will continue to increase, possibly even trebling by 2030. The aviation industry claims it is responsible for just 1.6–2% of global CO_2, but in certain countries it is much higher than this; in Britain the figure is 6%.

The Intergovernmental Panel on Climate Change (IPPC) says the real impact of aviation is 2.7 times that of CO_2 output alone, because other **greenhouse gases** are injected into the upper atmosphere. The 170 members of the International Air Transport Association (IATA) oppose inclusion of aviation in the European emissions-trading scheme. Kerosene (aeroplane fuel) is currently not taxed in a similar way to petrol on the forecourt. To reduce CO_2 emissions and to comply with the 1992 Kyoto Protocol, flying habits in the North will have to change.

Travel on the road network by car, moped and motorcycle

Car usage is highest in North America, Europe (especially the UK, Germany, France, Italy, Spain, Portugal, Belgium, the Netherlands, Switzerland and Austria), South Korea and Japan. Recently Malaysia and some of the other ASEAN nations have joined this group. Moped and motorcycle travel is very high in most of Asia (especially India, China, South Korea, Japan and South East Asia) and also in Europe. Europe, India and Japan have the most extensive road networks.

Tourism

Tourism movements and economics

According to the United Nations World Tourism Organization, international tourist arrivals grew on average 6.5% per year from 1950 (25 million) to 2005 (806 million).[4] Tourism, worth US$525 billion, accounts for 6% of global exports of goods and services. Transport and travel represent 52% of global export services. By 2020 over 1.6 billion international arrivals are anticipated annually, 1.2 billion being intra-regional and 378 million long-haul. So travel, in all its forms, is big business and is expanding.

Europe is the most popular destination and origin for tourists worldwide. Everyone wants to see Europe, the Mediterranean countries of France, Spain, Portugal, Italy and Greece being a real magnet for both European and non-European tourists. At the same time, Europeans, especially Germans and the British, want to see the rest of the world. In the Asia–Pacific region, Thailand is popular and Malaysia becoming surprisingly so. Malaysians are frequent tourists too, as are the Japanese and South Koreans. So it is incumbent primarily on the Europeans and Asians, the real globetrotters, to change their habits.

Who is making the money from tourism?

The countries bordering the Pacific and South East Asia (Australia, Malaysia, Thailand and Vietnam) and the Far East (China and Hong Kong) are making the most money from tourism. Many nations aren't making net profits from tourism, especially in the southern hemisphere and throughout Africa (South Africa excepted), but neither are they experiencing an exodus of currency that is being spent on tourism in other countries.

A country may suffer tourism net losses when its nationals travel extensively and inject large sums of money into other countries' tourist industries. In Europe this includes the British, Germans, Belgians, Dutch and Scandinavians. Elsewhere, citizens from the Middle Eastern states (especially Kuwait and UAE), South Korea and Japan are frequent outbound

tourists. All these frequent travellers carry a huge responsibility because they can forge positive change by choosing eco-travel destinations and modes of travel with lower environmental impacts. In this way they can contribute to genuine socio-economic benefits in the recipient country.

The tourism industry – friend or foe?

Trans-national and national corporations (TNCs and NCs) dominate the global tourism industry, from the big hotel chains (such as Accor, Forte, Hilton Hotels and Hyatt) to the airlines (including American Airlines, British Airways, KLM, Lufthansa and Japan Airlines) and travel agencies and tour operators (for instance, BA Holidays, Saga, Swire Group and Thomson). These companies exert huge power and control over the investment of capital, generation of revenue for their shareholders and orders for their suppliers. In the 1990s, 55–77% of gross tourism revenues in developing countries was actually lost to imports, that is, for every US dollar spent, only 23–45 cents were being spent in the host country.[5] What might appear to be a buoyant tourist industry in a destination might not be contributing significantly to the local economy. Every tourist thus needs to look more closely at where his or her hard-earned cash is actually ending up.

Key sustainability issues for travellers

Several key inter-related *sustainability* issues are colliding to pose huge questions to all travellers: *climate change*, *peak oil*, world population growth and poverty, the death of languages and culture and the destruction of ecosystems, plant- and animal life.

CLIMATE CHANGE

The link between the significant increase in atmospheric quantities of **carbon dioxide (CO_2)**, generated by anthropocentric activities since the beginning of the Industrial Revolution, and an increase in average global temperature seems to have been accepted by most, but not all, nations worldwide.[6,7] In November 2005 the indigenous people of the Carteret Islands in the Pacific Ocean, off Papua New Guinea, earned the unwanted moniker of 'climate change refugees', as rising sea levels contaminated their drinking-water supplies, forcing them to emigrate.

The eco-traveller asks, 'How can I reduce my carbon footprint and slow down global warming?'

PEAK OIL

In just over 120 years half of the world's accessible reserves of oil have been consumed by human activities. We are therefore at the peak of total consumption: 'peak oil' has been reached. Why is this important? Most of the travel by air, road and sea relies on oil and its derivatives. Does this imply that we might be nearing **peak travel** too? Is the recently heralded age of **hypermobility** to be short-lived?

The eco-traveller asks, 'How can I reduce my consumption of oil for travel (and other uses) to allow this valuable resource to be used by my grandchildren's children?'

POPULATION GROWTH

In 2000, the global world population reached 6.0 billion, as predicted by the landmark Limits to Growth report published by the Club of Rome in 1972. By 2008 a further 600 million people had been added to the population, giving a new total of 6.6 billion. By 2020 this could rise to 8 billion and by 2050 possibly to 10 billion. And, no doubt, all these additional people will need or want to travel.

The eco-traveller asks, ' How can I reduce my travelling in order that others not yet born might have the opportunity to do so?'

POVERTY

An estimated 1.5 billion people (23% of the world's population) live in poverty. The poorest 80% of the global population (5.3 billion) consume only 20% of global resources, whereas the richest 20% (1.3 billion, largely in the North) consume 80%. It is the same rich people who make up most of the 665 million tourists who circulate around the globe annually.

The eco-traveller asks, 'Can I somehow contribute to alleviating the poverty of others when I travel?'

DEATH OF LANGUAGES AND CULTURE

Our human ecology is under threat too. The homogenization of culture and fragmentation of communities that seem to follow globalization make it harder and harder for small but unique language groups to survive. Organizations such as Survival International help highlight the problems of tribal peoples.

The eco-traveller asks, 'How can I best contribute to helping people keep their language and communities alive and grow again?'

DESTRUCTION OF ECOSYSTEMS, PLANT- AND ANIMAL LIFE

Between 1950 and 1997 the world population of elephants declined 90% from 6 million to 0.6 million, mainly owing to destruction of suitable habitat and food sources, and to hunting and poaching. During the same period the global rainforest cover declined by 30% and its destruction is accelerating. The International Union for the Conservation of Nature (IUCN) Red List contains 41,415 species, up from 16,118 in 2006, of which 16,306 are threatened with extinction. Biomes are changing rapidly. Frozen since the last Ice Age, the permafrost in the Russian steppes is now melting and releasing **methane** as the peat soils decay. Methane is 22 times more powerful a greenhouse gas than CO_2, so will hasten global warming.

The eco-traveller asks, 'Can I somehow contribute to saving, conserving, preserving or helping to regenerate other living species and systems when I travel?'

This book hopes to provide some answers...

Is our current 'idea of travel' sustainable?

No, if our idea of sustainability is something that we can still hope to be doing at the end of the 21st century or beyond. The 'idea of travel' has to be tested according to the three underlying principles of sustainable development (SD), originally espoused by the Brundtland Commission's report, *Our Common Future*, in 1987, and articulated by the International Institute of Sustainable Development:

> Concern for equity and fairness – ensuring rights of the poor and of future generations
> Long-term view – applying the precautionary principle
> Systems thinking – understanding the interconnections between the environment, economy and society.

Perhaps we have to reframe 'development' as 'no growth' or **degrowth**. This implies setting new ambitions for the global, national and local economies while aiming to grow other things – responsible, eco-efficient business, ecotourism, social equity, social coherence, biological diversity, **ecosystem** health...and more.

The idea of **sustainability** implies, from an anthropocentric viewpoint, negotiated trade-offs. A more **bio-centric** view (as taken by **deep ecologists**, who ascribe equity to all living things) is that humankind is the problem and not, as yet, the solution. Nature's models are eco-efficient, being solar-powered and cyclic, allowing the continuous recycling of nutrients. Human models need to follow suit. The transformation to more sustainable models will not happen overnight but we can all take a few small steps...

What can we do to mitigate the negative impacts of travel?

We can rethink our travel needs and wants. We can aspire to new ways of daily and long-distance travelling.

We need to rediscover the ancient art of travel and, specifically, the joy of walking. Walking is an act sustained simply by our daily intake of food energy. It is a universal democratic action available to all.

As an alternative to walking, we should seek out eco-efficient modes of transport that use renewable power (wind, solar, hydro) or that use fossil fuels (oil, gas) efficiently, including many public transport systems. We cannot reduce the negative impacts of travel if we simply accept 'business as usual'. Below are some suggestions for positive actions we can all take.

ECO-COMMUTING

Balancing time, money and other values

The pattern of home, work and leisure journeys is very different from just thirty years ago, thanks to sociological, technological and infrastructure developments. Today it is possible to live in London, UK, and commute to work in Paris, France, in just 2 hours 15 minutes on the high-speed Eurostar train. The bullet trains, Shinkansen, transport millions of people every day between Tokyo and other cities on Japan's main island of Honshu at speeds of up to 330 kph (205 mph). These are the lucky commuters. Hundreds of millions journey to work by car or other motor transport on overcrowded roads for up to two hours a day. There are some real disadvantages to commuting by car[8]: between 1980 and 2002 UK roads have become 73% more congested; pollution-related asthma has risen fourfold in the last thirty years; 1 in 17 people will be seriously injured or killed in a road crash; annually 24,000 people die on UK roads; there are 31 million private cars and still increasing (representing about one car for every two people)[9]; over one third of car journeys cover less than three kilometres, contributing to a rise in obesity. Traffic speeds in many major conurbations and cities have not improved since the era of the horse-drawn cart.

Human-powered options

Walking – There are many ways to get to school without resorting to the car, for example, the 'walking bus'. As the name suggests, there is an adult 'driver', children walking side by side and an adult 'conductor', safely shepherding the rear end of the 'bus'. Commuters in UK cities can find the best walking route by using Walk It. Slow Cities in Italy encourages traffic-free days at the weekends, and there is a weekly No Drive Day in Seoul, South Korea.

Micro-scooting and skateboarding – Consider a micro-scooter or skateboard if you find walking just too slow. These mobility products are easily stowed under your desk at work and don't require special clothing. However, do be prepared to be a commuter 'outlaw' and brace yourself for the irritation of all other pavement and road users.

Cycling – The sheer range of folding bikes available today, from micro- to compact and full size, is fantastic (see Part 3, 'Eco-products', pp. 276–317), enabling anyone to switch easily from car, bus or train to bike. Improvements in national and metropolitan cycleways in Europe, such as Sustrans (UK) and Véloland (Switzerland), coupled with the recent resurgence of city bicycle-hire schemes (Copenhagen – the original City Bike scheme started in 1997 has encouraged other cities to follow: Barcelona – Bicing, Berlin – Callabike, London – OYBike, Lyon – Vélo'v and Paris – Vélib) give a wide variety of options for commuters and tourists. There's a resurgence of modern trishaws, with seven companies and 350 rickshaw drivers in London, many using Pedicabs. There are Pedicab operators in many US and international cities.

Eco-efficient motorized travel

Two wheels – The range of electric mopeds and motorbikes is diverse, with improved battery power giving travel distances of 30–80 kilometres (18–50 miles) per charge. Confident commuters might want to opt for the two-wheeled, gyroscopically balanced Segway.

Three wheels – The options are improving. See the petrol-engined Piaggio MP3 (p. 284) motorcycle

3. SUSTRANS has promoted the cause of cyclists and taken a significant role in extending the UK cycling network.

with two wheels at the front and the prototype micro-car CLEVER (p. 288) with two wheels at the rear. The chassis of these vehicles permits the vehicle to lean as you are cornering, improving road-handling.

Four wheels/cars – The world's motor-car manufacturers have seen the writing on the wall, particularly European Union directives on the end-of-life vehicle (ELV) and energy-use products (EuP), so there is a general rush to reduce the carbon footprint of new car models and make them more easily recyclable. The trend is most marked in small four-person compact cars (Part 3, 'Mobility Products', pp. 278–293) using the latest diesel engine technologies, computerized fuel consumption software, hybrid petrol-electric motors or electric-only motors. There is even a new hybrid electric/solar/wind-powered prototype, the Venturi Eclectic, being developed by a French company. Owning a car is becoming more expensive, with oil prices currently rising dramatically. Car-on-demand schemes are available in a number of metropolitan areas, including StreetCar, City Car Club and Whizzgo in UK cities; Zipcar in many US cities and various

eco-limousines at airports; PlanetTran and OZOcar. Car-sharing schemes are often encouraged by not-for-profit enterprises and local government authorities, which facilitate communication between owners and passengers via their websites, for instance, Carplus in the UK.

PUBLIC TRANSPORT
Bus
There are two aspects to the efficacy of a bus system: the eco-efficiency and carbon footprint of the bus itself and how effectively timetabling and

4. BICING in Barcelona, a success story for city bike hire.

access points to the system maximize its usefulness for passengers. European bus manufacturers are conscious of improving fuel efficiencies demanded by operators for economic reasons. Improvements in diesel, compressed natural gas (CNG) and hybrid technologies tend to lead the way. MAN Group in Germany utilizes the efficient common rail higher-pressure injection system, double turbocharging, exhaust-gas recirculation and improved particulate-matter catalytic filters to meet current EU emissions standards. MAN is working with Neoplan on liquid hydrogen-fuelled buses, having trialled these buses at Munich Airport since 1999. There are also developments in CNG and hydrogen-fuel-cell buses. Scania's OmniCity diesel or optional ethanol-powered bus features an aluminium body and all-through low floor for universal access. Weight savings of 600 kilograms permit an increased passenger complement. Ethanol-fuelled buses can cut CO_2 emissions by up to 90%, meeting Europe's most stringent emissions levels (Euro 5 and EEV), and a fleet of twelve is expected to start service in Sweden in 2008. The Citaro hybrid by Daimler–Chrysler uses a smaller diesel engine to power a lithium-ion battery pack, the electric motors in the wheel hubs and axles kicking in to give efficient power for standing starts and at low speeds.

Effective bus systems are being facilitated by reducing car traffic with fiscal penalites (such as London's congestion charge), no-car days (Seoul's weekly No Drive Day), but the biggest improvements are in simple things like 'bus lanes', effective digital timetable and communication systems, low-polluting fuels (such as ethanol-powered buses in São Paulo, Brazil, and ethanol-petrol mixes in Stockholm, Sweden), comfortable bus shelters and investment in rapid transit systems that link effectively with other transport modes (for instance, Bogotá's Transmilenio bus rapid transit, BRT, linking with 340 kilometres (211 miles) of dedicated cycle paths).

Train

Various eco-efficiency experiments are being conducted around Europe. Italy launched the first solar-power-assisted train, the PVTRAIN project, in 2003. Virgin Trains in the UK has tested bio-diesel fuel mixes for its diesel Voyager trains since June 2007, although research reveals that this type of train emits twice the CO_2 of a standard electric train supplied from the UK national grid. In Japan, Hitachi have produced a 'hybrid' battery-assisted, diesel-electric engine unit, in which the electric motor provides efficient torque from standing start to up to 50 km/h (31 mph) before the diesel engine takes over.

Good connections to other transport systems contribute to the effectiveness of train travel. Seat61 permits you to search for and price journeys around Europe by train. Eurostar and SNCF are working with seven European rail companies under Railteam to create a seamless high-speed rail network effective at competing with air travel.

Aeroplane

Increases in passenger air travel and air freight movements predicted for the next decade vastly overshadow any efficiency gains brought by technological developments. Flybe, a small but

5 .A SCANIA OMNICITY ethanol-powered bus helps reduce urban pollution.

growing player in European low-cost flights, uses modern turboprop Bombardier Q400 planes that leave carbon footprints closer to those of trains than of jet aeroplanes. Airbus claims their new A380 superjumbo, capable of holding 525 passengers, has emissions of just 75 grams of CO_2 per passenger per kilometre when full to capacity, 17% less than earlier Boeing 747s, but not as good as a Boeing 747-8 (71 grams). These figures look good against emissions of 95–100 grams from aeroplanes typically used for short-haul budget flights. However, these figures do not include CO_2 associated with the reality of flying. The Aviation Environment Federation (AEF) campaign group quotes figures of 300–460 grams CO_2 per kilometre for short-haul flying and 210–330 grams for long-haul. There seems a strong imperative for a transparent, effective carbon label.

Eco-efficiency is desirable but distracts from the real challenge. AEF estimates that fuel efficiencies are increasing at only 1–2%, while global flights are increasing at 5% or more per annum (domestic flights increased 8% in the Asia–Pacific region, 5% in Europe and 3% in the USA).[10] Reducing flying, in combination with reductions in other high-intensity carbon activities (driving cars, space-heating at high ambient temperatures, sourcing of high-carbon-intensity food), appears to be the only way forward.

Boats and ships

Since 2001 the German company Kopf has been using solar-powered ferries, showing the feasibility of quiet commuter transport by boat for European cities. Earthrace, a bio-diesel trimaran with sci-fi looks, is aiming to break the world circumnavigation speed records. More realistic are the tests being made on the 10,000-tonne Beluga fitted with a

SkySail, a 160-square metre (1,722-square foot) kite tethered to a rail around the ship. Savings of 10–35% of heavy fuel oil costs are projected for shipping.

Worldwide, some 15 million passengers boarded a cruise ship in 2006, compared to just 0.5 million in 1970. Some cruise companies are trying bio-fuels but it is a token gesture. The campaign group Bluewater Network claims that a week-long voyage by an average ship is responsible for generating 4.5 million litres (1.2 million gallons) of greywater, 50 metric tonnes of rubbish, over 200,000 metric tonnes of sewage and 160,000 litres of oil-contaminated water. Wherever this stuff ends up, and a lot goes straight to the sea, it creates local disposal or pollution problems. Cruise ships seem to have an ambivalent impact on the communities they visit too, as few significant tangible benefits reach the locals.

6. SKYSAIL pulls along the 10,000 metric tonne Beluga, promising potentially significant fuel savings to the world's shipping.

BUSINESS TRAVEL

Corporate initiatives

Improving the eco-efficiency and social benefits of business travel depends on cooperation between the employee and employer, freelancer and client, business and business. Whereas an individual might be committed to reducing his or her carbon footprint, this concern has to be shared with the wider business world to facilitate making that difference. At a very basic level, this might involve provision of showers for the workforce to encourage them to cycle to work. IKEA gave 9,000 of its UK employees Raleigh fold-up bikes as Christmas presents in 2006 and a 15% subsidy on public transport. Google copied this gesture, giving 2,000 of its European, African and Asian employees (why not American?) the Dahon Curve folding bike; it also operates a free shuttle bus in Silicon Valley that runs on bio-diesel. These measures help companies to meet their **corporate social responsibility (CSR)** agendas or carbon-reduction measures.

Encouraging your employer – or examining your own business – to reduce the carbon footprint by seeing how it fits into your personal footprint (see 'Calculating Your Carbon Footprint', pp. 320–322) is the first step in enabling the work culture change that the marketplace will ultimately require.

Letting the train take the strain

The real issue for business travel is that old chestnut, 'time is money', so flying might be the only option for intercontinental travel. Fortunately, the fly, drive or train choices in Europe and Japan provide genuine options because development of the high-speed train network makes it faster or just as favourable as air travel. Seat61 is an amazing resource to enable individuals to book cross-national European rail journeys. Railteam's consortium of European train operators is trying to facilitate intercity communication by rail. Eurostar claims travelling by its trains is ten times less polluting than flying.

Aside from any eco-efficiency gains of rail travel, the train can be your office: many operators offer good telephony and Wi-Fi connections to the internet and mobile phone networks, plus power points for recharging laptops. Another option is working more from home (see 'Virtual Travel', below) and using more teleconferencing to reduce face-to-face meetings.

RESPONSIBLE HOLIDAY TRAVEL AND ECO-TOURISM

Tourism is the 'practice of travelling for pleasure'. **Ecotourism** meets the additional criteria of providing for environmental conservation, including meaningful community participation, and ensuring enterprises that are profitable and can sustain themselves.[11] The International Ecotourism Society (TIES) defines ecotourism as 'responsible travel to natural areas that conserves the environment and improves the well-being of local people'. Lonely Planet talks about **responsible tourism** as 'travel that takes into consideration **triple bottom line** issues: environmental, socio-cultural and economic. As a traveller, responsible tourism is about accepting responsibility for your actions, attitudes and impacts...'[12]

Perhaps the ideal eco-holiday is one where we give as much as we receive, where what we have inadvertently taken away (our **ecological footprint**) we can give back in other ways (our social or conservation contribution). See Part 4, 'Resources' (pp. 318–342) for comprehensive information and tips for the eco-traveller, including how to calculate

and reduce your carbon footprint, what to think about before and during travelling, and more.

Slow travel

There is a movement focused on the idea of **positive slowness**, that is, being slow or going slowly gives you something valuable that much contemporary (fast) culture just can't provide. The Italian Slow Food and Slow Cities movements, from 1986 and from the mid-1990s respectively, celebrate the special qualities of local food and wine and encourage 'car-free' days in the city, actually trying to disrupt the 'fastness' of the road network. In the UK, Reclaim the Streets famously blocks busy roads, whereas Critical Mass takes a more gentle position by encouraging weekly meetings of cyclists who cycle slowly on a route. A similar phenomenon is promoted by Go Slow in Switzerland. Slow travel has empathy with these movements but is perhaps less activist and more personally focused – see Ed Gillespie's Slow Travel log – and obviously requires that you have time on your side. It embraces ethical travel, volunteer holidays and gap years on conservation or socially beneficial projects. It involves trying to consume in more benign ways, as advocated by the international network of Greenmaps, and by patronizing local makers and shops in your destination.

For slow travellers, the journey is as important as the act of arriving at the destination. Slow travellers might opt for sedentary modes of travel – lazing along the canals of Europe by barge, cycling or circumnavigating the globe, riding a horse-drawn gypsy caravan, exploring Europe by train, hitchhiking on ocean-going freighters or 'couch surfing' via social networking on the internet.

When you are walking, you are experiencing that positive slowness: you are, literally, grounded in the visceral reality of now. Brian Eno notes, 'We have the frame we operate in which we call "now". "Now" is all the things that are affecting me. All the things I can affect in a certain time frame I shall call "now".'[13] 'Now' is what the American architect Bruce Goff referred to as the 'continuous present', neither past nor future but linked to both. The slow traveller strives for that link and as a result directly experiences what Common Ground calls 'local distinctiveness'.[14]

Virtual travel

The advances of telephony, satellite communication and the internet (an estimated 1.3 billion people, 20% of the world, now have access to the internet) mean that we don't have to leave the comfort of our homes to 'travel' or to work. Information communications technology (ICT) gave birth to another acronym, SOHO, the solo home office, equipped with a personal computer, an internet connection and a desktop printer. Thanks to 'free' internet telecoms services, such as Skype and video-conferencing software applications, we can, in theory, avoid face-to-face meetings. Leisurely travelling and socializing on the internet take many forms, from viewing intimate details of the planet on Google Earth to 'visits' to chat rooms, blogs, social networking sites and even virtual sex experiences. In more recent years the games industry has spawned new virtual worlds online. The best-known example is Second Life, a '3D digital world imagined and created by its residents'. Registered users create a virtual person, an avatar, and 'travel' around the simulated 3D landscape, chatting with others or cooperatively creating new events, products and elements in the landscape. The 'population' of Second Life has doubled from 6 million in mid-2007 to 12.7 million by March 2008, with 'tour operators' offering 'virtual holidays'. Here is a chance to be transported to another world, gaze on fresh scenes and socialize with new people – in short, to relax without leaving home. This seems a guilt-free way of travelling, yet even a virtual holiday has an ecological footprint, for energy is required to manufacture the hardware, run the software and store all the information-hungry servers.

1   D. Dorling, M. Newman and A. Barford (2008) *The Atlas of the Real World: Mapping the way we live*. London: Thames & Hudson.
2   Worldmapper, see *http://www.worldmapper.org* by the University of Sheffield, UK, and University of Michigan, USA, with additional support from the Leverhulme Trust and the Geographical Association; accessed January 2008. See the Movement maps 19, 20, 21, 22, 25 and 26; see the Transport maps 27, 28, 29, 30, 31, 32, 35, 36 and map 142.
3   Methodology developed by Michael Gastner and Mark Newman. See M. Gastner and M. E. J. Newman (2004) 'Diffusion-based method for producing density equalizing maps'. *Proceedings of the National Academy of Sciences USA* 101, 7499–7504. Washington DC: National Academy of Sciences.
4   World Tourism Organization, *http://unwto.org/index.php*, accessed Feb 2007.
5   M. Mowforth and I. Munt (2003) *Tourism and Sustainability: Development and new tourism in the Third World*. Third edition. London and New York: Routledge, p. 175.
6   UN Framework Convention on Climate Change, Kyoto, Japan, 1997, known as 'The Kyoto Protocol'.
7   UN Climate Change Conference, Bali, 2007.
8   L. Hickman (2005) *A Good Life*. London: Transworld Publishers, p. 144.
9   This fact also brings the salutary realization that some 30 million people in the UK don't own cars. These citizens are often a neglected species when it comes to an equable share of investment by the government – of taxpayers' money – in pavements, cycleways and public transport. Somehow investment in roads for cars seems to take priority.
10 D. Adam (2007) 'Flights reach record levels despite warnings over climate change', *The Guardian*, 9 May 2007, p. 3.
11 R. Mader 'Exploring ecotourism', *www.planeta.com*, accessed 4 January 2007.
12 K. Lorimer (coordinating author) (2006) *Code Green: Experiences of a lifetime*. London: Lonely Planet, p. 9.
13 B. Eno and J. Thackera (2003) *Eternally Yours: Time in design*. Rotterdam: 010 Publishers, pp. 62–63.
14 S. Clifford and A. King (2006) *England in Particular: A celebration of the commonplace, the local, the vernacular and the distinctive*. London: Hodder & Stoughton.

PART TWO

Eco-destinations

The destinations featured here are diverse, from luxury beach resorts
and hotels to isolated mountain cabins, from large city hotel chains to
independently run eco-lodges, and from global corporate to family or
community operated businesses. Each destination has unique ecological
characteristics, from the architecture and the environmental management
of its buildings designed to reduce impacts, to its relationship with
the local culture and communities. Some destinations are certified by
independent eco-tourism authorities or organizations (see Part 4, 'Resources',
pp. 318–342), others are operated according to the motivating ethics of the
owners or managers. Standards vary from country to country but all are
trying in their own way to endorse tourism that treads more lightly and
gives rather than takes from the local people and places.

Key to symbols

 Eco-architecture and environmental management systems

 Benefits to local culture and environment

 Activities available at or near the eco-destination

What sort of eco-holiday do you want? In order to reflect changing demands in contemporary tourism, away from mass-packaged tours to individual, more flexible and personalized vacations, the destinations have been grouped into the following categories: Urban, Nature, Adventure, Leisure and Culture. Many of the destinations offer some or all of the facets implied by these categories (see Part 4, 'Resources', pp. 330–342, for more details and price bands). Whatever your final choice of destination, it is hoped that the detailed accounts of each destination alert you to the benefits and contributions you can make. 'Enjoy not destroy' is a challenge to us all, but with a little forethought and research, it is possible to strike a positive balance between pleasure and responsibility. How you do this remains your choice.

Urban   28

cycle racks, wooden floors, car shares, rooftop solar panels, low-VOC paints, recycled fibre carpets, local butchers, low-flow showers, restaurant food sourced locally, restored buildings, city campsites, converted green townhouses, boutique hotels, excellent insulation, muted natural tones, recycled polyester textiles, organic bath salts, chemical-free citrus cleaning products, hybrid airport transfers, green cabs

Nature   50

verandas, waterfalls, wildlife safaris, river lodges, marmoset monkeys, river dolphins, luxuriant jungle, tree houses, parrots, tented rooms on raised platforms, sustainable seafood supplies, bathing in local style, traditional recipes cooked on wood fires, oil-palm plantations, simple wooden constructions, leopards, irrigation systems, spotted deer

Adventure 122

mountain camps, microlight flying, paragliding, canvas pods, water-based kayaking, fishing for piranha, caving, offroading, motorbike riding, alligator-spotting, Himalayan resorts, working ranch holidays, birdwatching, foraging eagles, stud farm, cross-country ski communities, pumas, working ranches, crossing mountain waterfalls

Leisure 144

wildflower meadow walks, lagoon swimming, luxury spa, lake views, perfumed gardens, summer dining, chic coastal shacks, truffle-gathering, rustic farmhouse style, tranquillity, home-cooked food, spectacular coastal settings, miniature idylls, azure sea, essential oils, nestling between the groves, jacuzzis, world-famous oysters

Culture 240

holistic permaculture philosophy, community services, craft workshops, basket-weaving, learning Hindi, wall paintings, chilling in the *kasbah*, visiting the citadel, *salon de thé*, fortified villages, herb gardens, marriage ceremonies, music festivals, rice harvesting, pork cooked with oranges in a wood stove, carob trees, dancing, food gathering, medicinal gardens, village healers

urban

Most people don't think of city breaks when considering an eco-holiday,
but the sustainability challenge is changing the thinking in a few international
companies and independently operated hotels. Destinations are managed
to various environmental standards. They include historic and late
20th-century modern buildings that have been modified or new builds
to certified eco-standards. Have fun in the city and leave a light footprint.

Apex Hotels UK

Apex Hotels are part of a growing portfolio of hotels owned by the Apex group that are actively pursuing an environmental policy, reducing CO_2 emissions and resource depletion and increasing engagement with local communities. Decor is contemporary modern, with wooden surfaces, minimalist lighting and elegant colour schemes. There are five hotels in the group, in London, Edinburgh and Dundee.

> Eco-architecture: Apex Hotels have their own dedicated architect who is appraising each hotel to improve its performance by sustainable design. This includes a range of new and retro-fit features. Most hotels are in existing city-centre buildings or occasionally new builds on brownfield sites (for example, in Dundee). Energy losses are identified by thermographic imaging.
> Energy: Energy-efficient equipment such as lifts, boilers, air-conditioning; LED and other low-energy lighting managed by movement sensors; keycard system turns off unwanted lighting and heating.
> Water: Dual-flush water faucets; walk-in showers to encourage showers rather than baths.
> Consumables: Ozone rather than chlorine-treated swimming pools.
> Waste: Recycling of paper, plastic, cardboard, glass, CDs, polythene wrappers, mobile phones, polystyrene, waste cooking oil, toner cartridges and dry-cleaning coat hangers.
> CO_2 emissions: An offset package for each visitor's trip is offered via the Apex Hotels website in conjunction with ClimateCare; cycle racks to encourage cycling for employees and guests. Hotels encourage car sharing and provide information on local transport facilities.

> Conservation & community projects: As part of the local traders' association and local residents' association in Grassmarket, the Edinburgh hotel hosts a complimentary Christmas dinner party.
> Food supplies: Local produce for beverages, fish, meat, fruit, vegetables and dairy.
> Cultural events: Local community events and activities are posted in the hotel.
> Ownership: National commercial enterprise.

> Walking
> Swimming (some hotels)
> Gym exercise
> Golf
> Spa
> Theatre short breaks

Hotel Bougainvillea COSTA RICA

The 19th-century colonial town of Santo Domingo is the setting for this utilitarian modernist hotel that hosts a good range of facilities. It is surrounded by 4 hectares (10 acres) of its own tropical gardens, including some special ponds for the rare coffee frog. Bedrooms are fully functional, albeit in rather predictable international-style decor. Proximity to San José airport, the excellent local botanic gardens and the town's two stunning colonial churches make this a convenient base or stopover.

> The hotel holds a CST Certificado de Sostenibilidad Turística or Tourist Sustainability Certificate, fulfilling 60% of the criteria to achieve the equivalent three of five 'leaves' (stars).
> Water: Greywater is treated through a filtration plant.
> Consumables: Use of biodegradable cleaning agents.
> Waste: Recycling of paper, cardboard, plastic bottles and aluminium; oil and grease from the kitchen go to bio-diesel production; recycling of 100% of organic kitchen wastes (pig feed, fertilizers).

> Conservation & socio-cultural projects: The hotel's environmental and corporate social responsibility policies mean that it supports a number of projects, ranging from contributions to INBio (Instituto Nacional de Biodiversidad), the Tirimbina Biological Reserve, the local school and an Associación Solidarista for the provision of low-cost homes.
> Cultural events: Local events are always signposted; there's a good Saturday farmers' market.
> Employment: 85% of the 110 staff are from the local area.
> Ownership: Local commercial enterprise.

> Swimming, water sports

Gaia Napa Valley Hotel & Spa USA

Awarded a LEED (Leadership in Energy & Environmental Design) Gold rating, Gaia Napa Valley Hotel, just an hour north of San Francisco, was built to exacting environmental quality standards. LEED is overseen by the US Green Building Council; it awards ratings for the quality of the building's construction, its interior fit-out and its daily management operations to minimize its environmental footprint. There's even a real-time display in the lobby showing energy use and energy generated by the rooftop solar panels. All 131 rooms are painted with low-VOC paints and have recycled fibre carpets and an air-conditioning and heating unit that uses 15% less energy than a standard unit. The hotel's secular green philosophy reaches out into the bedrooms, each supplied with a Bible, a book of the Buddha's teachings and Al Gore's *An Inconvenient Truth*!

> Materials: FSC (Forest Stewardship Council) certified timber; recycled tiles and granites; low-VOC paints throughout.
> Energy: Low-energy air-conditioning and heating units in each room; solar roof panels.
> Water: Low-flush toilets reduce water consumption by up to 40% compared to standard units.
> Consumables: Fair Trade goods where possible; landscaped grounds are chemical-free.
> Waste: In-room recycling is encouraged.
> CO2 emissions: Green touchscreens show guests energy, water and carbon footprints (and savings).

> Conservation projects: The landscaped grounds of the hotel include a natural lagoon with resident swans and other wildlife, where no pesticide spraying is allowed. The hotel works with local environmental groups.
> Food supplies: California cuisine and Asian fusion menus stress organic and natural foods.
> Cultural events: Tours to local wineries (vineyards) and organic businesses in the Napa Valley.
> Employment: 100% local.
> Ownership: Local commercial ownership.

> Walking, trekking, hiking
> Cycling
> Swimming

Hotel Adalbert CZECH REPUBLIC

Hotel Adalbert sits in the grounds of the ancient Brevnov Benedictine monastery, right in the heart of the historic city of Prague – a setting of rare tranquillity for a hotel in a busy European city. The hotel was a former convent, which underwent a major reconstruction in the 18th century, hence the elegant proportions of the interior architecture. With such a pious history, the decor of the 44 bedrooms (singles, doubles and suites) is smart but a little spartan. Guided tours of the monastery can be arranged and Prague Castle is within walking distance.

> This is the first hotel in the Czech Republic certified to the EU 'flower' eco-label for tourist accommodation.
> Materials: This is a complex of old restored buildings.
> Energy: Focus on reducing energy consumption, helped by thick walls that obviate the need for summer air-conditioning.
> Water: Policy of reducing water consumption.
> Consumables: Use of low environmental-impact products with eco-labels, including washing powder and office paper.
> Waste: All waste is separated.

> Socio-cultural projects: The hotel supports a local school for disabled children.
> Food supplies: Locally sourced where possible, for instance, from a local bakery; Fair Trade tea and coffee.
> Cultural events: Prague is a busy cultural centre for entertainment, museums and more.
> Employment: 75–99% local staff.
> Ownership: Local commercial enterprise.

> Walking, trekking, hiking
> Historical city tours

Lane Cove River Tourist Park AUSTRALIA

Just 10 kilometres (6 miles) from Sydney city centre, the Lane Cove National Park is a mixed tourist park comprising permanent cabins and caravan and tent pitches. Certified to the Australian Ecotourism and Green Globe standards, this is a carbon-neutral destination. The park environmental management plan stresses habitat creation linked to encouraging populations of southern brown bandicoot, red-crowned toadlet, spotted marsh frog, southern water dragon, swamp wallaby and other fauna. Nature with a city on your doorstep.

> Materials: Additional insulation, skylighting and recycled materials for construction; certified forest products.
> Energy: Solar power and accredited Green Renewable Energy for all electricity supplies.
> Water: Toilets flushed with harvested rainwater; low-flush toilets; waterless urinals; water-saving showerheads – all with the objective of halving 2006 water consumption over the next five years.
> Waste: There are 18 recycling stations around the site for plastic, metal and paper; and large worm farms for food scraps.

> CO_2 emissions: The organization is carbon neutral and there is a voluntary offset system for visitors. Offsets are reinvested in solar and wind renewables and tree planting on site.

> Conservation projects: The organization is itself a national park supporting Sydney Metropolitan Wildlife Service, Kuring-gai Bat Society and a number of bush regeneration and diversity schemes in the Park. Active in local business groups and sponsorship of school environmental awards.

> Food supplies: Visitors are encouraged to source local food but food is not served on the site.
> Employment: 75–99% local employees.
> Ownership: State government, not-for-profit enterprise.

> Swimming, water sports
> Walking, trekking, hiking
> Conservation work, wildlife education, city tours

The Orchard Garden Hotel USA

This is one of San Francisco's newest hotels, near the shops, theatres and entrance to Chinatown. The Orchard Garden Hotel is an 86-room 'boutique hotel', one of the city's first hotels to obtain certification under the LEED (Leadership in Energy & Environmental Design) scheme. Excellent insulation of the building envelope reduces energy consumption overall while also making guest rooms very quiet. Rooms are in muted natural tones with wood surfaces and textiles made from recycled polyester. The Roots Restaurant serves local organic food.

> Designed by Architectural International, the building's framework, construction practices, guest- and public-room lighting and decor all contributed to the LEED award.
> Materials: Meet LEED specifications; all furniture is FSC certified; Luna Textiles developed fabrics for drapery, sheers, upholstery and shower curtains with recycled polyester; recycled paper, soy inks and carpets with recycled content are used.
> Energy: Low-energy building; compact fluorescent light bulbs; guest keycard energy-control system.
> Water: Low-flow water faucets and toilets.
> Consumables: Aveda organic bath products; chemical-free organic citrus cleaning products.
> Waste: In-room recycling system.
> CO_2 emissions: Hybrid airport transfers in green cabs; bike racks to encourage human-powered transport.

> Conservation & community projects: Groups such as Friends of the Urban Forest and Global Green are supported through special events and packages; since opening in November 2006 over 100 room nights have been donated to a wide range of not-for-profit causes including The Salvation Army, Gay & Lesbian Film and SF AIDS Walk.
> Food supplies: The Roots Restaurant uses local, organic and seasonal ingredients.
> Employment: 100% local.
> Ownership: International commercial enterprise.

> 'Eco-getaway' purchase includes a copy of the *Greentopia Guide* to green living in San Francisco, plus airport transfers and city tour by PlanetTran, an eco-car service.

Scandic Hotels SCANDINAVIA AND EUROPE

The Scandic Hotels group comprises 130 hotels in nine countries including Belgium, Denmark, Estonia, Finland, Germany, Lithuania, the Netherlands and Norway. The group has a comprehensive corporate sustainability policy, developed from 1994 onwards, that requires all its hotels to report monthly on whether they are meeting their operational targets to reduce impacts, especially energy usage. 66 of the group's hotels are certified by the Nordic eco-label scheme, the Swan, which requires significant reductions in environmental impacts and a monitoring system to ensure they are met. Rooms and public spaces offer a clean Scandinavian aesthetic. There is a policy to accommodate people with disabilities and special needs and smoking is not allowed in public areas.

> Buildings range from old historic ones to new builds with an emphasis on refurbishment and renewal. Over half the hotels are certified by the Nordic Swan eco-label for their operations and staff are trained in eco-responsibilities, which includes a standard list of 93 activities.
> Materials: Emphasis on eco-labels (Nordic Swan, EU flower, Bra Mijöval), Fair Trade and renewable materials such as wood, wool and linen.
> Energy: Renewable hydroelectric power used in Sweden and Norway; lighting sensors for auto turn-off/on; thermostat-controlled heating.
> Water: Low-flow taps and showers.
> Consumables: Eco-label dry cleaning of guests' clothing; eco-labelled products for cleaning; linen cleaned using low environmental-impact system.
> Waste: The underlying principle is re-use, recycle and renew, with waste-sorting bins in 23,000 rooms.
> CO_2 emissions: Over the last decade the group's emissions have been reduced by 31% and there is a target for zero emissions by 2025. Bikes and walking poles are available for loan at all hotels, plus maps with walking, cycling and running routes.

> Conservation & socio-cultural projects: Scandic founded the Stockholm Water Prize, is a member of the Swedish Fair Trade organization and of the Swedish Society for Nature Conservation. Each hotel runs a local 'Scandic in Society' activity, focusing on food for homeless people, children's hospital visits or similar social activities.
> Food supplies: Organic and health breakfasts; organic food in many restaurants. Purchase contracts include clauses relating to efficient transport of goods.
> Employment: Proportion of local staff varies according to the hotel.
> Ownership: International and national commercial enterprise.

> Urban nightlife

Radisson SAS UK

Situated halfway down Edinburgh's famous cobblestoned Royal Mile, between Edinburgh Castle and Holyrood Palace, this hotel is within easy reach of the old city, museums, galleries and diverse cultural activities. The substantial stone building accommodates 238 rooms, appointed in a modern style, with monochromatic decor and locally commissioned artworks. As befits an international-standard hotel, the facilities are wide-ranging and include a Leisure Club offering sauna, swimming pool, massage and aromatherapy.

> Certified by the Green Tourism Business Scheme to Gold award standards.
> Materials: Stone building.
> Energy: Use of energy-efficient light bulbs and appliances throughout, backed up by a staff policy of vigilance. Electricity use was reduced 10% in 2007; natural gas use is down by 44% since 2005.
> Water: Towels and bed linens are changed only every three days or on request, thus reducing laundry water usage.
> Consumables: Ecolab cleaning products only.
> Waste: Glass, aluminium, plastic, paper and cardboard are all recycled; guests are encouraged to recycle too.
> CO_2 emissions: The hotel offers a 'Green Room' rate to offset carbon emission associated with guests' accommodation; also offsets 53 kilograms of CO_2 for each event or delegate attendee, at no additional cost to the client, through Climate Change Scotland or Climate Care.

> Conservation & socio-cultural projects: Bird feeders and nesting boxes installed in the gardens. A reafforestation project, Carrifran Wildwood, in Dumfries and Galloway, is supported. Partner with Spectrum Charity to support homeless people in skill-building and job-seeking. Unwanted furniture is donated to a local charity.
> Food supplies: Produce from a nearby cheese shop and local butchers; coffee, sugar are Fair Trade, organic and Rainforest Alliance certified. A 'Fair Trade Coffee Break' offers chocolate, bananas, fruit bars and dried fruit.
> Cultural events: Every September the hotel sponsors a number of local events to raise awareness about environmental issues, including a movie night open to all.
> Employment: 25–49% local staff.
> Ownership: International commercial enterprise, part of The Rezidor Hotel Group.

> Swimming, water sports
> Gym

Sofitel Amsterdam THE NETHERLANDS

This centrally located hotel, just five minutes' walk from the Central Station, Dam Square and the Royal Palace, is housed in three conjoined buildings dating from the 13th, 14th and 19th centuries. Behind the elegant façades are 148 rooms decorated in traditional, rather than modern contemporary style. Facilities include a sauna and solarium, a restaurant serving fusion and French cuisine and the Duke of Windsor, a bar and brasserie in the style of an Orient Express train.

> This Sofitel is the only one certified to Green Key standards in Europe. An environmental management system is in place to meet the requirements of the hotel group, Accor, which has 13 brands and 4,000 hotels.
> Energy: Features include monthly monitoring, regular maintenance of equipment, high thermal insulation, turning off of appliances not required, fitting of low-energy light bulbs, lowest possible thermostat settings.
> Water: Monthly monitoring, low-flow equipment where possible (toilets 6-litre flush, showers 9 litres per minute, taps 8 litres per minute or less); treatment of all waste water.
> Consumables: Non-chlorine-bleached paper or eco-label paper.
> Waste: All waste must be separated and staff are responsible for appropriate recycling or disposal.

> Conservation projects: Hotel is a member of the local wildlife and conservation association.
> Food supplies: Max Havelaar coffee, local meat and Eko-bread.
> Employment: 50–74% local staff.
> Ownership: International commercial enterprise.

> Amsterdam tours

Hotel Jolie ITALY

There was a time when the Adriatic resort town of Riccione was known as 'The Green Pearl' for its numerous parks and green spaces. Modern development has threatened that nickname, but some hotels have tried to revive the concept, albeit in a modest way. This clean, modern and typically Italian hotel is endorsed by two eco-labels. It is just minutes from the beach, where glamour and Wi-Fi internet access are *de rigueur*, and is within easy reach of numerous theme parks, ancient monuments and castles.

> Certified to the Italian Legambiente Turismo eco-label and the EU 'flower' eco-label, it displays its multi-language environmental policy in each room.
> Energy: Low-energy lighting; guest guidelines for energy conservation.
> Water: Water-saving devices are installed; guest guidelines for water conservation.
> Waste: Guests are invited to help separate waste to facilitate recycling of packaging, paper, food, batteries and even corks.

> Conservation projects: Near by is a sea-park, Olremare, where Cetacea, an Italian association to conserve dolphins, is based.
> Food supplies: Most food is sourced locally and guests are advised about which places to visit; cookery classes by arrangement.
> Cultural events: The beach is where Italian life unfurls in the summer months.
> Employment: 100% local.
> Ownership: Local commercial enterprise.

> Food and cookery classes
> Swimming, water sports
> Walking, trekking, hiking
> Trips to wineries, Italian language classes

Koidulapark Hotell ESTONIA

This early 20th-century building on the site of the old fortified town of Pärnu, on the Gulf of Riga, was restored and converted into a hotel in 2002. Its 39 rooms overlook mature oak trees and Koidula Park, named after a famous Estonian poet, Lydia Koidula. Behind the elegant wooden façade, the decor blends original features with modern international style. This is an ideal base for exploring the historical centre of this Baltic coast city.

> Certified to Green Key label for environmental management system, including giving advice to guests on how they may help.
> Energy: Conservation measures.
> Water: Conservation measures.
> Consumables: Policy to reduce use of chemicals and other environmentally damaging substances.
> Waste: Policy to reduce and recycle.
> CO_2 emissions: Guests are offered a guided city tour on foot or by bicycle.

> Food supplies: A 'Green Key' package includes a healthy breakfast.
> Employment: 100% local staff.
> Ownership: National commercial enterprise.

> Walking, trekking, hiking

Hotel Alexandra DENMARK

This central city hotel cooperates with the Danish Design Centre to celebrate the talents of internationally renowned designers such as Arne Jacobsen, Hans Wegner and Finn Juhl. Of the 61 rooms arranged over three non-smoking floors, one floor is designated 'allergy-free' for sensitive guests and 13 'design' rooms house Danish design classics and art. The hotel retains many original features and cleverly mixes an early 20th-century and modern ambience.

> Certified to Green Key label environmental management system.
> Materials: Policy to source materials from managed or certified sources.
> Energy: Conservation policy involving staff and guests.
> Water: Water-saving policy involving staff and guests.
> Consumables: Environmentally damaging detergents are avoided; packaging is preferred that is biodegradable, recyclable or returnable.
> Waste: Sorting of biodegradable, recyclable and returnable refuse.
> CO_2 emissions: Policy to try to minimize CO_2 emissions.

> Food supplies: Supply of local food encouraged where possible; organic food at the breakfast buffet.
> Employment: 75–99% local staff
> Ownership: Local commercial enterprise.

> Cycling around the city on the hotel's free bicycles
> Tour of the classic and vintage Danish design shops

Hotel del Rey BRAZIL

The city of Foz do Iguaçu in the state of Paraná is on the Brazilian–Argentinian border near the spectacular Iguaçu Falls. Rising in the Serra do Mar mountains 1,320 kilometres (820 miles) away, the Iguaçu River in full spate plunges over 275 waterfalls, the largest 19 falls providing the main attraction. Just 30 minutes from the falls, Hotel del Rey has 40 apartments with modern decor plus the usual international facilities. The area offers an amazing array of tourism activities, from waterfall jumping and white-water river trips to strolling around the local bird park or visiting local churches, a Buddhist temple, a mosque and a casino.

> Certified by the Brazilian eco-tourism authority, PCTS.
> Energy: All rooms fitted with services to control energy; lighting is low-energy fluorescents.
> Water: Consumption is reduced by re-use.
> Consumables: Biodegradable products are used for laundry services.
> Waste: Daily sorting and correct disposal of garbage.
> CO_2 emissions: The hotel cars are all powered by ethanol.

> Conservation & socio-cultural projects: Hotel supports trade unions for sanitation projects and people with hearing impairments, as well as the Cancer Institute.
> Food supplies: Sourcing of local food is encouraged.
> Cultural events: Local events are advertised to guests, who are also encouraged to buy locally.
> Employment: 100% local.
> Ownership: Local commercial enterprise.

> Adventure sports
> Cycling, mountain biking
> Swimming, water sports
> Walking, trekking, hiking

Stayokay THE NETHERLANDS

This is a Dutch chain offering 7 city venues, 11 rural or small-town and 12 coastal or waterside hostels in a range of buildings varying from historic houses to ultra-modern new builds. Try the manor houses at Heemskerk, Scheemda or Utrecht–Bunnik for country living. Urbanites should head for canalside hostels in Amsterdam (Stadsdoelen) or The Hague or the famous Amsterdam Vondelpark. Those preferring the wilder, windblown north can stay on the offshore islands of Ameland, Terschelling or Texel. The new Sneek is set near the sheltered waters behind the inland sea, or Ijsselmeer. The emphasis is on stylish yet economical accommodation, where careful design brings out the best from each building and introduces some quirky features, producing a mix of conviviality and modernity. Many outdoor nature and cultural activities are available and bicycle travel is encouraged.

> The whole group is certified to European eco-label standards and several hostels are certified to Green Key eco-tourism standards. Many of the hostels are unique buildings that are part of the varied Dutch architectural heritage, although some are new builds.
> Materials: Use of renewable resources and less hazardous substances is favoured.
> Energy & water: The group maintains a policy of energy and water conservation and reduced usage; some hostels have solar power generation; all hostels buy electricity from renewable sources (wind, bio-gas, solar power).
> Consumables: Eco-label or other low-impact products.
> Waste: Reduction of waste production is combined with recycling.
> CO_2 emissions: Bicycles are often included in hostel packages.

> Conservation & socio-cultural projects: Guided tours are offered of the Waddensee's marshland; beach-cleaning holiday activities at Milieujutten on Terschelling Island; field-study packages at Gorssel. Environmental education is promoted as part of the group's activities. Recently 600 marginalized or poor families had a free weekend in ten of the hostels as part of the group's corporate social responsibility (CSR) activities.
> Food supplies: Part of the food supply chain is usually local.
> Employment: 95% of the 800 employees are local.
> Ownership: National not-for-profit enterprise.

> Cycling, mountain biking
> Swimming, water sports
> Walking, trekking, hiking

Casa Camper SPAIN

In a quiet side street of the old Raval district, just a couple of minutes from the bustle of Barcelona's famous Las Ramblas, there is a boutique hotel behind a historic façade. Casa Camper is a brave new venture between the well-known contemporary Spanish shoe manufacturer Camper and renowned designers Vinçon. There are two types of accommodation: '1+1', a quiet, rear-facing bedroom and bathroom separated by a corridor from a lounge area; and suites where all the rooms are connected. Strong, vibrant, warm colours fill the rooms, complementing the carefully chosen furniture and lighting. The rear courtyard houses a vertical garden of aspidistras, while to the front is a shaded roof terrace with spectacular city views.

> An ideal destination for culture vultures, this restored and converted old town house mixes solid 'passive' vernacular architecture with innovative new features.
> Materials: Emphasis is on durable, high-quality fixtures, fittings and materials.
> Energy: Good natural lighting in the bathrooms and natural ventilation reduce energy demands.
> Waste: Novel, self-service food system reduces waste potential.

> 'Bicing', the local Barcelona hire scheme, is nearby
> Walking, trekking, hiking

> Food supplies: There is a 24-hour snack bar where you can select and make your own hot or cold snacks, inclusive in the room cost; some organic products; herbs from the rooftop terrace.
> Cultural events: Barcelona is on your doorstep!
> Employment: A mixture of local and international staff.
> Ownership: Joint-venture commercial enterprise.

nature

Safari camps, lodges, retreats, hostels, mountain huts and more – these destinations offer you an abundance of wildlife on your doorstep, treks and excursions by experienced guides and opportunities to get involved with local conservation projects. These locations are for the dedicated naturelover and those who want to experience the 'wild'.

Tongabezi Lodge ZAMBIA

Situated on the Zambian side of the Victoria Falls, this was the first upstream river lodge, established in 1990. Tongabezi is a discrete complex of small houses and cottages, each with its own unique name and atmosphere, all enjoying amazing river views. A mix of African and colonial aesthetic frames the verandas, windows and deckings, which allow visitors a close-up riverside experience. Catering for those who want intimacy and privacy, yet with more than a hint of decadence, Tongabezi permits you to enjoy the waterfalls of the Mosi-oa-Tunya ('the smoke that thunders') as the Zambezi River cascades over many precipices.

> Materials: Local timber, thatch and other building materials suited to the locality.
> Energy: Naturally ventilated rooms throughout the lodge.
> Water: Enjoy hot bucket baths on nearby Sindabezi Island accommodation.

> Conservation & educational projects: The Tongabezi Trust School, founded by Vanessa Parker, wife of one of the founder-owners of Tongabezi, now accommodates 100 children; guests are asked to bring old toys, books, videos and writing materials to donate to the school.
> Ownership: Privately owned and operated.

> Swimming, water sports
> Wildlife safari

Amazon Yarapa River Lodge PERU

Set on the banks of a tributary of the Yarapa River in the Peruvian Amazon jungle, near the former boomtown 'rubber capital' of Iquitos, the lodge shows exemplary practice in sensitive eco-tourism, encouraging guests and local tribespeople actively to conserve the rainforest together. Here you can see the pygmy marmoset monkeys, smell the hoatzin bird or watch the pink river dolphins. The jungle intimately embraces the lodge with its sensory experiences. Take a river canoe trip and watch spear fishing, then enjoy the local cuisine.

> The emphasis is on local architectural design and the minimal use of machinery during construction to avoid disturbance of local wildlife. The building footprint is kept as small as possible.
> Materials: Local thatch and timber.
> Energy: Solar panelling provides 95% of electricity needs.
> Waste: Composting and flushing toilets; greywater and sewage are contained in septic tank system to avoid contamination of river water.

> Conservation & socio-cultural projects: The Yarapa River Rainforest Reserve, 26 square kilometres (10 square miles) of virgin rainforest, was created in partnership with the neighbouring village of Jaldar and Cornell University. It is hoped that this reserve forms the seminal idea for a new national park. Local tribespeople are encouraged to fish using traditional weapons (bows, fish spears) rather than modern ones. Emergency medical support is provided for lodge guests and local people, including a local aeroplane service landing at nearby Lake Ubu.
> Cultural events: Guests are educated about the sensitive balance between

tourism and the local tribes. The local chief is one of the lodge's best guides.
> Food: Vegetarians are catered for.
> Employment: 100% local – owners, managers, guides and cooks.
> Ownership: Local, not-for-profit.

> Craft workshops
> Dance, music
> Volunteer work
> Walking, trekking, hiking
> Wildlife safari
> Conservation work

Don Enrique Lodge ARGENTINA

Hemmed in between the Uruguay River (Brazil) and the Paraná River (Paraguay), this remote part of Argentina is about 285 kilometres (117 miles) equidistant from airports to the north and south in the province of Misiones. The effort to reach it is worthwhile, as Don Enriques Lodge sits on the banks of the Paraíso River and abuts a reserve of luxuriant jungle called the Yaboti Biosphere Reserve. The area is renowned for its waterfalls, including the great Moconá Falls. There are three good-sized cabins, each with a capacity for four people, and yet there is plenty of space to circulate, dine and relax.

> Materials: The lodge is simply constructed using local timber and stone, with shaded verandas and decking.
> Consumables: Natural shampoos and soaps are provided for guests to use; other products are forbidden because of close proximity to the bio-reserve.

> Food supplies: Cuisine is local, regional, colourful and full of flavours. The lodge has its own orchard.
> Cultural events: Visits can be made to the Guaraní Indian villages to see local craftsmen at work.
> Employment: Local Guaraní guides for jungle walks.
> Ownership: Local enterprise.

> Swimming, water sports
> Walking, trekking, hiking

Dantica Lodge & Gallery COSTA RICA

Situated in a private cloud-forest reserve under supervision of the Ministry of the Environment and Energy (MINAE), Dantica Lodge overlooks the valley of San Gerardo and the Los Quetzales National Park. This mountainous region supports diverse primary forest, populated by pumas, tapirs, deer, coatis and otters, and is ideal for nature enthusiasts or those looking for a leisurely break in a temperate climate. Bungalows, separated by trails, lawns and forest, dot the lodge area. Each two- to four-person bungalow offers an almost Scandinavian aesthetic, with wooden floors, huge floor-to-ceiling panoramic windows, lightness and brightness, and a south-facing terrace, ideal for some armchair birdwatching. A modernist restaurant perches on the hillside, some 300 metres (984 feet) above the river. A large gallery celebrates the work of artisans and craftspeople.

> Energy: Solar gain from large glass windows.
> Water: Natural spring water.
> Waste: Organic waste is separated and composted on the premises; other waste is taken off-site to a city disposal facility.

> Conservation & community projects: Employees for the newly recognized Los Quetzales National Park are given free workshops on ecotourism and conservation.
> Cultural events: There is a large art gallery celebrating handicrafts from indigenous and rural communities.
> Employment: 75–99% local but wildlife guides are exclusively local.
> Ownership: International commercial enterprise.

> Craft workshops
> Volunteer work
> Walking, trekking, hiking

Danta Corcovado Lodge COSTA RICA

Costa Rica has an enviable reputation for tropical ecotourism. Danta Corcovado Lodge reveals how this culture of ecotourism has penetrated to the heart of everyday operations. Situated in a 35-hectare (86.5-acre) farm in Guadalupe, just 8 kilometres (5 miles) from the Corcovado National Park and the Guaymi Indigenous Reserve, the lodge emphasizes the importance of local flavour and enterprise. A unique feature is the organic-style stick and tree-trunk furniture, which shows off the beauty of timber harvested from the estate. After a day's exertions, guests are treated to authentic Costa Rican dishes.

> The lodge is a remodelled house built 25 years ago, with additions using local timber.
> Materials: Mainly locally sourced.
> Energy: Guests are encouraged to save energy (and water); natural materials and passive building design enhance cooling; only energy-saving light bulbs.
> Water: Projects for 2007–8 included a rainwater-harvesting system and purifying black- and greywater with artificial lagoons and a bio-digester to create natural gas.
> Waste: Garbage is separated into paper, plastic, glass, aluminium and organic.

> Conservation & cultural projects: The lodge is a founder-member of ASEDER (Entrepreneur Association for Responsible Development) and invests time, materials and services in local initiatives and community projects.
> Food supplies: Local and seasonal.
> Cultural events: Visits and interaction with the people of the Guaymi Indigenous Reserve.
> Employment: 100% local; training and education given.
> Ownership: Locally and nationally owned commercial enterprise.

> Craft workshops
> Dance, music
> Farm work
> Swimming, water sports
> Volunteer work
> Walking, trekking, hiking
> Horse riding

Paperbark Camp AUSTRALIA

Just two hours from Sydney, Paperbark Camp could be a thousand kilometres away. This small, minimal-impact tented camp was inspired by the safari camps of Africa, but has a distinct Down Under flavour. Set on the edge of Currambene Creek in the Jervis Bay National Maritime Park, the camp combines a genuine bush experience with the calm, relaxed minimalist decor of tented rooms, raised off the ground to minimize disturbance to the forest and protect from flooding. While not totally roughing it, guests can get pretty close to nature on land and underwater. Almost ten years on from its original eco-pioneering concept, Paperbark seems to retain its essential character – simplicity in a natural world – and is now one of many eco-destinations that succeed because they make ecological and economic sense.

> Achieved Accreditation with the Ecotourism Association of Australia in 1999, and Advanced Accreditation in 2005.
> Materials: Bush furniture and some structural timber from local paperbark trees off the property; lightweight, high-tech materials for luxury tents.
> Energy: Solar-powered lighting.
> Water: Low-flow showerheads are fitted; a change of towels is provided only upon request or after three days; signage advises guests to conserve water; rainwater tanks are to be installed and used for irrigation and firefighting.
> Waste: All effluence is removed from the site in order to preserve the delicate wetland environment and the nearby Marine Park.

> Conservation projects: Extensive regeneration of the local bush has been undertaken. Cars are parked in a central area away from accommodation and facilities to minimize noise disturbance. No feeding of animals or birds is allowed and visitors are educated about the damage these practices may cause.
> Food supplies: Local organic produce is purchased where possible, as well as local sustainable seafood supplies, such as farmed oysters and mussels. The camp hosts fundraising events for the bi-annual Sea Change Festival and participates in the annual Huskisson Food & Wine Festival.
> Cultural events: Aboriginal bush-tucker tours are organized for guests, as well as campfire talks with local Koori people, who teach about Aboriginal culture, in particular the importance of the natural environment to them, as well as how music and the playing of the didgeridoo help communicate this relationship to the next generation.
> Employment: Local.
> Ownership: Local family enterprise.

> Adventure sports
> Swimming, water sports
> Walking, trekking, hiking

Hapuku Lodge & Tree Houses NEW ZEALAND

Hapuku Lodge represents a rare combination of cutting-edge, contemporary, luxurious eco-design and a stunning landscape. Situated on New Zealand's South Island between the Kaikoura Seaward Mountain Range and Mangamaunu Bay, the building complex is surrounded by a deer farm and an olive grove and comprises a lodge with six guest rooms, an apartment, various multi-use rooms and five tree houses in the canopy of a native Manuka grove. The lodge's designer-owners, Tony and Peter Wilson, exhibit attention to detail in every facet of the building and its immediate landscaped grounds, providing a haven for quiet indulgence or a base for energetic adventures.

> Materials: Certified local and recycled timbers; high-specification insulation with double-glazed windows.
> Energy: Keycard system to turn off room lighting and facilities when guests exit; solar hot-water heating; ultra-efficient log-burning fires; energy-efficient light bulbs.
> Water: Recycling under development.
> Waste: Recycled, composted or used as animal feed.
> CO2 emissions: To offset carbon and restore native vegetation, a tree is planted for every guest who stays at the Lodge.

> Conservation projects: Between July and November 2007, 1,452 trees were planted locally; 10,000 have been planted over the lifetime of the Lodge. There is an opt-in carbon offset scheme for all guests.
> Food supplies: Organic certified produce is often used, with an emphasis on local seafood, venison and vegetarian dishes.
> Cultural events: The Lodge supports a local 'roots' music event and local musicians on-site.
> Employment: 50–74% local. Local guides are used for swimming with seals and dolphins and for whale-watching tours. Most staff are New Zealanders or international staff who have relocated to New Zealand.
> Ownership: Commercial local and international enterprise.

> Farm work
> Volunteer work
> Conservation
> Walking, trekking, hiking
> Marine safari

Rose Gums Wilderness Retreat AUSTRALIA

Set in over 90 hectares (222 acres) of bush bordering the World Heritage-listed Wooroonooran National Park, Queensland, and with views of the state's highest mountain, Mt Bartle Frere, in the cool Cairns Highlands, the lodge is an ideal centre for exploring endless walks in pristine rainforest interspersed with creeks. Established in 1994, this former dairy farm has been transformed into a biodiverse refuge. Developed with sustainability in mind, the lodge has a number of handcrafted pole and timber tree houses, each comprising two bedrooms, spa bath, bathrooms, wood-burning stove and private deck suspended in the canopy.

> The lodge is independently audited to ISO14001, an environmental management system (EMS) and is accredited with the Advanced Ecotourism Australia certificate. Environmental design considerations included site gradient, drainage, exposure, aspect, privacy and no removal of trees.
> Materials: Sustainably managed timber sources; durable materials; insulation.
> Energy: Passive thermal mass; natural ventilation via orientation and high ceilings; 80% of lighting system is low-energy fluorescents; no dishwashers or air-conditioning used; low-energy appliances sourced.
> Waste: All recycled.

> CO_2 emissions: Independently audited, including travel by guests, to identify where savings may be made. The lodge is carbon-neutral, having around 300,000 kilograms of carbon credits as a result of a 12-year tree-planting programme.

> Conservation & socio-cultural projects: The lodge is a registered 'Land for Wildlife' property, a state government-listed nature refuge. A member of local conservation group TREAT (Trees for the Evelyn and Atherton Tablelands). Rose Gums helps the local indigenous people, the Dulabed, to maintain their local sacred trail.
> Food supplies: There is a local community vegetable garden and local food supply is encouraged.
> Employment: 100% local.
> Ownership: Local commercial enterprise.

> Walking, trekking, hiking

Inn at Coyote Mountain COSTA RICA

Enjoying a rainforest location in central Costa Rica's coffee and ranching area, this 28-hectare (70-acre) private nature reserve offers stunning views from its observatory tower. The four-bedroomed lodge offers commodious accommodation and authentic connections with the land, culture, flora and fauna – look out for hummingbirds, sloths and coyote. Visitors can enjoy the courtyard pool, leisurely gourmet dining, Spanish and Creole cooking lessons and visits to the coffee fields. More adventurous souls can visit the nearby Arenal Volcano, Carrara National Park or the Central Valley for more strenuous activities.

> Materials: Sustainable lumber used in construction.
> Energy: Wind turbine on site; no energy-hungry air-conditioning; low-energy light bulbs; solar-powered landscape lighting.
> Water: Gravity-fed water system using local spring water.
> Consumables: 100% recycled paper products; bulk dispensers in all rooms.
> Waste: Greywater system feeds fruit orchard.
> CO2 emissions: No air-conditioning; car pooling encouraged.

> Conservation projects: Orchid protection and reafforestation programme on site.
> Food supplies: Inn grows own fruit and vegetables and uses local farmers' market; caters for vegetarians.
> Employment: 100% local including wildlife and conservation guides.
> Ownership: International commercial enterprise.

> Adventure sports
> Food and cookery classes
> Volunteer work
> Walking, trekking, hiking

Tree Tops Jungle Lodge SRI LANKA

Established in 1991 originally as a nature retreat and centre for environmental activism, this rustic mud-and tree-hut retreat is situated in the Weliara wilderness north of Yala National Park in south-east Sri Lanka. The lodge encourages conservation of the jungle and secondary forest and scrub to maintain biodiversity. Guests bathe in local style and eat meals cooked on a wood fire, enjoying a back-to-nature experience of intimacy with the landscape and wildlife of the area, which includes elephants, spotted deer, hundreds of bird species and the occasional leopard. This is also an ancient landscape, with irrigation systems originating in the 2nd century BC and Buddhist monuments from the 10th century AD.

> Materials: Rustic timber, mud-brick and vernacular building techniques create an empathy with the local landscape, which is the source of the materials. Tree huts are inspired by traditional chena tree huts used by farmers to watch their cultivated plots.
> Energy: There is no electricity.

> Conservation projects: The presence of the Lodge deters poaching and has encouraged interest in conserving biodiversity. The Lodge is closed ten days a month to respect nature's needs.
> Food supplies: All local, using traditional recipes cooked on a wood fire.
> Employment: Local, including the expertise of local jungle guides.
> Ownership: Owner-operated commercial enterprise.

> Walking, trekking, hiking
> Wildlife safari

Ulu Ai Project MALAYSIA

Borneo Adventure, a specialist tour company, has encouraged small group tours of the two East Malaysian states of Sabah and Sarawak on the island of Borneo since 1987. This three-day tour, commencing at the Sarawak capital, Kuching, takes you overland and upriver to the Ulu Ai Project, where you are accommodated in a jungle lodge of simple wooden construction. Facilities are basic but comfortable. From here treks are made along rainforest trails to Enseluai waterfall and a local longhouse belonging to the Iban ethnic group. Here you can see regional handicrafts and imbibe the communal and cultural way of life in these traditional buildings. Tourist income helps to protect the habitat and these indigenous communities from expansion of logging and oil-palm plantations.

> Materials: Timber, corrugated tin and plants for thatch, flooring and walls.
> Energy: Kerosene lamps, no generator.
> Water: Gravity-fed water.
> Waste: All recycled.

> Conservation & community projects: Assistance is given for a school clinic, buildings, water piping, sewage system and even a bridge; plus a scholarship for young people.
> Food supplies: Local fruit and vegetables.
> Cultural events: Exposure to life in a traditional Iban longhouse.
> Employment: 50–74% local.
> Ownership: A mixed local, national and international partnership.

> Craft workshops
> Dance, music
> Swimming, water sports
> Volunteer work
> Walking, trekking, hiking

Three Rivers Eco Lodge DOMINICA

Waterfalls, rivers, warm rain and a tropical sea guarantee this family-run lodge in Dominica is a genuine aqua paradise teeming with life. Accommodation varies from dormitories to cabins, cottages and a tree house. Sustainability underlies the whole ethic of the lodge, from overall concept to detail, and guests and the local community come together to understand and further sustainable living principles. Visits to discover traditional herbal medicines and bush teas, coffee and cocoa picking, traditional dance classes and a renewable energy workshop all help achieve this aim, thereby earning the lodge Green Globe certification. Here is a place to swing your hammock, seek out the unique sisserou parrots or simply commune with nature.

> Materials: Forest accommodation is made wholly from local renewable materials in traditional building styles.
> Energy: Lodge runs entirely on renewable energy from solar, hydro and wind power; the lodge truck runs on used vegetable oil; hot water from solar collectors.
> Water: Extracted from the river with a solar pump, then filtered with a carbon candle system.
> Consumables: Only biodegradable cleaning products are used.
> Waste: All organic waste is composted.

> Conservation & cultural projects: A joint project with the University of Vermont and an NGO called the Sustainable Living Committee (SLIC), which also runs sustainable living courses, aims to set up a bio-diesel plant on the island.
> Food supplies: There is a large organic garden.
> Cultural events: Three Rivers is extensively involved with all aspects of the local community.
> Employment: 100% local.
> Ownership: Naturalized local commercial enterprise plus not-for-profit NGO.

> Craft workshops
> Dance, music
> Farm work
> Food and cookery classes
> Swimming, water sports
> Volunteer work
> Walking, trekking, hiking
> Workshops in renewable energy

Quilálea Island MOZAMBIQUE

On the north-east coast of Mozambique, not far from the Tanzanian border, sit the old Portuguese and Arab trading towns of Quissanga and Pemba. Offshore in the nearby Quirimbas Archipelago is the 14-hectare (34-acre) private resort island of Quilálea, a refuge for humans and wildlife alike. Nine luxuriously appointed villas, each built to high standards of craftsmanship using local materials and makuti thatch, offer stupendous Indian Ocean views The sea-life is plentiful, thanks to the establishment of Quilálea Marine Sanctuary. Dugongs graze seagrass meadows, fish eagles sit patiently in the mangroves, turtles laze on the beach and humpback whales swim in the waters. So this is an outstanding place for diving (there is a PADI dive centre) and other tropical water sports or simply to lap up the relaxed atmosphere and enjoy *lala*, a Swahili word meaning 'sleep'.

> An environmental management system helps minimize any impacts.
> Materials: All construction materials, including a seawater-cement mix, were locally sourced and the architecture is in tune with vernacular traditions.
> Water: Desalination to provide potable water.
> Consumables: Low-environmental-impact cleaners and detergents in pump-action dispensers.
> Waste: Recycling of greywater; septic tanks.

> Conservation projects: The island and surrounding area constitute a marine sanctuary and a 'Zone of Total Protection', which encouraged the creation of the Quirimbas National Park, supported by the WWF. Guides are trained with the WWF. Over 500 mainly indigenous trees have been planted.
> Food supplies: All fish is supplied by local fishermen; a lot of fresh produce is bought locally, including honey.
> Employment: 75–99% local.
> Ownership: Commercial enterprise.

> Swimming, water sports
> Diving, kayaking
> Walking, trekking, hiking
> Bird watching

Cristalino Jungle Lodge BRAZIL

The lodge is set in a private natural heritage reserve bordering the Cristalino State Park in the state of Mato Grosso, in the southern part of the Brazilian Amazon. It is a birdwatcher's paradise: 1,800 species, representing almost one-third of Brazil's birds, live in and around the reserve. There are many trails and a 50-metre (164-foot) high canopy platform allowing guests an intimate experience of the jungle and its riches. Accommodation nestles in a forest clearing and varies from bungalows to shared twin-bed rooms. Facilities include a butterfly-filled flower, vine and orchid garden, lounge and dining rooms, a natural history library and a floating deck for swimming and relaxing.

> The Lodge has an environmental management system based on Brazil's Instituto de Hospitalidade system, the leading eco-tourism label. Many of the lodge's features are based on permaculture principles.
> Materials: Thatch or tile roofs with brick or timber structures; preference for certified eco-products.
> Energy: Hydrokinetic power plant to run the freezers; diesel generator; solar-heated showers.
> Water: Extracted from the Cristalino River and treated to be potable.
> Waste: Waste water is used for banana cultivation; organic materials are composted; other materials are transported back to facilities in the city of Alta Floresta for recycling.

> Conservation projects: The owner is president of the Fundação Ecológica Cristalino (FEC), dedicated to conservation projects, environmental education and scientific research in the Amazon region. All tourists visiting the lodge pay a donation to the foundation. Various research projects are supported and a range of workshops are held for secondary and university students at the Escola da Amazônia.
> Food supplies: Fruits and vegetables from the organic gardens of Alta Floresta; fish from nearby farms. Vegetarians catered for. Local dishes prepared on a wood-fired stove.
> Cultural events: Local festivals and plays are supported.
> Employment: All staff are local, including wildlife guides.
> Ownership: Local commercial enterprise.

> Adventure sports
> Swimming, water sports
> Volunteer work
> Walking, trekking, hiking
> Conservation work
> Birdwatching

La Laguna del Lagarto Lodge COSTA RICA

Journeying to the lodge, in the north-east of Costa Rica, is a pleasure in itself, as you go from tarmac roads to ever smaller gravel tracks. You pass the side of the Poás volcano, known for its huge crater, gaze at beautiful coffee *fincas* (farms) and fruit and flower nurseries and, in the warm lowlands of San Carlos, see sugar cane, yucca, pineapple and many citrus fruits. Set in remote virgin tropical rainforest, the lodge offers peace and calm, abundant bird life, including the great green macaw, and 10 kilometres (6 miles) of marked rainforest track to enjoy it all.

> The Lodge is certified by CST (Certification in Sustainable Tourism) to four stars (out of five).
> Materials: A cluster of wood-built cabins.
> Energy: Ceiling fans rather than air-conditioning units; rooms oriented towards cooling breezes.
> Waste: Paper, plastic and bottles are recycled.
> CO2 emissions: 180 hectares (445 acres) of rainforest provides a CO2 sink.

> Conservation projects: 40 hectares (99 acres) are being reafforested. Hunting is forbidden on the entire estate of 220 hectares (544 acres). The Lodge contributes to the organization that protects the green macaw.
> Food supplies: Fruit and hearts of palm are grown on the estate; eggs, yucca and tubers sourced locally.
> Employment: Guides are from the local village and trained at the lodge by overseas volunteers.
> Ownership: Local nationalized citizens own the commercial enterprise.

> Walking, trekking, hiking
> Birdwatching

Saunders Gorge Sanctuary AUSTRALIA

Sitting under the shade of a Red River gum tree in the rugged Adelaide Hills, South Australia, will fill your senses with the sights and sounds of the ancient bush. This 1,364-hectare (3,370-acre) sheep station, just a 90-minute drive from Adelaide, is slowly being converted into a wildlife refuge and conservation area. Scattered over the Saunders Gorge Sanctuary is a variety of accommodation in the Boundary Cottage, Hideaway Cottage and Nature Lodges (pictured below). The latter have panoramic views over the floodplain of Saunders Creek and are of a low-energy design, equipped with double beds and small pot-bellied wood-burning stoves. A main attraction is the huge diversity of plant life and fauna, including birds, kangaroos, wallabies, possums, geckos and goannas. Conservation aficionados can find plenty of volunteer work here and city dwellers can go bush.

> Materials: Timber sourced from plantation-grown forests.
> Energy: Solar power for the four Nature Lodges and Hideaway Cottage.
> Water: Rainwater harvesting on all buildings, supplemented with spring and creek water; low-water-use fittings and low-pressure overhead tanks to minimize water usage.
> Waste: Main house, restaurant and four Nature Lodges recycle greywater to irrigate trees and shrubs around buildings.

> CO_2 emissions: Over 500 trees and shrubs are planted annually for carbon offsetting; main 4WD vehicle runs off LPG; motorbike favoured for local trips.

> Conservation projects: Profits from the business go back into conservation work on the Saunders Gorge Sanctuary to convert old sheep-station land into a wildlife refuge. To date one-third of the property has been converted.

> Food supplies: Where possible local suppliers are used in sourcing food for the restaurant.

> Conservation work

Finca Rosa Blanca Country Inn COSTA RICA

On a hillside above coffee plantations and orchards at 1,000 metres (3,280 feet) in the central valley of Costa Rica, this lush tropical retreat, set among massive higuerón trees, embraces the guests. Built on sustainable ideals, the hotel pursues a holistic approach to create a distinctive aesthetic and to demonstrate that biological, architectural, educational and social responsibility can go hand in hand with tourism and maintaining biodiversity. Accordingly, it has gained the accolade of 'five green leaves' from Costa Rica's Certification in Sustainable Tourism (CST), endorsed by the International Ecotourism Society (TIES). Finca Rosa Blanca has given much to the local community, with which it is interdependent.

> Francisco Rojas Chaves, an advocate of sustainable architecture, supervised the architectural construction, giving considerable attention to maximizing light but minimizing heating, the creation of an organic aesthetic and a small footprint for the building.
> Materials: Mainly local, some sourced from the estate.
> Energy: Cross-breezes and strategically placed ceiling fans are used for passive cooling; solar laundry for drying.
> Water: Rainwater is harvested and applied to fruit cultivation; potable water is from a natural well.
> Consumables: Biodegradable cleaning agents only.
> Waste: All organic waste is composted and used to create a vermiculite-based manure; synthetic and other wastes are collected in separate streams and recycled.
> CO2 emissions: A carbon offset programme was due to start in December 2007.

> Conservation projects: Since 1985 the number of bird species on the property has grown from 56 to over 130, encouraged by planting of native trees, climbers and flowers, with sensitive zoning of activities. Profits from waste recycling and 5% of bar and restaurant sales are donated to the local Barrio Jesús School, the Children's Food Bank, and to encourage employees to take educational courses and environmental excursions. Two new recycling centres have been developed for local communities.
> Food supplies: Organically grown on the property or purchased from local suppliers. Coffee produced on the estate is certified organic by the Rain Forest Alliance and the National Institute.
> Employment: 100% local.
> Ownership: National owners.

> Dance, music
> Farm work
> Swimming, water sports
> Volunteer work
> Walking, trekking, hiking
> Agrotourism

Le Parc aux Orchidées GUADELOUPE, FRANCE

Individual wooden chalets or bungalows sit in a luxuriant, flowering paradise, framed by towering Royal Palm trees, coconut palms, diverse fruiting trees and orchids by the thousand. This specialist botanical park in the French Caribbean was established by Jean-Claude Rancé on the slopes of an old volcano and is now nurtured by the Gautier family. The prolific vegetation attracts hummingbirds, butterflies, geckos and frogs, so there is always a natural orchestra in the background. Guests can amble around, visit working plantations or just head for the beach.

> Materials: All construction is made according to local wooden tradition.
> Energy: Solar heating for water and further solar energy harvesting was planned in 2008.
> Water: Extracted from the river, then treated; freshwater pool and jacuzzi.
> Waste: Controlled waste disposal and composting.

> Conservation projects: Owner is an associate member of the botanical conservatory of the French West Indies and also of the Conservatoire des Collections Végétales Spécialisées for wild orchids of Guadeloupe. The park supports the Soleil d'Argent association, a local community project.
> Cultural events: Owner belongs to a local association of the district and city, hence is involved with local culture.
> Employment: The lodge trains local guides.
> Ownership: Local commercial enterprise.

> Swimming, water sports
> Walking, trekking, hiking
> Birdwatching

The Lodge at Big Falls BELIZE

This 12-hectare (30-acre) smallholding provides a series of octagonal cabanas set in a managed and natural landscape beside the Rio Grande in the Toledo district. This is an area of Mayan culture with more than forty Mek'chi or Mopan Maya villages. Birds, butterflies and iguanas are your companions. Local tours vary from dawn birdwatching to visits to an organic cocoa plantation, medicinal rainforest, ancient Mayan ruins and a craftsman who continues to make the Mayan harp.

> Materials: Thatch for cabana roofs; sisal hammocks.
> Energy: Passive cooling of cabanas by louvred windows, overhanging verandas and insulating thatch; solar and low-voltage lighting.
> Water: River water is pumped and treated.
> Waste: Composting; heavily packaged supplies are avoided.

> Conservation & cultural projects: The lodge provides a base for the Aguacaliente Wildlife Sanctuary, an important wetland eco-system, 16 kilometres (10 miles) from the resort. Jaguar, tapir and paca find refuge in the sanctuary as pressures from commercial farming continue. Since October 2001 the lodge has been involved in replanting trees after damage by Hurricane Iris.
> Food supplies: Food is purchased from the market in Punta Gorda with a view to incorporating more local dishes in the menu.
> Employment: 100% local Maya.
> Ownership: International commercial enterprise.

> Adventure sports
> Craft workshops
> Dance, music
> Swimming, water sports
> Walking, trekking, hiking
> Birdwatching

SarapiquíS Rainforest Lodge COSTA RICA

The ethos underlying the Centro Neotrópico SarapiquíS (CNS) complex is a respect for vernacular building traditions and the ecology and cultural history of the area. It is situated in the foothills of the Cordillera Central mountains, just 85 kilometres (52 miles) from San José, right by the Tirimbina Biological Reserve, and accessed by a 260-metre (850-foot) suspension bridge over the Sarapiquí River. The layout of the lodge represents a pre-Columbian village, using round palenques (or ranchos) covered with palm-thatched roofs. Each palenque, whose apex soars up 18 metres, houses eight deluxe rooms; further accommodation gives a total capacity of 36 people. On the doorstep are a museum, a unique archaeological park, lush gardens, an orange orchard and spectacular rainforest.

> Traditional construction techniques dating back to pre-Columbian times ensure the buildings have a low environmental footprint. Certified to CST eco-tourism label.
> Materials: Thatch, roundwood.
> Energy: Solar panels for hot water; low-energy lighting.
> Consumables: Use of biodegradable products.
> Waste: A bio-plant for treating waste water; an ionizing system to purify the swimming pool; a recycling system.

> Conservation & socio-cultural projects: The lodge cooperates with the Tirimbina Biological Reserve.
> Food supplies: Local and vegetarian dishes are served, including spices served in pre-Columbian times.
> Cultural events: The museum celebrates the architectural and cultural traditions of the indigenous people.
> Employment: 75–99% local.
> Ownership: International commercial enterprise.

> Adventure sports
> Craft workshops
> Swimming, water sports
> Walking, trekking, hiking
> Wildlife safari

Xandari Resort & Spa COSTA RICA

This 22-villa resort is set within a private plantation, botanical gardens and natural forest high in the Central Valley, at an altitude of 1,200 metres (3,950 feet), where the climate is pleasantly cool. 4 kilometres (2½ miles) of trails through the diverse vegetation link up several waterfalls. The admirably designed, carefully oriented villas vary in size and facilities but each has high ceilings and a private terrace. A central spa village offers some personal pampering. The international and Costa Rican menu uses organic fruit and vegetables produced on the estate. Among the active pursuits here is gliding down the rainforest-canopy zip-line.

> Certified by Costa Rica's most respected scheme, the Certification in Sustainable Tourism (CST).
> Energy: Low-energy and solar lighting.
> Water: Reduced water usage for laundry.
> Consumables: Chlorine-free swimming pools.
> Waste: There is a recycling centre.
> CO2 emissions: Guests and local children join a tree-planting programme.

> Conservation projects: There is an orchid house and a natural planting scheme that encourages birdlife; the resort supports Zoo Ave, a local refuge that rehabilitates animals, and SASY (Stop Animal Suffering).
> Food supplies: Organic fruit and vegetables grown in own greenhouse.
> Employment: 100% local.
> Ownership: International commercial enterprise.

> Swimming, water sports
> Walking, trekking, hiking

Mowani Mountain Camp NAMIBIA

Mowani Mountain Camp, set in the fascinating geology and archaeology of Damaraland, inland from the western coastal park zone, offers a variety of accommodation, from luxury tents, with their own private wooden deck, to well-appointed suites of rooms in perfectly conical thatched buildings perched on a rocky outcrop, offering amazing mountain views. Butler service is available for each suite. Trekking is plentiful around the rugged desert mountain landscape or excursions can be made to Twyfelfontein, which houses more than 2,500 rare Bushman engravings and paintings. This is just the place for a pampered and leisurely wilderness experience without the dirt under the fingernails.

> Materials: Tents are built on raised platforms to minimize impact. Local vernacular techniques and materials used for the conical roofed buildings.

> Food supplies: The supply of local food is encouraged.
> Employment: 75–99% local; guides from local tribes are employed for game drives.
> Ownership: National commercial enterprise, Visions of Africa Safari Company.

> Swimming, water sports
> Walking, trekking, hiking
> Game drives

Onguma Safari Camps NAMIBIA

On the eastern side of Etosha National Park is a range of camps to suit all wildlife enthusiasts, varying from basic, through intermediate, to outright luxury accommodation in the Tented Camp. In the basic campsite you get a pile of firewood, a shower and a place to pitch your tent. The intermediate Bush Camp comprises six en-suite bungalows around an open *lada* lounge. The Tented Camp is at the edge of a waterhole in the Onguma Private Nature Reserve, home to more than 30 species of African game, including giraffe, eland, lion, leopard, hartebeest and zebra. The tented bedrooms open to private wooden platforms where you can savour the earthy connection with the landscape, then cool off in the well-appointed bathing room or visit the plunge pool. The sight of thousands of migrating birds in the temporary wetlands is one to remember. No wonder: *onguma* means 'the place you don't want to leave' in Herero, the local language.

> Materials: Combinations of natural materials – timber, stone, thatch.
> Waste: Sewage is treated with an Australian septic-tank system that produces only biodegradable products and toxin-free water.

> Conservation projects: The whole 20,000 hectares (49,500 acres) of the Onguma Private Nature Reserve is managed for biodiversity and conservation.
> Employment: 75–99% local.
> Ownership: International and nationally owned commercial enterprise, Visions of Africa Safari Company.

> Swimming
> Wildlife safari
> Game drives

Shenandoah National Park Lodgings USA

Not far from the heady politics of Washington, DC, lies another world, in the Blue Ridge mountains of Virginia and Shenandoah National Park. The lodgings, arrayed along the Skyline Drive scenic route, range from the guest rooms of the Skyland Resort to the 1939 Big Meadow Lodge and the authentic Lewis Mountain cabins in a wooded area. Take a park guide on a trek over the famous Appalachian Trail, get on your bike, get on a horse or stay in the kitchen and learn some local and regional recipes using sustainable ingredients. Or stock up at one of the Wayside stores and head for the southern, more remote part of the park known as the backcountry. Autumn is the time to savour the changing landscape, but remember the park is closed from December to March.

> Certified to Greenseal eco-label standards, USA.
> Materials: Bamboo and hard-surface flooring.
> Energy: Compact fluorescent light bulbs, dark-sky outdoor lighting; Energy Star-rated appliances; high-efficiency propane heating equipment.
> Water: Water-saving devices.
> Consumables: Products with high recycled content, from gifts to furniture.
> Waste: There is a recycling programme.
> CO_2 emissions: Local and green energy offsets are purchased for 100% clean power.

> Conservation projects: The lodgings support all the park's conservation programmes.
> Food supplies: As local as possible.
> Employment: 50–74% local; Shenandoah guides are all local.
> Ownership: Corporate commercial enterprise.

> Craft workshops
> Dance, music
> Food and cookery classes
> Swimming, water sports
> Walking, trekking, hiking
> Conservation work

Ecolodge San Luis & Research Station
(University of Georgia, UGA, Costa Rica Campus) COSTA RICA

This is a research centre where academics rub shoulders with eco-tourists in the beautiful cloud forest of Monteverde that is a habitat for over 300 bird species, 100 different mammals and 3,000 plants. The varied campus accommodation includes casitas, cabinas, bungalows and dormitories for both permanent and visiting staff and guests. There is an extensive programme of recreational and learning activities on and off campus.

> Certified under the Costa Rican CST ecotourism scheme. Campus policy is to 'design and practise programmes that promote sustainability of our bio-physical environment'. Architecture embraces vernacular features.
> Materials: Plantation wood, tin roofs and concrete.
> Energy: Monitoring of energy conservation measures and support of the San Luis Development Board for energy services.
> Water: Monitoring of water conservation and management.
> Consumables: Use of certified biodegradable cleaning products.
> CO_2 emissions: The newly established UGA Costa Rica Carbon Program aims to minimize emissions.

> Conservation projects: Among other research and conservation projects aimed at maintaining the ecological stability and protecting the flora and fauna of natural areas, the centre chairs the Monteverde–Gulf of Nicoya Biological Corridor project. Locally supports community projects for infrastructure development and an educational English-language programme.
> Food supplies: On-site organic farming supplies 30% of the vegetables; milk from farm cows; policy to purchase as much local food as possible.
> Employment: 80% local.
> Ownership: International not-for-profit organization.

> Craft workshops
> Dance, music
> Farm work
> Food and cookery classes
> Swimming, water sports
> Walking, trekking, hiking
> Wildlife safari
> Ecology & wildlife courses
> Horse riding

EcoHotel L'Aubier SWITZERLAND

L'Aubier sits on the mountainside with grand views of Neuchâtel town, the Lac de Neuchâtel and the distant Swiss Alps. This 25-bed hotel has a large public restaurant serving organic food from its own 14-hectare (35-acre) bio-dynamic farm founded in 1979. Bedrooms in the main building have individual names and characters; an adjacent pavilion offers simpler yet still modern, functional accommodation. A team of four coordinates the cooperative that runs L'Aubier, involving hundreds of people who share the common philosophy of ecological awareness and responsible consumption. L'Aubier also runs a smaller hotel and café in an elegant period townhouse in Neuchâtel. This successful partnership is a viable model for any aspiring eco-hotel. The surroundings offer diverse recreational pursuits and there is volunteer work on the farm too.

> OE-PLUS certified and top-rated at 'five ibex' classification.
> Materials: All materials were selected for minimal ecological impact (including FSC materials) and impact on human health.
> Energy: Half of the hotel's energy is generated on site, the rest is purchased from 'Naturalmade Star'; automated local-wood heating system; energy recovery from fridges and ventilation system.
> Water: Rainwater for all the toilets and laundry.
> CO2 emissions: Measures to reduce CO2 are in place.

> Conservation & socio-cultural projects: Supports a schools project on local selection of wheat.
> Food supplies: This is a strictly bio-dynamic kitchen with food products from the farm certified to Demeter, Bio-Suisse, Goût-Mieux and KAG-Freiland standards.
> Employment: 100% local.
> Ownership: Local enterprise with participative partnership.

> Adventure sports
> Farm work
> Swimming, water sports
> Walking, trekking, hiking

Hotel Fazenda Baia das Pedras BRAZIL

The Hotel Fazenda, in Brazil's Mato Grosso region, is the ideal place from which to explore the extraordinary landscape of the world's largest inundated plain, the Pantanal. Straddling Brazil, Bolivia and Paraguay, the Pantanal experiences dry and wet seasons, creating a nature-lover's paradise with an unrivalled diversity of species, including over 3,500 plants, 124 mammals, 177 reptiles and 423 birds. The farm itself is a comfortable, refurbished 1960s building with a hammock lounge, balconies and five guest bedrooms. Tantalizing smells of local organic food emanate from a wood-burning stove, which produces such typical regional fare as carreteiro rice and a pantaneiro barbecue, perfect after a day's horse riding or canoeing on the many freshwater lakes.

> Certified by the Brazil Sustainable Tourism Programme (PCTS), a joint venture between the Hospitality Institute and the Brazilian Council for Sustainable Tourism.
> Materials: From managed certified resources and eco-labels where possible.
> Energy: Consumption targets to reduce energy use are set and monitored.
> Water: Devices to reduce water usage and control waste water.
> Waste: Management to prevent damage to the environment, segregate waste streams and re-use or recycle where possible.

> Conservation & socio-cultural projects: The lodge is a partner of the Pantanal National Park and is involved in projects to conserve and study wild pigs and caimans. It also supports a nearby farm school.
> Food supplies: The lodge is a member of ABPO (Organic Products Brazilian Association) and produces organic meat, vegetables and fruit.
> Cultural events: The traditional dances of the Pantanal are supported.
> Employment: 100% local.
> Ownership: Commercial enterprise.

> Farm work
> Swimming, water sports
> Walking, trekking, hiking
> Wildlife safari
> Horse riding, fishing

Jungle Bay Resort & Spa DOMINICA

Dominican-born property developer and sustainable development activist Samuel Raphael and his wife, Glenda, set about creating a resort that would enhance the natural environment and generate wellness for guests, staff and local communities. Developed along guidelines of the International Ecotourism Society (TIES), the 22-hectare (54-acre) Jungle Bay site borders the Morne Trois Pitons National Park, a UNESCO World Heritage Site. Minimum disturbance during construction was deemed essential, so each of the 35 hand-built cabins and cottages is set on stilts above the forest floor, giving an intimate relationship with surrounding forest.

> Materials: Sustainably managed greenheart timber from Guyana; local volcanic stone; locally crafted Kalinago (Carib) furniture and artworks.
> Energy: Supplied by the national grid, which is 40% hydro-power; the resort currently uses only 35–40% of the electricity of a conventional resort, according to US Energy Star calculations; energy-efficient light bulbs; fans instead of air-conditioning units; solar systems being tested, including solar collectors on 15% of cottages for hot water; minimal pathway and landscape lighting.
> Water: A spring-fed stream; gravity-fed system.
> Waste: Food waste is composted.
> CO_2 emissions: Current energy strategy uses 20,000 kilograms less CO_2 per year than previous system.

> Conservation & socio-cultural projects: Encouraged the Turtles for Tourism initiative to convert hunters into guards and rangers to save the turtles; guides are trained and certified to talk about wildlife and biodiversity and the healing properties of Dominica's herbs; a research project with SETDC (South East Tourism Development Committee) is cataloguing plant life in south-east Dominica; the resort helped fund schooling for over 200 Carib high school students; Friends of Jungle Bay given seed money for the development of the community House of Hope.
> Food supplies: 75–95% purchased from local organic farmers and small fisheries. Local Dominican Bello coffee. Red meat is not served at the restaurant.

> Adventure sports
> Dance, music
> Food and cookery classes
> Swimming, water sports
> Walking, trekking, hiking
> Drumming, meditation, yoga

Tui Nature Reserve Wilderness Park NEW ZEALAND

The views over Pelorus Sound, in the northern part of New Zealand's South Island, from the cottage or wooden chalets, make the journey by mail-boat (Fridays only), water taxi or float plane worthwhile. The remote Tui Nature Reserve, set on a forest plateau, is a conservation and eco-accommodation project that embraces the concept of treading lightly. There are no roads here and transport is generally on foot or by water, so tranquillity is guaranteed.

> Materials: Low-impact, re-used materials and low embodied-energy (EE).
> Energy: Solar-powered cabins; cottage will be solar-powered in the future.
> Water: Rainwater harvesting from all roofs.
> Consumables: Biodegradable cleaning products.
> Waste: Vegetable waste composted for use in the organic garden.

> Conservation projects: Projects have been running for twelve years on the estate land of 42 hectares (104 acres) and have now been extended to the rest of the peninsula, with an active pest-control programme to help native vegetation and wildlife flourish, including the Marlborough green gecko.
> Food supplies: An organic garden, homemade bread and local produce.
> Ownership: Local family-owned enterprise.

> Craft workshops
> Swimming, water sports
> Volunteer work
> Walking, trekking, hiking

Wilderness Lodge Arthur's Pass NEW ZEALAND

An uneconomic New Zealand high-country farm was purchased in 1994 and transformed into a 600-hectare (1,480-acre) nature reserve, 600-hectare merino wool farm and a 20-room hotel-cum-lodge, where every room is suffused with the atmosphere of the mountains. You can take a walk with a knowledgable guide into McKay Moa Forest and Wild Boar Hill, through protected shrubland and beech forest with rare red-flowering mistletoe; watch the sheepdogs mustering the merinos against the dramatic backdrop of the snowy Southern Alps; or explore the rivers and lakes by kayak.

> Materials: Stone, wood, steel; timber from plantations managed on a renewable basis.
> Energy: Design includes thermal mass storage of solar energy; double glazing; energy-efficient lighting throughout; all electricity is sourced from hydro-power suppliers.
> Water: Showers prevent excessive water usage.
> Consumables: Emphasis on using New Zealand products such as Manuka soap.
> CO_2 emissions: Helicopter or jet-boat operations are not permitted.

> Conservation & cultural projects: There is constant attention to regeneration of the native forest, and guests sometimes help plant new seedlings. The development of Arthur's Pass has helped significantly to raise conservation issues in the region, yielding various projects including rescue of the endangered orange-fronted parakeet. Projects are developed in consultation with the Maori people at the nearby Kura Tawhiti reserve.
> Food supplies: Encourages the use of South Island foods and applies NZ Forest and Bird Society guidelines when sourcing for the restaurant.

> Cultural events: Learning about sheep husbandry.
> Employment: 50–74% local.
> Ownership: Local commercial enterprise.

> Farm work
> Swimming, water sports
> Walking, trekking, hiking
> Wildlife safari

Ullapool Youth Hostel UK

Ullapool Hostel sits in a relatively sheltered spot on the shore of Loch Broom on the wild north-west coast of Scotland, a dream location right in the heart of a characterful town full of seafood restaurants, pubs and cafés. Social evenings, often including music, are guaranteed. Ferries head off to even more remote destinations – the Hebrides and the windswept isles of Lewis and North and South Uist. Enjoy a maritime wildlife tour or just amble along the coast to find some real peace and quiet.

> Certified by the Green Business Tourism Scheme, scoring an overall Gold Standard against 60 criteria, from complying with environmental legislation and improving environmental performance and management to a commitment to social involvement and communication.
> Materials: FSC wood products are encouraged.
> Energy: Efficient combination of lighting, heating, appliances, insulation and renewable energy use; new boilers have been installed.

> Water: Well-maintained low-consumption and low-flush appliances; rainwater harvesting.
> Consumables: Products made from recycled materials, eco-cleaners.
> Waste: Follows 'eliminate, reduce, re-use, recycle' principles; has supplier take-back agreements; recycling and composting.
> CO_2 emissions: Aims to minimize visitor car use by promoting local and human-powered transport.

> Conservation projects: All visitors are informed about the hostel's responsible green charter, work with the local community and use of local resources. The hostel values corporate social responsibility reporting.
> Employment: 25–49% local.
> Ownership: Not-for-profit national enterprise.

> Walking, trekking, hiking
> Wildlife safari

Moinhos da Tia Antoninha PORTUGAL

A labour of love reclaimed this rural retreat from an abandoned farm and mill to the south of the Douro River in northern Portugal, in a region famed for its wines and local fare. An apartment and six rooms are dotted around the complex, each with its own colourful, tasteful furnishings to complement the natural stone, wood and tiles. A unique feature is the natural swimming pool fed from the stream that bisects the property. This is rural Portugal at its best. You can learn about the local cuisine and try your hand at the recipes, or work up an appetite on assorted activities, from walking, horse riding, birdwatching and mountain biking to hunting on special reservations.

> Certified by the Green Key European eco-label. Plans include reviving a rural bakery and traditional water mill activities.
> Materials: Stone, pantiles and traditional materials in harmony with the local environment. Timber was sourced from a supplier using sustainably managed forests. Natural textiles were used where possible.
> Energy: The complex is autonomous, using solar photovoltaic 'field' and hydro-power from the mill stream, with an occasional support generator.

> Conservation projects: The owners work with UTAD, a conservation body, and local authorities on conservation projects.
> Food supplies: Fair Trade supplies of vegetables and meat, organic- and bio-products where possible sourced from the nearby village.
> Cultural events: Promotes local craftwork.
> Employment: 100% local.
> Ownership: Local commercial enterprise.

> Adventure sports
> Farm work
> Food and cookery classes
> Swimming, water sports
> Walking, trekking, hiking
> Local history, antiquities

Lochmara Lodge NEW ZEALAND

This multipurpose lodge, surrounded by pristine bush on Lochmara Bay in the beautiful Marlborough Sounds, in the far north of the South Island of New Zealand, is reached by water taxi. Comprising accommodation in twin or double ensuite rooms and one- and two-bedroom luxury chalets, with a café, restaurant, in-house massage therapist and spa pool, this is a TV-free retreat for serious relaxation. Guests can enjoy walking and mountain biking on the stunning Queen Charlotte Track or leisurely kayaking around the local waters.

> The lodge is certified to Green Globe ecotourism standards.
> Materials: Some local reclaimed building materials were sourced from Marlborough and Nelson.
> Consumables: 100% plant-based Eco-store detergents.
> Waste: 70% of waste is recycled, transported to Blenheim; pigs get the food scraps.

> Conservation projects: The Marborough Sounds Wildlife Recovery Trust operates a centre at Lochmara Lodge, which offers a rehabilitation, education and protection programme for injured wildlife and endangered species such as the gecko, kakariki (parrot) and weka (wood hen), work supported by 5% of the admission fees to the Arts Centre.
> Employment: Local.
> Ownership: Local commercial enterprise.

> Bungi jumping, mountain biking
> Swimming, water sports
> Walking, trekking, hiking
> Whale watching

Mombo Camp BOTSWANA

Situated on an island in the Okavango Delta, in the Moremi Game Reserve, Mombo Camp is one of many camps operated by Wilderness Safaris, which, for the last 25 years, has been actively involved in protecting 2.6 million hectares (6.4 million acres) of wild landscapes for the benefit of the wildlife, local communities and visitors. This is a continual balancing act, but vital for the maintenance of biodiverse carbon sinks. Mombo provides top-quality amenities, but in an intimate setting. Nine luxuriously furnished tents are raised off the ground and connected by an elevated walkway that weaves among the trees. Morning and afternoon safaris by 4WD vehicle give visitors a close-up view of the floodplain and its diverse wildlife, including lion, leopard, cheetah, buffalo, hyena, giraffe, wildebeest and more. A simple plunge pool, outdoor showers and the shady trees afford welcome cool. This kind of high-income, low-volume tourism offers the well-off visitor an insight into a unique wild world while also ensuring that it is conserved for future generations and that locals can earn a living in conservation.

> Materials: Aimed at minimizing visual and aural impact of a camp in this undisturbed wilderness area.
> Energy: Diesel generators run off a computerized system to maximize efficiency.
> Waste: Sewage is broken down using enzymes in an above-ground system, allowing the 'back water' to be safely returned to the ground; all waste is separated into organic and inorganic, and recyclables, such as paper, plastic, glass and tin, are removed from the site to Maun by truck.
> CO_2 emissions: Solar-powered facilities are in the planning stage, with a view to running all the Wilderness Safaris camps on hybrid systems by 2012, halving emissions.

> Conservation projects: Wilderness Safaris and the Botswana government cooperate on conservation of the white and black rhinos.
> Cultural events: A traditional evening is held weekly observing local Setswana customs and enjoying local food.
> Employment: The company's 'localizaton programme' employs 683 people from local communities, including local guides.
> Ownership: Local and other owners.

> Wildlife safari

Chumbe Island Coral Park TANZANIA

The island, not just the accommodation, is the real eco-destination here. Chumbe Island Coral Park Ltd (CHICOP) is a not-for-profit private conservation project that in 1991 created probably the first private marine park in the world. Although operations follow commercial principles, the objectives of CHICOP are non-commercial, supporting conservation, research and environmental education for local fishers, schoolchildren, their teachers and all other visitors (only 14 of whom are allowed to stay on the island at any one time). Chumbe has many biodiversity achievements to its credit, including one of the most pristine coral reefs in the region and a forest reserve representing one of the last undisturbed semi-arid 'coral rag' forests in Zanzibar. It is a sanctuary for the critically endangered endemic Ader's duiker and the rare coconut crab, listed in IUCN Red Book, as well as for the rare roseate tern, which has been bred on Chumbe. This is a small but beautiful and truly eco-luxuriant location.

> All buildings on Chumbe Island were constructed on state-of-the-art eco-architecture lines.
> Materials: Local materials and techniques, including high-insulation thatch with naturally ventilating roof space.
> Energy: Solar water heating and photovoltaics provide for all energy needs; cooking is by gas and efficient wood-burning stoves.
> Water: Integrated systems of rainwater catchment, composting toilets, greywater and vegetative filtration. At night, walkways and beach areas are not illuminated to protect nocturnal wildlife from light pollution.

> Conservation projects: Chumbe Island Coral Park was registered in Zanzibar (1992) for the purpose of conserving uninhabited Chumbe Island and creating a model of sustainable park management, where ecotourism supports conservation and environmental education. Over 15 years, CHICOP has developed Chumbe Island into a fully managed conservation area. The west coast reef of Chumbe Island was gazetted a Reef Sanctuary, and the island forest declared a Closed Forest by the Zanzibar government in 1994. This is the only privately established and managed Marine Protected Area (MPA) in the world. Chumbe relies solely on revenue from small-scale ecotourism. Permitted uses of the marine park include recreation (swimming, snorkelling), education and research. Diving is allowed only for research, and fishing, anchorage and collection of specimens are forbidden. Chumbe has also promoted environmental clubs in many schools and well over 2,100 schoolchildren and 440 teachers have visited Chumbe Island.
> Food supplies: Bought directly from fishers and farmers in local markets.

> Employment: Local people are given preference. A third of the 41 employees are directly involved in conservation management and education, which offers direct economic benefit by protecting their natural resource for long-term subsistence and livelihood.
> Ownership: Locally registered not-for-profit company owned by non-nationals.

> Craft workshops
> Swimming, water sports
> Volunteer work
> Walking, trekking, hiking
> Marine safari

Adelaide Hills Wilderness Lodge AUSTRALIA

The lodge is next door to the Mylor Conservation Park and the Mount Lofty ranges, just an hour's drive from Adelaide. It offers a range of basic but comfortable facilities, ranging from bunk-bed dormitories to group or family suites and rooms, accommodating solo visitors, small groups and large parties (up to 100). The adventurous might like to try sleeping under canvas in the tipi. An ideal base for bushwalkers and nature-lovers, it is also an educational facility for schoolchildren, which includes a wildlife sanctuary for reptiles and kangaroos.

> Eco-certified by the Australian authorities to 'Advanced' ecotourism status, the lodge operates an environmental management system.
> Materials: FSC and other certified sources where possible.
> Energy: Buildings all designed to maximize energy efficiency.
> Water: From local borehole.
> Consumables: Sometimes Fair Trade goods.
> Waste: Waste treatment plant.
> CO_2 emissions: A tree-planting programme to offset some emissions.

> Conservation projects: The wildlife sanctuary, tree-planting and local conservation programmes.
> Food supplies: Local food supply encouraged.
> Employment: 100% local.
> Ownership: Local commercial enterprise.

> Adventure sports
> Food and cookery classes
> Swimming, water sports
> Volunteer work
> Walking, trekking, hiking
> Environmental education

Eco Hotel Uxlabil Atitlán GUATEMALA

In the heart of the San Juan community on the shores of Lake Atitlán, this is a simple, low-key eco-hotel that offers tranquillity and immersion in Guatemala's culture and nature. Rooms are basic but open on to a balcony or veranda with lakeside views. There are also two discrete bungalows. You can meet the local *tejedoras* (weavers) in their colourful textiles and visit weavers to learn basic techniques. Outdoor activities embrace everything from horse riding, swimming from the private waterside jetty and canoeing on the lake to taking a hot sauna. Bird, insect and amphibian life is abundant, including many different lizards and frogs. At mealtimes, local fish and crabs are accompanied by fresh vegetables straight from the garden.

> Materials: Stone-crafted and built by local stonemasons.

> Socio-cultural projects: The hotel supports and encourages the local weaving community in the production of traditional handicrafts, using natural dyes, and offering weaving lessons for tourists.
> Food supplies: Vegetables and medicinal plants from the hotel garden; local crustaceans and fish.
> Employment: 100% local.
> Ownership: Local commercial enterprise.

> Craft workshops
> Swimming, water sports
> Walking, trekking, hiking
> Horse riding

Ard Nahoo IRELAND

Situated in the North Leitrim Glens in the north of Ireland, Ard Nahoo offers a number of recently constructed eco-cabins, sleeping 2–10 people; 'eco', 'yoga' and 'mammas & papas' retreat packages are available at the adjacent health farm. Here you can relax by using the steam room, detox box sauna and hot tub, by joining yoga and meditation sessions in a specially constructed studio or by just indulging in a bit of night-time stargazing. There are plentiful opportunities for outdoor pursuits such as hiking, mountain climbing, swimming, kayaking and even surfing around Sligo Bay.

> Certified to the European eco-label standard.
> Materials: All new building work on the eco-cabins is timber-framed, with local cedar cladding from sustainable forestry projects; minimal use of concrete and no petrochemicals. Hemp insulation and eco-paints used throughout.
> Energy: Wood-pellet stoves provide the space heating.

> Dance, music
> Farm work
> Swimming, water sports
> Walking, trekking, hiking
> Yoga, health farm

> Conservation projects: Ard Nahoo is part of the international WWOOF (World Wide Opportunities on Organic Farms) organization. Litter-picking and other conservation projects for nearby Loch Nahoo. Local tree-planting.
> Food supplies: All food provided for 'retreats' packages is locally produced, vegetarian and organic where possible. Cultural events: A Celtic nature trail describes native trees and plants and their role in Celtic myth, legend and folklore; it forms part of the Meditation Mandala, a contemplative walking circle. Visitors are encouraged to attend local cultural events, such as traditional Irish music sessions around Dromahair.
> Employment: 100% local.
> Ownership: Local commercial enterprise.

Uig Youth Hostel UK

Sample the austere beauty of the north of the legendary Isle of Skye, off Scotland's west coast. Now accessible by a dramatic toll road bridge, the island's scenery takes the breath away. The 60-bed hostel overlooks the Little Minch channel towards the Western Isles and, if the fancy takes you, there is a daily ferry service to spirit you across the waters to Tarbert on Harris or Lochmaddy on North Uist. Skye is true walking country, with a wealth of landmarks to aim for, such as the Fairy Glen, the Pinnacles of the Quiraing or Old Man of Storr.

> Certified by the Green Business Tourism Scheme, scoring an overall 'Gold Standard' against 60 criteria.
> Materials: FSC wood products are encouraged.
> Energy: Efficient combination of lighting, heating, appliances, insulation and renewable energy use; new boilers have been installed.
> Water: Good maintenance of low-consumption and low-flush appliances; rainwater harvesting.
> Consumables: Products made from recycled materials; eco-cleaners.
> Waste: 'Eliminate, reduce, re-use, recycle' practices minimize waste; supplier take-back agreements; glass, cardboard, tin, paper recycling.

> CO2 emissions: The hostel aims to minimize visitor car use by promoting local or human-powered transport.

> Conservation projects: All visitors are informed about the hostel's responsible green charter and the importance of working with the local community and using local resources. The hostel regards corporate social responsibility reporting as a priority.
> Food supplies: Much is sourced from local butchers, bakers and contractors.
> Employment: 25–49% local.

> Ownership: Not-for-profit national enterprise.

> Walking, trekking, hiking

Refúgio Ecológico Caiman BRAZIL

Founded twenty years ago, the Caiman Ecological Reserve (CER) celebrates and actively contributes to the conservation of the unique and vast area of wetland called the Pantanal, straddling Brazil, Paraguay and Bolivia. The CER is a symbiotic operation involving a 53,000-hectare (131,000-acre) beef cattle-raising farm, Estáncia Caiman, the Caiman eco-lodge, a private nature reserve of 5,600 hectares (13,800 acres) and an extensive ecological research programme. CER lies on the road between the state capital, Campo Grande, and Corumbá in Mato Grosso do Sul, south-western Brazil. There are three lodges: Sede (25 people), Baiazinha (12 people) and Cordilheira (16 people), each equipped with hot showers, other modern facilities and swimming pools. Guests are allocated to a lodge upon arrival. Common areas feature brightly coloured sofas and walls blending with natural materials and ranch-style furnishings. With three main seasons – rainy, intermediate (*vazante*) and dry – the Pantanal changes from a landscape of lakes to dry savannah, giving it an extraordinary richness of flora and fauna. Take an excursion on horseback or canoe with a local guide to see the birdlife and, if you are lucky, an endangered hyacinth macaw or even a prowling jaguar or puma.

> Certified to Brazil's eco-tourism standard, PCTS.
> Energy: Solar panels for hot-water heating; employees are encouraged to keep to monthly consumption targets in their accommodation.
> Water: Guests are encouraged to conserve water.
> Consumables: Biodegradable detergents and soaps; recycled paper; non-disposable cups for guests to take on tours.
> Waste: There is a recycling programme developed with the local community to separate inorganic waste, such as aluminium cans, paper, glass and PET, and to generate revenue for the community from selling it.

> Conservation & socio-cultural projects: The lodge helps local associations such as REPAMS (Associação dos Proprietários de Reserva Particular do Patrimônio Natural) and the WWF Hyacinth Macaw Project. In 2004, the 5,600-hectare (13,800 acre) Private Reserve of the Natural Patrimony (PRPN) 'Dona Aracy', within the land husbanded by the Caiman Ecological Reserve (CER), received official recognition. A permanent exhibition in the environmental interpretation centre reveals and celebrates the natural and socio-cultural riches of the Pantanal. CER is currently involved in 12 different research and conservation projects.
> Food supplies: All food is sourced from within 50 kilometres (30 miles) of the refuge.
> Cultural events: All guests experience firsthand the culture of the Pantaneiros who live and work in this amazing biome.

> Employment: All Pantanal tours use local guides with good knowledge of natural history. The project's aim is 100% local employment.
> Ownership: National commercial enterprise.

> Cycling, mountain biking
> Farm work
> Swimming, water sports, canoeing
> Walking, trekking, hiking
> Wildlife safari
> Horse riding, cattle driving

Hog Hollow Country Lodge SOUTH AFRICA

Sitting on the edge of the Tsitsikamma mountains near the edge of the Matjies river gorge, this lodge comprises 15 luxury suites in a private reserve that is being restored to indigenous trees and shrubs. Here in the renowned Garden Route of South Africa, nature is really on your doorstep. Rooms are furnished to a high standard, mixing contemporary modern with African detailing. Various leisure activities, from hiking to elephant riding and roaming the nearby beaches, vie with a lazy day by the pool. Local wildlife includes monkeys, baboons, bush pigs, porcupines and a diverse bird life. The communal facilities by the main house are an ideal place to relax by telling stories in front of the *boma* (open fire).

> Energy: Lighting is low-energy and set to timers.
> Water: Greywater is used to irrigate the gardens; rainwater tanks for lodge supply.
> Waste: Biodegradable materials are recycled via a local pig farm; paper, glass and cardboard are recycled.

> Conservation & community projects: The Lodge supports ORCA, a marine conservation organization that monitors the coast between Tsitsikamma and Robberg Nature Reserves. Wattle is slowly being replaced on the estate by indigenous trees and shrubs. A local soccer team is sponsored and an extra teacher funded at a school for the Kids of Kurland project.
> Food supplies: Ad hoc local food until the supply chain improves, but emphasis is on quality.
> Employment: 100% from local villages.
> Ownership: Local commercial enterprise.

> Swimming, water sports
> Walking, trekking, hiking

Eco-cottages at Mohua Park NEW ZEALAND

At the southernmost tip of New Zealand's South Island lies the area known as the Catlins. Here bird-rich beech and podocarp forest flourishes alongside farmland. In this sub-Antarctic climate it is possible to see Yellow-eyed penguins, petrels and sealions. The solitude and wildness make an ideal setting for four energy-efficient eco-cottages at Mohua Park, Tawanui, an 8-hectare (20-acre) native forest reserve. To sit on the veranda of one of these simple, well-insulated, solar-powered dwellings is to experience something of rural Kiwi life. The self-catering cottages sleep two people, perfect for nature enthusiasts or city-dwellers seeking a peaceful getaway. The cottage managers offer a number of wildlife treks and volunteer conservation work.

> Catlins Wildlife Trackers operate a comprehensive environmental management policy, manifest in the buildings and surroundings.
> Materials: Timber, solar panels.
> Energy: Passive solar-energy design with fully glazed north wall, double glazing, double-door heat lock; energy-efficient heat pumps; water heating by Solartherm panels.
> Water: Gravity-fed rainwater collected from roofs and filtered.

> Conservation & community projects: The Sutherlands have run an eco-tourism operation in the Catlins for eleven years, encouraging diverse conservation projects in cooperation with the Department of Conservation. The couple are also involved in and contribute financially to a variety of heritage, conservation and wildlife organizations locally.
> Food supplies: Local food suppliers preferred.
> Employment: 100% local.
> Ownership: Local family-owned commercial enterprise.

> Volunteer work
> Walking, trekking, hiking

Sadie Cove Wilderness Lodge USA

The accolades for this amazingly sited wooden lodge are impressive, with endorsements from the International Ecotourism Association, Green Globe, Co-op America and Condé Nast's top ten green US destinations. Just 16 kilometres (10 miles) from the Alaskan town of Homer, set on a forested waterside in the Kachemak Bay State Park on the Kenai Peninsula, this small, exclusive lodge is a dream location for leisure tourists, adventure seekers or serious nature-lovers. Guest numbers are deliberately kept below ten to minimize impacts on the wildlife and environment. The hosts, the Iversons, offer warm hospitality, whether visitors want to pursue energetic sports such as 'glacier' kayaking, sailing, skiing or snowshoeing or stay on terra firma to watch bears and mountain goats. Take a whale-watching trip and you are likely to see bald eagles while out at sea. Visit native villages, where indigenous arts, crafts and cookery skills are retained.

> Green Globe 21 benchmark, certified in 2006.
> Materials: The lodge was hand-built from driftwood and other natural materials, including a salvaged wooden boat.
> Energy: 100% alternative energy from hydroelectric system.
> Water: From mountain springs and steams.
> Consumables: Detrimental chemicals are avoided.
> Waste: Grey- and foul-water all treated before being allowed back into the hydrosphere; all possible materials recycled through the Alaskan Materials Exchange.
> CO2 emissions: A blue spruce or white birch tree is planted for every guest who stays in the lodge.

> Conservation projects: The lodge is working on a project to create a mountain goat sanctuary; supports local conservation organizations.
> Food supplies: Organic produce from the lodge gardens, wild Alaskan salmon and local organically reared meat; Fair Trade coffee.
> Employment: 100% local, including guides.
> Ownership: 100% locally owned and operated enterprise.

> Adventure sports
> Cycling, mountain biking
> Swimming, water sports
> Volunteer work
> Walking, trekking, hiking
> Wildlife safari

Camp Denali & North Face Lodge USA

No one can fail to understand the true meaning of the word 'wilderness' in the spectacular environs of Camp Denali and North Face Lodge, plumb in the middle of 6 million hectares of the Denali National Park, near Mount McKinley (also known as Denali) in Alaska. The former comprises 17 wooden cabins, each with a wood-burning stove, scattered over 27 hectares (67 acres) of open landscape. Not far away, near Moose Creek, is a former converted homestead that now is a cosy lodge housing 15 rooms with a convivial central space. With both these options in the same vicinity, you can choose extreme adventure in the Alaskan peaks or sunbathing on the patio, marvelling at the natural grandeur. Fresh vegetables emanate from the lodge's own greenhouses and are accompanied by Alaskan wild berries and produce.

> The company aspires to 'promote the integrity of Alaska's public interest lands through the philosophy, policies, and practice of environmental stewardship'.
> Materials: 'Green-building', locally made and recycled materials and products, such as 'Green Seal'.
> Energy: All electricity generated from a mixed system of fuel oil, propane, wood, trash, solar panels and hydroelectricity; the sites practise energy conservation; buildings are oriented to the south for solar gain.
> Water: Low-volume showerheads; bed linen changed twice weekly, not daily, reducing water and energy demands.
> Consumables: Environmentally safe cleaning products.
> Waste: Recycling of tin, plastic, glass, cardboard and mixed paper; wax-coated paper for starting the wood stoves; composting.
> Conservation projects: Guides are encouraged to follow the principles of 'leave no trace'.

> Food supplies: Priority is to source as much organic and Alaskan-grown produce as feasible; some food from own commercial greenhouse heated by waste heat from generator.
> Cultural events: The 'local' community is 145 kilometres (90 miles) away!
> Employment: Alaskan naturalist guides are hired; staff 25–49% local.
> Ownership: Local commercial enterprise.

> Cycling, mountain biking
> Swimming, water sports
> Walking, trekking, hiking
> Wildlife safari
> Nature photography
> 'Active learning' courses

Posada Amazonas PERU

Your adventure starts on the journey to Posada Amazonas, a community-built and part-owned lodge on the banks of the Tambopata River in the Amazonian jungle of Peru. Short flights from Lima or Cuzco take you to Puerto Maldonado, with daily buses to Infierno River port, where 6-metre-long boats take you 45 minutes upriver to the 30-bed lodge. The welcoming, open-space, communal dining room is ventilated by cool river breezes; individual rooms breathe naturally through the cane and clay walls. Activities include an ethnobotanical trail, learning local crafts and general wildlife observation, including from a canopy tower. Attractions include giant river otters, harpy eagles and macaws. This is an ideal place for a first visit to the rainforest. Keen nature-lovers can extend their visit at the nearby Refugio Amazonas (24 beds) or Tambopata Reserve Centre (18 beds).

> Materials: Traditional native materials (wood, palm fronds, wild cane, clay).
> Energy: Lighting by kerosene lamps, candles and wind-up lights only; refrigerators are gas-powered; generator is powered once a day for essential services.
> Consumables: Biodegradable soaps, shampoos and laundry products.
> Waste: All biodegradable material is composted on site; all glass recycled; all other waste transported by boat to town dump.

> Conservation & community projects: Rainforest Expeditions, the tour company managing Posada Amazonas, has a strong conservation ethic and is allied with research and monitoring programmes to preserve wildlife diversity. Guides from the native community receive conservation training. The presence of the lodge has encouraged improvements in infrastructure for health, education and transport while raising the human capital and skills in the community.

> Food supplies: Food is sourced from nearby Puerto Maldonado where possible; if not, it has to come in from distant Cuzco.
> Cultural events: The venture works with the local community in specific projects such as the ethnobotanical garden and the farm.
> Employment: 75–99% local, with emphasis on training and improving skills.
> Ownership: The lodge was built by the community and is jointly owned by the Ese Eja community of Infierno within their private reserve. The community receives 60% of the profit. Local and national mix of owners in a mixed cooperative and commercial enterprise.

> Dance, music
> Swimming, water sports
> Walking, trekking, hiking

Natural Lodge Caño Negro COSTA RICA

In the north of Costa Rica, near the Nicaraguan border, is an amazing area of wetlands recognized by UNESCO as a unique habitat of international importance. The Caño Negro National Wildlife Refuge, bounded by the Caño Negro lagoon and the Frio River, is home to over 350 species of birds, river turtles, caimans and more. This lodge has grown from small beginnings into a 22-bed complex of low-lying, salmon-red buildings set among the trees in the wetlands. A wide variety of tours is offered by boat, canoe or on foot, to experience the extreme biodiversity of the area and learn about the indigenous peoples. On your trips you are likely to encounter howler, white-faced and spider monkeys, as well as sloths and iguanas.

> Holds a Certificate for Sustainable Tourism (CST) award, three out of five 'leaves'.
> Materials: Certified resources or eco-labels are obtained where possible.
> Energy: Policy to reduce energy consumption.
> Water: Policy to reduce excessive use of drinking water.
> Waste: Recycling of waste materials is coordinated with a local school and women's group.

> Conservation & socio-cultural projects: The lodge is aware of its sensitive location within the reserve and supports its designation as one of the 'Ramsar' areas registered on an international database of wetlands sites under the Ramsar Convention Secretariat. Supports a reafforestation programme and local craft project.
> Food supplies: Local and international cuisine.
> Employment: 100% local.
> Ownership: International commercial enterprise.

> Swimming, water sports
> Volunteer work
> Walking, trekking, hiking
> Wildlife safari

Yelverton Brook Eco Spa Retreat & Conservation Sanctuary AUSTRALIA

Set in the wine-growing area of the Margaret River, just three hours south of Perth in Western Australia, is a group of one- and two-bed chalets in their own private, 40-hectare (100-acre) wildlife sanctuary. Each chalet is equipped with its own hydrotherapy spa. Although close to the white beaches of the Indian Ocean, huge karri forests and vineyards, you might just choose to stay within the reserve and watch the fascinating variety of wildlife that comes right up to your door. The hosts provide special food for the indigenous animals, which include woylies (small rat-kangaroos, also known as brush-tailed bettongs), possums, over 30 species of birds and more. Here is a slice of convivial Australian life, all in a Mediterranean climate.

> The establishment has held an Advanced ecotourism certificate with the Ecotourism Association of Australia since 1999.
> Materials: Local plantation timber where possible; handmade mud bricks.
> Energy: Chalets are oriented to maximize passive solar cooling and heating; well-insulated; energy-efficient lighting; efficient reverse-cycle air-conditioning units.
> Water: Water-saving taps and showers; own water supply from bore hole.
> Consumables: Recycled paper products only.

> Conservation projects: This is a conservation sanctuary for Australian bush life. Other efforts include sponsorship of a programme of breeding endangered species, ring-tailed possums and woylies, and other conservation, environmental and local programmes.
> Food supplies: Local produce for breakfast; hosts try to use mainly Western Australian suppliers, source organic food where possible and are in the process of setting up an organic vegetable garden.

> Employment: 100% local, family-run operation.
> Ownership: Local commercial enterprise.

> Farm work
> Walking, trekking, hiking
> Conservation work

Papillote Wilderness Retreat DOMINICA

Established over three decades ago, this verdant mountainside retreat is a botanical garden, guesthouse, public restaurant and volcanic spa pool, which is a beacon of responsible tourism in Dominica. Although close to the Dominican capital of Roseau, the lodge is secreted in a secluded and tranquil river valley. There are four-poster beds in most of the rooms or suites, the decor of which reflects the involvement of the local community, from the handicrafts and furniture to quilts, all set off by fresh flowers from the garden. Flowing water and lush plant life caress the gardens, which conceal several hot mineral volcanic pools surrounded by moss-covered stone carvings. Orchids, butterflies and abundant bird life cohabit this haven of relaxation. Just 15 minutes away by jungle trail are the Trafalgar Falls, a refreshing place to swim, and within easy reach are beaches, whale watching and some island-hopping.

> Energy: Hydroelectric power supplies the electricity; hot water comes from the local volcanic rocks; solar-powered and low-energy light bulbs.
> Water: Piped spring water is the source of bountiful drinking water and is also used for laundry.
> Consumables: Biodegradable soaps only.

> Food supplies: Creole food made from local market ingredients. The restaurant serves guests and locals alike.
> Cultural events: Papillote has a strong relationship with the local village of Trafalgar and encourages guests to explore and buy locally.
> Employment: 100% local.
> Ownership: Local commercial and not-for-profit enterprises.

> Conservation & socio-cultural projects: Papillote Tropical Gardens is a not-for-profit company supporting community development, education, job creation and awareness of indigenous plant conservation by establishing a seed bank. Collaborative research is undertaken with the Smithsonian Institution in Washington, DC, and Clemson University in South Carolina. In the wake of Hurricane David in 1979 the lodge became a focus of activity for retraining the community and formed a skills workshop called Pumpkin.

> Swimming, water sports
> Walking, trekking, hiking
> Wildlife safari
> Volcanic spa

Pousada Vale das Araras BRAZIL

The *pousada* is near the town of Cavalcante some 320 kilometres (200 miles) north-east of Brasilia in Goiás state. The area is characterized by savannah-like vegetation, known as *cerrado*, and table-top mountains (*chapadas*). Several waves of development have taken place over the last couple of hundred years – first gold, minerals and crystals, then cattle, and now, because of the inherent beauty of the landscape, the Chapadas dos Veadeiros National Park, it is becoming an ecotourism destination. Nine chalets are dotted around the lodge, which sits in its own private reserve. Each chalet is in muted natural colours with wooden features, simple, clean and close to nature. A glass of *chacaça*, sugar-cane spirit, will round off your day with nature.

> Guests are encouraged to recycle and conserve energy and water. The guesthouse and lodge are certified by the PCTS scheme.
> Materials: Brick, tiles, timber.
> Energy: There are no air-conditioning units or TVs in the chalets; 95% of the lighting system uses compact fluorescents; motion timers control certain areas.
> Water: Underground water is pumped to reservoirs and gravity-fed; toilets are low-flush at 6 litres (2 gallons) per flush.
> Waste: All garbage is separated and recyclable items donated to supplement income of those who sell on to recycling companies. Food waste goes to local farms or is composted; other waste is safely disposed of via the municipality.

> Conservation projects: The Brazilian government created a scheme in 2005 to enable private landowners to set up a private natural heritage reserve on 31 hectares (77 acres) of native *cerrado*, to offer environmental education for school groups and possibly to provide a refuge for injured or mistreated wild animals. New planting has been made.

> Food supplies: Some food is produced on the *pousada*; the rest comes from local producers.
> Employment: Local guides' association provides services, most being IBAMA (the Brazilian environmental agency) accredited. Staff are 100% local.
> Ownership: National commercial enterprise.

> Swimming, water sports
> Walking, trekking, hiking
> Birdwatching

Iona Hostel UK

Bracing westerly winds and a sense of beautiful remoteness are guaranteed at the private hostel on this 24-hectare (59-acre) croft with the lovely name of Lagandorain ('the hollow of the otter'), on the island of Iona, off the Isle of Mull in western Scotland. Accommodation is in five bedrooms, each sleeping two to six people. There is a well-equipped communal kitchen and dining area. An evening ferry service daily between April and August brings the tourists, who head to Iona Abbey and contemplate the rigours that St Columba must have endured in this centre of Christian learning dating from AD 600. Today's visitors find a landscape of wild flowers, grazed pastures, curious black Hebridean sheep and plentiful fresh air.

> Gold Award in the UK's Green Business Tourism Scheme. The hostel owners are members of Tourism Concern and Responsible Travel.
> Materials: The building treads lightly on the land with a non-load-bearing foundation, utilizing sixteen old wooden telegraph poles and reclaimed timber from the whisky industry; marmoleum is a natural linoleum floor covering.
> Energy: Insulated beyond building regulation requirements; triple-glazed windows; future option to source energy through a local group.
> Consumables: Biodegradable and safe cleaning products are used.
> Waste: Paper, glass, metals are recycled.

> Conservation & socio-cultural projects: A large part of the croft is in an Environmentally Sensitive Area (ESA) and the owners work with the National Trust on the Corncrake Scheme.
> Food supplies: The owners are active members of Slow Food and promote the supply of local, regional and organic foods, including eggs from their own ducks. Iona has just become a Fair Trade island.
> Employment: Run by local owner.
> Ownership: Local commercial enterprise.

> Swimming, water sports
> Sea activities
> Walking, trekking, hiking
> Local businesses offer a range of activities

Country Hotel Anna ICELAND

The clutch of buildings that forms Country Hotel Anna nestles together for comfort in the dramatic and starkly beautiful landscape of Moldnúpur under the watchful eye of Eyjafjöll – 'The Island Mountains'. With just five rooms, this is an intimate, congenial hotel that allows you to explore the vast open spaces of the Icelandic terrain. Traditional Icelandic meat soup, lamb, salmon and trout make for a nourishing menu to set you up on those walking expeditions. Here you can experience deep quietness in spectacular surroundings.

> The hotel is Green Globe 21 certified.
> Energy: Energy use is monitored using own electrical power and heating plant.
> Waste: All waste is recycled.
> Consumables: Environmentally tested soaps and detergents.
> CO_2 emissions: Trips to obtain local supplies are reduced in frequency to limit CO_2 vehicle emissions.

> Conservation projects: Tree-planting annually on the 200 hectares (495 acres) surrounding the hotel, which is all dedicated to wildlife.
> Food supplies: Local supply chains are supported through a scheme called Farm Holidays.
> Cultural events: Woollen garments made locally or by family relatives are sold. The local history, including the work of the renowned Icelandic writer Anna of Moldnúpur, and walking in the area are promoted.
> Employment: 75–99% local.
> Ownership: Local commercial enterprise.

> Walking, trekking, hiking

Hoopoe Yurt Hotel SPAIN

You may rub your eyes as you try to reconcile these Mongolian and Afghani yurts with your location in Andalusia, southern Spain. In a new trend sweeping western Europe, these authentic nomad dwellings are rooting themselves all over the countryside. Here at Hoopoe, surrounded by three hectares (seven acres) of olive groves, the Grazalema mountains visible in the distance, it is possible to dream. All yurts are lavishly furnished in Mongolian style, each one with a different atmosphere according to setting and detailing. Spring visitors will enjoy the wildflower meadows, which include orchids and a wide range of migrating birds and birds of prey such as the black kite.

> Materials: Traditional willow, chestnut poles, felt; traditional embroidery; stone platforms with wooden floors.
> Energy: Solar-powered camp.
> Water: Solar hot-water showers; freshwater pool.
> Waste: Composting toilets.

> Conservation projects: The olive groves, cork oak trees and meadows are being slowly managed to maximize biodiversity.
> Food supplies: All from a kitchen garden or locally produced.
> Employment: Partner-operated.
> Ownership: Small enterprise with overseas partner.

> Swimming, water sports
> Walking, trekking, hiking
> Birdwatching

Hotel Bourazani GREECE

Hotel Bourazani, set in the snow-capped Pindhos mountains in the north-western mainland Greece, took a significant step in its evolution as an educational wildlife park when the second generation of the Tassos family transformed a sheep farm into a wild game farm in 1974. Since then, the concept has grown and now the 205-hectare (507-acre) park is a model biodiversity project, the Bourazani Environmental Education Park, which organizes daily tours around the many trails. The park is home to 850 wild animals, including deer, wild goats and boar, and 690 flower species, including 50 orchids. Guest rooms are crisp, clean and traditional.

> Materials: Local vernacular stone buildings.
> Energy: Gas is used to reduce oil consumption in the kitchen.
> Water: Local source.
> Consumables: Biodegradable and safe cleaning agents are used.
> Waste: Waste is recycled. There is a liquid-waste treatment plant.

> Conservation projects: Local wildlife projects are supported in cooperation with universities in Greece and international organizations. The watermill of Bourazani was restored and transformed into the Centre of Water Movement, which grinds wheat and washes clothes.
> Food supplies: All food is locally sourced and guests are encouraged to take gastronomy tours to visit some of the suppliers.
> Cultural events: Guests are encouraged to take part in the Fiesta for Tsipouro (a local *eau-de-vie* drink) Distillery in Molivdoskepasti village each November. Traditional music and dance is supported.

> Employment: 100% local.
> Ownership: Local commercial cooperative.

> Adventure sports
> Craft workshops
> Dance, music
> Food and cookery classes
> Swimming, water sports
> Volunteer work
> Walking, trekking, hiking

Finca Esperanza Verde NICARAGUA

Situated in central Nicaragua at an altitude of 1,200 metres (3,930 feet), 'Green Hope Farm' is an eco-lodge comprising a variety of cabins set in a working organic coffee farm and nature reserve. This international cooperative won the Virgin Holidays Responsible Tourism Awards 2007 in the Small Hotel/Accommodation category as an exemplary practice of sustainable tourism that has generated local economic and community development. At any one time there is room for up to 26 guests in the cabins, with camping and options for homestays in the nearby town of San Ramón. An important development is a fully fledged organic cooperative coffee farm, bringing much-needed income to the area. Visitors can join in the coffee production and see how the beans are sundried, sorted and processed. Nature-lovers can enjoy a specially created butterfly farm, birdwatching and trekking with local guides. In the absence of light pollution, stargazing in the clear mountain air is a real bonus.

> Materials: Basic brick construction and local materials to enhance shading and natural ventilation.
> Energy: All cabins are equipped with solar power with deep-cycle batteries; hydro-generator is used during the rainy months when solar panels are less productive.
> Water: Spring-fed, certified potable water.
> Consumables: Low environmental-impact detergents and soaps.
> Waste: Waste water from the accommodation and coffee production is channelled to sedimentation ponds for cleaning; toilet facilities connected to septic tanks.
> CO2 emissions: Via reafforestation projects but not audited.

> Conservation projects: Many visitors come for the wildlife, especially birds such as toucans, mot-mots and weaver birds. The farm supports projects for reafforestation, school education and prevention of illegal logging. 10% of all earnings go to community development projects.
> Food supplies: Coffee production on the *finca* is certified organic by Bio-Latina and by the Rainforest Alliance and Fair Trade. Most food is produced in the local region; only wine is imported. Vegetarian food provided.
> Cultural events: A bonfire night with Nicaraguan music is held; and cooking classes are offered.
> Employment: 100% local staff including wildlife guides specializing in birds and butterflies.
> Ownership: A US-founded international cooperative, the Sister Communities of San Ramón, Nicaragua.

> Craft workshops
> Farm work
> Food and cookery classes
> Volunteer work
> Walking, trekking, hiking
> Conservation work

Esquinas Rainforest Lodge COSTA RICA

This venture is an example of cooperation between the people of Austria and the Costa Rican government leading to a viable model for ecotourism, conservation, research and community development. Situated 300 kilometres (185 miles) south of the capital, San José, in the Piedras Blancas National Park, near the Golfo Dulce and the Panamanian border in the south, the lodge is just a few kilometres from the Interamerican Highway. Rooms are decorated with panels woven by the indigenous Guaymi and Boruca Indians and can accommodate one, two or three people. The lush vegetation surrounding the lodge, including a hectare of tropical gardens and ponds, blurs the boundaries between inside and outside and ensures that the music of the cicadas, frogs and birds is omnipresent. Many wildlife and adventure tours enable visitors to explore every dimension of this amazing habitat.

> Certified to CST, the Costa Rican standard for sustainable tourism.
> Materials: The main building is thatched with palm on a wooden frame.
> Water: The Quebrada Negra stream borders the property, feeding the pool and other amenities.
> Consumables: No chemicals are used in the swimming pool.
> Waste: All solid wastes are separated and recycled; plastic bottles and metal cans are avoided where possible; organic waste is composted using worm culture; bio-system waste-water treatment ponds; special septic tanks.

> Conservation projects: Rainforest of the Austrians, the mother organization of Esquinas Lodge, has purchased and donated many properties to the Costa Rican government. Over 3,200 hectares (7,900 acres) have been incorporated into the Piedras Blancas National Park, which has two salaried wardens. The University of Vienna runs a project to reintroduce scarlet macaws. There's also a fund for the local village, where the first project involved installation of a water system for 70 houses. A women's craft and cosmetics cooperative also receives support.
> Food supplies: Organic vegetables and fruit are grown on the property, and additional fruit, vegetables, eggs and cheese are purchased from the local village of La Gamba; organic coffee from a cooperative in Coto Brus; fish from the Golfito fishermen.
> Employment: Guides for horse-riding and boat tours are local, as are the operators; staff are 75–99% local.
> Ownership: International commercial enterprise.

> Adventure sports
> Cycling, mountain biking
> Farm work
> Swimming, water sports
> Volunteer work
> Walking, trekking, hiking
> Wildlife safari
> Conservation work

La Cusinga Eco-Lodge COSTA RICA

Set within the 250-hectare (620-mile) nature reserve of the Finca Tres Hermanas, La Cusinga Eco-Lodge is dedicated to the wildlife and ecology of the wild southern Pacific coast of Costa Rica. Accommodation is provided in ten simple but carefully crafted cabins made from trees taken directly off the land, varying from the 'honeymoon suite' to double, single or shared dormitory rooms, all with sea vistas. A commitment to treading lightly is evident in the ethos and fabric of the lodge, which takes its name from the fiery-billed aracari, just one of the hundreds of birds that can be seen from the extensive primary forest trails. The location on the border of the Ballena Marine National Park, designated to protect the humpback whales, gives unique access for international and local visitors alike.

> Materials: Local trees, stone, shells and sand.
> Energy: 100% solar collector for hot water and micro-hydroelectric supplies.
> Water: There is no pool at Cusinga as the sea is already there. Guests are taught the value of water conservation. There is always local filtered fresh water to drink.
> Consumables: Refillable containers are used where possible and disposable drinks containers avoided.
> Waste: Recycled, composted or taken for safe municipal disposal. Black- and greywater is treated.

> Conservation & socio-cultural projects: The lodge is a member of ASOPARQUE, which manages the Ballena Marine National Park, WWF, TIES and many others, and is involved in conservation activities on land and water, hosting educational programmes and fun days for schools and communities. Projects have encouraged reafforestation and wildlife conservation over three decades.
> Food supplies: Come mainly from the farm and garden, local suppliers and organic products.
> Cultural events: La Cusinga and Finca Tres Hermanas have been deeply involved with the local communities for over thirty years and can suggest and advise on cultural activities.
> Employment: More than 90% local volunteers.

> Swimming, water sports
> Volunteer work
> Walking, trekking, hiking
> Birdwatching

Rawnsley Park Station AUSTRALIA

Just five hours by road from Adelaide, South Australia, on the southern side of Wilpena Pound, sits the 2,500 hectare (6,180-acre) Rawnsley Park Station. Here the landscape bears testimony to 150 years of settlers' struggles to pastoralize the wild landscapes near the Flinders ranges. Today, thanks to the present owners, the land supports a burgeoning biodiversity of flora and fauna while maintaining a stock of 600 sheep. The modernist luxury eco-villas blend Outback vernacular with the latest eco-tech thinking, incorporating wooden floors, traditional verandas and a retractable ceiling for stargazing. Accommodation also includes a caravan park and camping. Bushwalking, horse riding, mountain biking and guided 4WD-tours form part of the experience.

> Certified to Advanced grade by Ecotourism Australia. The eco-villas incorporate features for passive cooling (verandas, overhanging eaves), all on a suspended-thermal-mass concrete slab to reduce temperature fluctuations.
> Materials: Rendered straw bales, concrete, recycled timber, double-glazing.
> Energy: Passive solar design reduces energy demand.
> Waste: A Biolytix waste-water treatment system generates water for sub-surface irrigation.
> CO_2 emissions: The resort audits CO_2 emissions with Carbon Planet.

> Conservation projects: Owners and the South Australian Department of Environment & Heritage jointly manage 1,000 hectares (2,500 acres) of the property. Rangers from the Flinders Ranges National Park near by help control feral animal populations (goats, rabbits, foxes, cats) while monitoring vegetation and kangaroo populations. The family is involved in many local community and tourism initiatives.
> Food supplies: Native foods are used wherever possible.
> Cultural events: Events such as the Hawker Race Meeting, sporting clubs

and area school are supported.
> Employment: 100% local, including three guides.
> Ownership: Local commercial enterprise.

> Swimming, water sports
> Walking, trekking, hiking
> Scenic flights, horse riding, guided walking tours

Hotel Hellnar ICELAND

Those with a penchant for moody, dramatic landscapes that are full of elemental power should head straight for the Snæfellsnes coastline of Iceland and the stripped-back aesthetic of this timber hotel-cum-guesthouse. This is the habitat of the Arctic fox and a plethora of bird life, with a landscape affording stunning panoramic sea, volcano and glacier views during the long days of summer. A welcoming interior, with vibrant yellows, provides a comforting contrast to the landscape, which blooms only briefly in the summer months. Different, refreshing and, like many modest but inspiring eco-destinations, this is the incarnation of one person's vision.

> The first hotel in Iceland certified by Green Globe 21.
> Materials: Sustainable certified timber, high insulation-value materials.
> Energy: All hydroelectric.
> Water: The policy is 'use water sparingly'.
> CO_2 emissions: There is a policy to minimize CO_2 footprint and use local, sustainable, certified materials and consumables where possible.

> Conservation projects: The owner worked with the municipalities in the Snæfellsnes peninsula during the certification process and supports the communities by contributing regularly to the Snæfellsnes Environmental Fund which he set up for the communities. The owner also frequently plants trees.
> Food supplies: Fish and eggs sourced from local suppliers.
> Employment: Employees mainly drawn from areas of high unemployment.
> Ownership: Local commercial enterprise.

> Adventure sports
> Walking, trekking, hiking
> Whale watching

adventure

Destinations included here have a strong focus on outdoor adventure
sports, such as trekking, climbing, snowboarding, skiing, kayaking
or other energy-intensive activities. Other destinations include those
where day-to-day physical activity is embedded in the experience.
This accommodation is often sited in dramatic and remote landscapes.

Ecocamp Patagonia CHILE

Ecocamp Patagonia, set in the heart of the dramatic granite peaks of the Torres del Paine National Park, was the first tourism company in Chile to obtain ISO14001 Environmental Management certification. Its geodesic domes, housing a maximum of thirty guests at any one time, echo the traditional Kawesqar hut dwellings of the nomadic peoples who used to roam this part of the coastline. The entire lodge is thus portable. Sightings of guanacos, foxes, chinchillas, skunks, wild rabbits and pumas are virtually guaranteed. Horses roam around freely, as the camp complex is not fenced. Long days, bracing winds and a sense of wilderness are the essential ingredients of this remote Patagonian experience.

> Eco-architecture: Lightweight, light-footprint; celebrating former indigenous designs; domes constructed on platforms above ground.
> Materials: Domes include galvanized iron frame, canvas and pine wood; decorated with local traditional materials and artworks.
> Energy: Solar lamps to light platforms and walkways; solar power for toilet chute fans; propane gas for heating water and cooking but wood calderas (kettles) and stoves may be installed.
> Waste: Composting toilets separate biodegradable solids and liquids; all other waste compacted and taken off-site for disposal.
> CO_2 emissions: Once a year the emissions generated by the guests' travel by air and by vehicle from Punta Arenas are offset.

> Conservation & community projects: Support of small local businesses.
> Food supplies: Some products from local farms.
> Employment: 75–99% local.
> Ownership: Local commercial enterprise.

> Adventure sports
> Walking, trekking, hiking
> Wildlife safari

Tiger Mountain Pokhara Lodge NEPAL

Kathmandu has long been a trekking centre for international travellers but development has not always respected the region. Tiger Mountain Pokhara Lodge offers a fresh, sustainable perspective with its stone-built cottages following vernacular practices and hospitable common facilities. You can dine off the land with organic local vegetables, jams, honey and spicy eggs for breakfast, while feasting on the incredible vista of Himalayan peaks in the distance. On treks and walks, hundreds of species of bird and butterfly provide continuous entertainment. More adrenaline-charged activities include microlight flying and paragliding. Either way, you'll find pure mountain air coursing around your lungs and toughened calf muscles at the end of your stay.

> Materials: Local vernacular materials, stone, timber.
> Energy: Nepal Electricity Authority provides electricity from hydro-power; solar heating of water in some rooms.
> Water: From a local spring, by agreement with the local community.
> Waste: Recycled or composted as much as possible.

> Conservation & cultural projects: With an affiliated charity, the International Trust for Nature Conservation (UK-registered), supports community forestry projects via the Community Support Partnership, which is also involved in local schools. Guides raise conservation awareness and monitor wildlife populations.
> Food supplies: Organic garden; local farm produce.
> Employment: 100% local.
> Ownership: Joint venture between local and foreign shareholders; commercial enterprise.

> Adventure sports
> Food and cookery classes
> Walking, trekking, hiking
> Birdwatching
> Yoga, massage

Whitepod SWITZERLAND

Alpine ski resorts are synonymous with high environmental-impact tourism, so it is refreshing to see a resort determined to show that there is another way. Nine geodesic pods, 1,400 metres (4,600 feet) up in the Swiss Alps, are dotted around a century-old central lodge, which provides all eating, bathing and spa facilities. The canvas pods literally 'tread lightly', suspended on a wooden platform, which also acts as a terrace. Each is heated by a wood-burning stove and lit from rechargeable batteries or using traditional storm lamps. The double-bedded Expedition pod and Pavilion pod are respectively 25 and 50 square metres (269 and 540 square feet), whereas the Group pod, which sleeps eight, measures 55 square metres (590 square feet). Open between 1 December and 30 April, Whitepod offers an intimate experience with nature on its private ski runs. For its well-publicized eco principles, it has won the First Choice Responsible Tourism Award.

> Materials: For the pods: timber, canvas, natural materials for interior decor; lodge refurbished using local materials.
> Energy: Wood-burning stoves, wood from sustainably managed Swiss forests.
> Consumables: Ecover cleaning products.
> Waste: All waste is either composted or recycled.
> CO_2 emissions: Partnership with Cool Earth to offset all carbon emissions on the resort, including guests' travel. Discounts are offered to guests making all or part of the journey by train.

> Conservation & community projects: Whitepod has opened a grocery store for residents and a ski lift for schoolchildren. Furniture is sourced from a small local 'atelier protégé' (protected workshop), an enterprise for people with special needs.
> Food supplies: Swiss cuisine based on local produce delivered in returnable wooden crates. Priority to organic or Fair Trade produce and Whitepod works with a local food and wine association.
> Cultural events: A visit to the Whitepod refuge at 1,800 metres (5,900 feet).

> Employment: 100% local.
> Ownership: Local commercial enterprise.

> Adventure sports
> Craft workshops
> Dance, music
> Food and cookery classes
> Walking, trekking, hiking
> Wildlife observation tours
> Observation tours

Aurum Lodge CANADA

Close to Banff and Jasper National Parks in the Canadian Rockies, the lodge is at an elevation of 1,350 metres (4,430 feet) overlooking Abraham Lake and surrounded by forests and mountain peaks. Tumble out of the door to find yourself in a natural all-season playground for leisurely strolls or serious trekking, for example, in the Kootenay Plains Ecological Reserve. The choice of site, passive solar design, solar panels and renewable electricity suppliers help minimize the carbon footprint, and the hosts believe that their holistic 'educational' approach helps guests to rethink their own actions and habits while having instant access to outdoor activities.

> The development demonstrates a balance between passive architecture, suitable technologies and an appropriate day-to-day management system. A guest manual encourages low 'eco-footprint' behaviour.
> Materials: Locally available materials predominate.
> Energy: Solar renewable technologies produce 60–70% of needs, supplemented with energy sourced from renewable supplies.
> Water: Low-flow showerheads.

> Employment: Family-run.
> Ownership: Locally owned enterprise.

> Adventure sports
> Swimming, water sports
> Walking, trekking, hiking

Pousada dos Monteiros BRAZIL

This *pousada*, in the southern Mato Grosso region of Brazil, is set in the big skies, lakes, rivers and amazing biodiversity of the Pantanal, the world's largest freshwater complex. It is based at two distinct ranches of 20,000 hectares (49,400 acres), some 36 kilometres (22 miles) apart: the São Roque *fazenda* in the foothills of the Maracaju mountains, and the São João *fazenda*; both are for fattening Nelore and Brangus steers. The former farm has three apartments and the latter five, all simply furnished in rural Brazilian style. The activities list is huge – from kayaking, fishing for piranha and boat rides on the Correntoso River to watch the amazing flocks of egrets rise into the sunset, to horse riding, helping with the cattle or offroading on motorbikes. After a hard day in the saddle, slip into a hammock on the veranda and enjoy a local barbecue.

> The farm is registered with the Brazilian Ministry of Tourism, PCTS Sustainable Tourism Programme, encouraging local and collective supply-chain management to promote responsible practices.
> Water: Policy to reduce consumption and manage water quality.
> Waste: Preference is given to biodegradable and re-usable materials; employees recycle metal and glass in the city.

> Conservation projects: Trees are cultivated around new grass seeding.
> Food supplies: Local fruit, juices and vegetables are provided seasonally from the farm garden; manioc is locally grown; farm cheese, yoghurt and milk; meat from the cattle; eggs from the chickens.
> Cultural events: The local São Sebastião feast (patron protector of animals) is celebrated on 21 January.
> Employment: 100% local.
> Ownership: Family-run local commercial enterprise.

> Adventure sports
> Craft workshops
> Farm work
> Walking, trekking, hiking
> Wildlife safari
> Horse riding
> Kayaking
> Piranha fishing
> Birdwatching

Korubo Safari Camp Jalapão BRAZIL

An up-and-coming eco-destination is Jalapão State Park in the northern state of Tocantins, bordering Bahia, Maranhão and Piauí. This is Brazil's dry outback country, called *sertão*, through which run crystal-clear rivers and streams. This strange juxtaposition creates a unique environment, protected by man-made 'preservation units'. Korubo has pitched the perfect camp by the Novo River (Rio Novo), where ten double-bedroom tents nestle under the shade of cashew and mangaba trees. Here in this surreal scenery range panther, jaguar, wolf, fox and wild dog and the endangered bird *pato de penacho*, or Brazilian merganser. This is definitely the place for adventurous souls who don't mind some serious offroad travel and want to experience the dramatic landscape in a little-known area.

> This is an under-canvas holiday restricted to small groups and certified by the Brazilian Sustainable Tourism Programme (PCTS).
> Materials: Canvas tents.
> Energy: Solar panels for lighting and solar cookers.
> Waste: Chemical and composting toilets; all waste is separated and taken back to a municipality for recycling.

> Conservation & socio-cultural projects: Korubo has invested in the Rio Novo community and encouraged the craft of *capim dourado*, the weaving of hats, baskets and bags from a golden-coloured grass. Legal support is offered to families who have lived on the land for more than fifty years but are facing the possibility of expropriation by the government for 'conservation'.
> Employment: 100% local, including guides.
> Ownership: Local commercial enterprise.

> Adventure sports
> Swimming, water sports
> Walking, trekking, hiking
> Wildlife safari

Juma Lodge BRAZIL

The Lodge sits on the banks of the Juma River, a tributary of the Solimões or Amazon River. Manaus, the capital of the north-eastern state of Amazonas, Brazil's largest, is situated at the confluence of the Amazon with the Negro River. Here begins the 100-kilometre (62-mile) journey to Juma Lodge. The 16 stilt houses or bungalows, each with its own river views and balcony, are perched well above the waters in the dry season but during floods the water level can rise up to 15 metres (49 feet), totally transforming the experience (inundated forest is known here as *igapó*). The richness of the timber contrasts strikingly with crisp white bed linen. This is a full-on sensory experience, providing comfort and privacy, except from the ubiquitous monkeys, toucans and macaws, but also the chance to sleep in a jungle hammock, fish for piranha, spot alligators, play with the pink river dolphins and or enjoy a sunrise river excursion.

> Certified by the Brazilian Sustainable Tourism Programme (PCTS).
> Materials: Built by traditional techniques from local timber with thatch from the babaçu tree. Other resources certified by IBAMA, the government department responsible for preservation and conservation.
> Energy: A generator for electricity during dinner.
> Waste: Taken by boat to Manaus for safe disposal or recycling, except sewage, which is treated on site.

> Conservation & socio-cultural projects: The lodge works with a non-profit organization, Eco Amazonas, affiliated to the Federal University of the Amazon, and with 40 families to conserve nearby forest: 3,500 hectares (8,650 acres) have been restored. A census of Mura Indians is being undertaken and their tribal language and culture supported.
> Food supplies: From the markets in the surrounding villages.
> Employment: 75–99% local, plus guides from the Amazon region for wildlife safaris.
> Ownership: Locally and nationally owned commercial enterprise.

> Craft workshops
> Swimming, water sports
> Walking, trekking, hiking
> Wildlife safari
> Conservation work

Bateleur Camp at Kichwa & other safari lodges KENYA

Africa has long provided a backdrop for safari adventures, from the early days of colonial exploration to today's big-game watchers. An international company, Conservation Corporation Africa (CC Africa), is at the forefront of the challenge to balance the development of wildlife safaris with social and environmental issues, knowing that more and more people aspire to safaris that offer a modicum of luxury, yet that companies totally reliant on an abundance and diversity of wildlife have to protect this resource for locals and visitors alike. CC Africa runs a variety of locations throughout Africa, supporting conservation projects at each. Bateleur Camp at Kichwa is typical of the type of camps operated, with small numbers of accommodation units and/or tents, built mainly from local material and carefully sited among existing trees. Although the impact at each site can be managed, there are other less tangible impacts that need to be considered – frequent human presence in wild habitats, access with diesel or petrol 4WD vehicles and large transit distances by road or air for visitors and some supplies. This type of safari adventure is therefore naturally the preserve of the better-off and it remains 'exclusive' rather than 'mass market' ecotourism. Ironically, this can have some hidden benefits in the form of reduced human traffic and generous donations from wealthy visitors for local projects.

> Individual camps vary, but most aim to minimize their footprint by using hand construction, without disturbing existing trees, and to maximize their sensitivity to location. Eco-audits are undertaken at all camps and lodges to ensure best green practices are met.
> Materials: Local materials with minimal use of concrete.
> Energy: Energy-saving light bulbs in all locations; solar-power technologies in the company's East Africa lodges to reduce fossil fuel consumption in generators.
> Waste: All waste products are recycled.

> Conservation, education & health projects: A number of conservation measures are taken at Kichwa Tembo in Kenya, including protection of the riparian forest of the Sabaringo River

with fencing, ensuring rare species such as red-tailed monkey, Ross's turaco and Lühder's bushshrike can dwell in the diospyros and warburgia trees; to reduce the use of wood, fuel bricks are made from waste paper and coal dust; revegetation of the Sabaringo River by planting and protecting tree saplings cultivated in a nursery. Fast-growing figs and species that are less attractive to elephants and other browsers are selected. Extra saplings provide shade and prevent soil erosion in local villages. In western Kenya, CC Africa gives an annual grant to the Kakamega Environmental Education Programme (KEEP). Kakamega is Kenya's only true rainforest, with an enormous wealth of biodiversity, but is threatened by encroaching human settlement. KEEP promotes the value of Kakamega as an important water catchment, a site for renewable forest resources and a source of income. CC Africa donates

a significant amount of money annually, including donations from guests, to a partner not-for-profit organization, the Africa Foundation, for conservation and community projects, such as paying community landlords money for leases and buying services from local communities, including bush clearing and carpentry. Other initiatives include building of healthcare clinics, school classrooms and sponsorship of tertiary education, and small business development.
> Employment: 2,500 people, 90% from local communities.
> Ownership: International shareholders.

> Craft workshops
> Walking, trekking, hiking
> Wildlife safari

Loch Ossian Youth Hostel UK

Loch Ossian has more eco-design features than any other of the 63 hostels in the Scottish Youth Hostels Association. With no road access, this 20-bed hostel is strictly for serious walkers and trekkers who wish to experience the powerful scenery and relative isolation of Rannoch Moor, leading to the valley of Glen Coe (site of the infamous massacre in 1692), Ballachulish, Loch Linnhe and the Great Glen. The facilities are basic but more than compensated for by the all-encompassing experience of the natural setting. The whole hostel can be hired by individual groups.

> Certified to the Green Business Tourism Scheme, scoring an overall Gold Standard.
> Materials: FSC wood, bat-friendly paint!
> Energy: Efficient combination of lighting, heating, appliances, insulation and renewable energy use; wind and solar power generation.
> Water: Good maintenance of low-consumption appliances; rainwater harvesting.
> Consumables: Products made from recycled materials, eco-cleaners.
> Waste: 'Eliminate, reduce, re-use, recycle' principles; supplier take-back agreements; greywater treatment; dry composting toilet.
> CO_2 emissions: Hostel aims to minimize visitor car use by promoting local or human-powered transport.

> Conservation projects: All visitors are informed about the hostel's responsible green charter and the importance of working with the local community and using local resources. Hostel regards corporate social responsibility reporting as a priority.

> Food supplies: Some sourced from Fair Trade and the local estate.
> Employment: Only one employee but use of local wildlife guides is encouraged.
> Ownership: Not-for-profit national enterprise.

> Walking, trekking, hiking
> Wildlife safari

Capricorn Caves AUSTRALIA

A limestone rock formation with an above-ground complex of caves provides the unique setting for this camping, caravan and cabin park near Rockhampton in central Queensland. The two-bedroomed cabins are scattered through the bush, offering standard or deluxe accommodation in basic 'Outback style', with porches and verandas. There is plenty to explore in the caves, with guided tours for visitors or some serious wild caving adventures for diehard potholers. This is also an ideal place to absorb life in the bush and admire the local flora and fauna, including some rare ferns in the dry rainforest and bats in the caves.

> Advanced ecotourism certified by Ecotourism Australia.
> Materials: Sourced from renewable or recyclable materials.
> Energy: Deployment of efficient electrical equipment; use of natural light where possible; cooling provided by evaporative water system.
> Water: Rainwater harvesting off roofs; water minimization devices throughout the property.
> Waste: Minimization policy in place.

> Conservation & sociocultural projects: Control of feral animals to encourage local fauna; conservation of dry rainforest, including a rare fern, *Tectaria devexa*; conservation of caves, their bats and other fauna; special school camps are held and several cooperative tourism ventures are supported.
> Employment: 100% local.
> Ownership: Local commercial ownership.

> Adventure sports
> Walking, trekking, hiking
> Wildlife safari

Kalmatia Sangam Himalaya Resort INDIA

This resort in the Kumaon hills, near the Tibetan and Nepalese borders in northern India, lies 2,000 metres (3,280 feet) above sea level and nestles among cedars, pines, oaks, mimosa and wild cherry trees. A series of individually designed cottages is constructed in mixed colonial and Kumaoni style using predominantly local materials. Almost 400 kilometres (250 miles) of the snow-clad Himalayan chain can be seen from the patio of each cottage. Leisurely strolls can be mixed with serious trekking and birdwatching at the Binsar Wildlife Sanctuary, sightseeing at the 2nd-century BC temple of Kasar Devi or yoga under scented trees. Homestays in local villages can be arranged.

> No trees were felled in the construction of the resort.
> Materials: Handcrafted indigenous wood and stone.
> Water: In order to protect mountain springs, water-saving mechanisms are installed in toilets and rainwater is harvested in specially built tanks.
> Waste: Divided into biodegradable and non-biodegradable, most being composted or recycled.

> Conservation & cultural projects: The reserve is part of the Kalimat Estate, home to diverse birdlife as well as occasional leopards, jackals, hares, pine martens and foxes. Income from selling pashmina made by local women weavers is used to provide medical facilities for nearby Dina Hospital.
> Food supplies: Seasonal, organically grown local vegetables; salads from nearby villages.
> Cultural events: Local Kumaoni festivals include Nanda Devi, Ramlila, Raksha Bandhan and Bageshwar Mela, the latter also a national event.

> Employment: All employees are local except the resort manager. Villagers are trained as guides and occasionally take guests for homestays.
> Ownership: International commercial enterprise.

> Adventure sports
> Dance, music
> Walking, trekking, hiking

Estancia los Potreros ARGENTINA

This a 2,400-hectare (5,930-acre) working ranch (*estancia*) in the Sierras Chicas mountains, between the Andes and the Pampas. Four Anglo-Argentine generations have been custodians of the landscape since 1679. Accommodation comprises a shady colonnade linking individual rooms, which have beamed ceilings, whitewashed walls and a rustic simplicity. Los Potreros provides an insight into life tending cattle in the rural setting of the Cordoba hills, with daily opportunities to saddle the sure-footed Criollos or Paso Peruanos horses and explore or catch a game of polo. Herb-scented grassland provides food for foraging eagles, vultures and condors.

> Materials: Adobe mud walls.
> Energy: 90% solar heating and wind turbines; back-up generator; buildings face north to absorb sun.
> Water: Spring water and a policy to conserve.
> Waste: Bottles and plastics recycled.

> Conservation projects: The ranch is operated on a 'sustainable farming memorandum' to harmonize beef cattle production, a stud farm and local eco-systems. The farm management works closely with provincial park wardens and there is a no hunting and no shooting policy so that the puma is safe. The ranch supports a local school financially.
> Food supplies: The farm has an organic garden. Local and Fair Trade food is promoted.
> Employment: 100% local.
> Ownership: Local commercial enterprise.

> Swimming, water sports
> Horse riding
> Walking

Nipika Mountain Resort CANADA

Set up in the Rocky Mountains near Kootenay and Banff National Parks, Nipika is an operational logging lot, the unusual features being that all felling is selective and done with horse power and that visitors can go and watch. The rustic but comfortable cabins and most of the furniture were lovingly hand-constructed from locally worked lumber in the lodge's own woodworking shop, and the cabins are fitted with wood-burning stoves. This is an ideal summer base for gentle or strenuous wilderness activities, from wildlife spotting to white-water rafting. Alternatively, visit in winter and you'll be rewarded with plenty of cross-country skiing in the expansive, crisp mountain air.

> Materials: All locally felled timber.
> Energy: All generated via solar and micro-hydro-power; self-sufficient in energy.
> CO_2 emissions: Motorized vehicles are not allowed on any of the trails.

> Conservation & cultural projects: The Nipika Wildlife Foundation was formed as a non-profit agency to support sustainable and conservation practices in the forestry landscape to encourage biodiversity. Nipika Naturalist Guides are renowned. The resort supports the local cross-country ski community and the Wings Over the Rockies Bird Festival.
> Food supplies: Guests cook their own meals.
> Employment: 100% local.
> Ownership: Local commercial enterprise.

> Adventure sports
> Cycling, mountain biking
> Swimming, water sports
> Volunteer work
> Walking, trekking, hiking
> Winter sports, horse riding

leisure

Accommodation ranges from luxury designer villas to modest chill-out places, from beaches to mountains, all aiming to induce maximum relaxation. Here, the key ambition is to make the most of local offerings, customs and culture, while striving to tread a little more lightly. Sensitive hedonism is attainable in local and faraway destinations.

Bird Island SEYCHELLES

As the name suggests, this lodge is situated on a spectacular coral island swarming with bird life, just a short chartered flight from Seychelles International Airport at Mahé, 100 kilometres (62 miles) to the north. Established in 1973, Bird Island offers 24 chalets and a lodge complex with a crisp, spartan, but tropical aesthetic. This is not a glamorous five-star resort — there are no TVs, air-conditioning, room telephones or swimming pools — but there are 70 hectares (172 acres) and a 5-kilometre (3-mile) beach to explore, as well as friendly social evenings with other guests.

> Materials: Passive design to enhance shading and make the most of sea breezes.
> Energy: Mainly from generators.

> Employment: All local; some have been working there for over 25 years.
> Ownership: Partner-owned enterprise.

> Conservation projects: Conservation is at the heart of Bird Island. Whereas in 1967 just 18,000 pairs of sooty terns existed, now the colony is up to a million pairs. Two sea turtle species, threatened globally with extinction, sometimes nest on the island's beaches. Currently the lodge is the only member of Green Globe in the Seychelles.

> Swimming, water sports
> Walking, trekking, hiking
> Birdwatching, fishing

Hotel Posada del Valle SPAIN

This is a certified organic farm, situated near the north coast of Spain in the Asturias, which breeds rare Xalda sheep, Asturcon (or Asturian) ponies and Pita Pinta chickens. Wildflower meadows, a newly planted orchard and stock grazing on the hillside complete this rural idyll. Bright, colourful walls combine with exposed stone and wooden beams to create a modern feel to this traditional farmhouse. This is an excellent base for a walking holiday in a green, hilly corner of Spain.

> Materials: Originally the hotel was an Asturian farmhouse built out of stone and wood in 1899. New furniture is sourced from Forest Stewardship Council certified managed forests.
> Energy: Passive solar heating by south-facing glass areas; low-energy light bulbs; renewable energy supplied by Electra Notres; solar panels for hot water were installed in 2007.
> Consumables: Eco-label cleaning products.
> Waste: The hotel chooses supplies with minimal packaging and composts organic waste.

> Food supplies: Whenever possible the hotel uses local and organic produce from the rural Asturias.
> Employment: 100% local.
> Ownership: Local commercial enterprise.

> Farm and vineyard work
> Walking, trekking, hiking

Jean-Michel Cousteau Fiji Resort FIJI

This pioneering eco-luxury resort is carefully landscaped into 7 hectares (17 acres) of old coconut plantation overlooking the pristine waters of Savusavu Bay, on Vanua Levu, the second-largest island in Fiji. As one would expect from a resort that bears the famous Cousteau name, this destination displays a unique combination of environmental vision and cultural sensitivity. A full-time marine biologist and a Fijian guide and medicine man are employed to promote the resort's aims. Guests are encouraged to explore the forests, lagoons and beaches to learn about the ecology. The accommodation, all sensitively dovetailed into an elegant palm-tree landscape, comprises 24 Fijian-style thatched-roof *bures* with ocean or garden views. There is also an exclusive 168-square metre (1,808-square foot) villa – a multi-level decked construction with several rooms, pool and spa tub – the height of Fijian luxury.

> The villa on the resort was designed, using a mix of modern and traditional Fijian architecture, by the resort's general manager, Karen Taylor.
> Materials: The bures use thatch and stone, and decks are made of recycled wood product.
> Energy: Ceiling fans are used rather than air-conditioning units; solar power.
> Water: The resort constructed Fiji's first water-reclamation plant, using crushed coconut husks and recycled plastic water bottles to provide surfaces for aerobic breakdown of waste and filtration media. Water exiting the treatment plant irrigates wetland ponds and fruit trees.
> Waste: Composting on site.

> Conservation projects: The Namena Marine Protected Area, funded by the resort, has some of the most outstandingly diverse coral reefs in the Pacific and a calving site for the humpback whale in Fiji. Recreational activity here is restricted. The local village, not the government, controls the rights to the reef, including the world-class diving on the outer reef.
> Food supplies: An organic garden.
> Cultural events: A resident Fijian guide, Niumaia Kavika, takes guests to the local medicinal plants. The resort funded the Savusavu Community Foundation and encourages cultural activities for the guests, including traditional meals, market visits, coconut husking and learning basic Fijian language.

> Swimming, water sports
> Walking, trekking, hiking

La Lancha Resort GUATEMALA

Part of Francis Ford Coppola's Blancaneaux Resorts group, La Lancha is a collection of spacious jungle *casitas* connected by winding paths. The bright decoration of each *casita* is inspired by local artisan culture and decks and verandas offer spectacular views of the beautiful and unspoilt Lake Petén Itzá. Expect visits from the local howler monkeys. Tikal, one of the archaeological wonders of the world, is near by. Careful and sympathetic siting of all the buildings ensures a sense of seclusion, yet the resort is a mere half an hour by road from Flores International Airport.

> Materials: Most construction materials are locally or regionally sourced, especially sustainable hardwoods, Caribbean pine, bamboo, bayleaf thatch and ceramic and *saltilla* tiles.
> Energy: Good passive design means that no air-conditioning is necessary; low-energy light bulbs throughout; wind-up torches for guests.
> Water: Choice of locally adapted species for landscaping reduces watering requirements.
> Consumables: Local organic toiletries are used.

> The resort follows a sustainable tourism policy operated by Blancaneaux Resorts, covering in detail everything from design to everyday operations.
> Conservation & educational projects: La Lancha is a privately owned 'green zone' helping to maintain forest for the critical survival of howler monkeys. It is also part of 'Alimza Verde', a local conservation group encouraging low-impact tourism.
> Food supplies: The resort group has a policy of growing or obtaining supplies of organic and local food.
> Employment: 98% of staff are local.
> Ownership: International commercial enterprise.

> Wildlife safari, birdwatching
> Walking, trekking, hiking
> Swimming and other water sports
> Fishing

Levendi's Cottages & Estate GREECE

Perched on a hillside on the northern tip of the legendary Ionian island of Ithaca is the three-hectare (seven-acre) gated country estate called Levendi's. Guests can stay in the farmhouse or in private houses, each sleeping up to five, in the grounds. Four generations of the same family have produced organic olive oil from the ancient gnarled trees in this spectacular coastal setting. Tranquillity prevails, as guests leave their cars at the boundary of the estate. Perfumed gardens and summer dining areas on vine-strewn patios complete this miniature idyll. Enjoy a stroll through the landscape, a swim in the azure sea or a therapeutic massage, or dine on produce harvested from the organic garden. Various cafés and services are available in nearby villages. Where better to read a Homerian tale?

> Materials: Timber from sustainable managed forest on the estate.
> Energy: Solar power currently being installed; passive construction, maximizing cooling effects of sea breezes, negates need for air-conditioning.
> Water: Water is gravity-fed; greywater is used to water orchards.
> Consumables: All cleaning products homemade using natural materials and essential oils, as are personal care products.
> Waste: Organic waste composted.

> CO2 emissions: All guests are offered an option to offset their flights, have trees planted on the estate or donate to a Greek national reafforestation programme.

> Food supplies: Local organic produce whenever possible.
> Cultural events: Guests are introduced to local families to enhance cultural exchange.

> Employment: 100% local. Employees are all family members.
> Ownership: Family-owned commercial enterprise.

> Olive harvest
> Food and cookery classes
> Swimming, water sports
> Walking, trekking, hiking

Jake's JAMAICA

Vogue magazine once described Jake's as 'the chicest shack in the Caribbean', an accolade supported by its unique location and roll-call of celebrity visitors. This boutique hotel on Jamaica's south-west coast, near the fishing village of Treasure Beach, is actually a collection of 38 individualistic cottages that morphed out of an earlier backpacker haunt. It is the creation of the bohemian artist Sally Henzell. The cottages, each resplendent in its own ice-cream shade of paint, are set on diverse micro-sites – from wind-bracing rocky outcrops to secluded lush botanical gardens – so guests can feel their experience is genuinely unique. This laid-back retreat is part of a larger group of hotels around the Caribbean under the Island Outpost brand, but each retains its own distinctive local flavour. At Jake's this means jerk chicken, porridge, ackee with saltfish, fresh prawns and lobster.

> Materials: Local and organic materials.
> Energy: Solar-energy facilities.

> Conservation & socio-cultural projects: Jake's supports training of local farmworkers in organic husbandry; involved in raising money for the local BREDS Foundation to support community activities including IT and sports facilities for schools.

> Food supplies: Encourages local food supply from farms and fishermen.
> Cultural events: Mixing it up with the locals in Duggie's Bar.
> Employment: 100% local, including fisherman guides.
> Ownership: Local commercial enterprise.

> Craft workshops
> Dance, music
> Farm and vineyard work
> Food and cookery classes
> Swimming, water sports
> Volunteer work
> Walking, trekking, hiking
> Conservation work

Ponta dos Ganchos BRAZIL

Set in 3 hectares (7 acres) of lush vegetation on a privately owned peninsula jutting into the Atlantic on the southern 'Emerald' coast of Brazil, Ponta dos Ganchos is a luxury eco-resort comprising 20 discrete bungalows in rustic-chic style. Bungalows offer a variety of studio arrangements comprising bedroom(s), a living room, bathrooms, dry sauna and/or jacuzzi in single or split levels with private verandas. Activities range from water and adventure sports, including diving, and seeing the amazing marine diversity at the Brazil–Malvinas Confluence (of Atlantic currents), to trekking, walking and exploring the old Azorean Portuguese towns. Mussels from the local district of Governador Celso Ramos and Santa Caterina's world-famous oysters promise a seafood feast, along with varied Brazilian fare. There is even an annual gastronomic festival. Caressed by warm sea breezes, this idyll is strictly for hedonists.

> The resort was built horizontally to merge with the existing vegetation; bungalows are all freestanding; only 5% of the land is built on; traditional verandas and cross-flow ventilation provide good natural cooling. It is certified by the foremost Brazilian ecotourism scheme.
> Materials: Predominant use of timber.
> Energy: Local energy supply.
> Water: Local water supply.
> Waste: All sewage and greywater is cleaned and used for irrigation.

> CO2 emissions: Over 3,000 trees have been planted during the last six years; only electric cars are used on the resort.

> Conservation projects: None supported at the moment, but tree planting continues on the estate.
> Food supplies: Products are purchased from certified organic farms and producers.
> Employment: 89% local.

> Ownership: Local and international commercial enterprise.

> Adventure sports
> Swimming, water sports
> Walking, trekking, hiking

Locanda della Valle Nuova ITALY

Nestling in the well-tended countryside near Urbino, a medieval town on UNESCO's World Heritage list, is the 75-hectare (185-acre) organic farm that is the setting for the Locanda. An old renovated farmhouse provides diverse accommodation, from B&B rooms to self-catering apartments and a villa. Ancient oaks in the nearby woodlands are protected and nurture a rich flora and fauna. The output of the farm goes straight to the table, so guests can feast on the freshest of ingredients, including truffles from the woods. The spacious and colourful rooms are full of character. Here you can enjoy a wide variety of countryside activities, from horse riding to walking to joining the local dance. Rural Italy at its best.

> Materials: A traditional farmhouse built in the 1920s using local materials; restored in 1998 with double glazing and full insulation.
> Energy: High thermal insulation, plus solar collectors and a wood-burning stove (using own wood from farm); low-energy light bulbs; ceiling fans, not air-conditioning units.
> Water: Toilets with low-flush option.
> Waste: Recycling bins provided for cans, plastic and paper. Edible waste fed to the pigs.

> CO2 emissions: This is an organically run farm, so emissions are significantly lower than those typical of modern agricultural systems.

> Conservation projects: Being an organic farm in itself encourages biodiversity. Hunting is forbidden on the farm.
> Food supplies: 70% of the food served is produced on the organic farm; the rest is bought from other local farms.

> Cultural events: Basket-weaving courses, truffle hunting.
> Employment: 100% local.
> Ownership: Local commercial enterprise.

> Craft workshops
> Dance, music
> Swimming, water sports
> Walking, trekking, hiking
> Horse riding

L'Ayalga Posada Ecologica SPAIN

This homestay in Asturias, the green north-west corner of Spain, offers a space where people come together to eat home-cooked food and enjoy the simple pleasures of life. Restoration of this hundred-year-old country house has been executed with much attention to detail, applying bio-building and bio-climatic principles to exclude any potential pollutants. There are five rooms with wooden floors and beams complementing the functional furniture. Near by are the famed mountains of the Picos de Europa National Park and the Redes Nature Reserve, so you can go mountain walking or do some serious climbing.

> Materials: Lime mortar; natural oiled woods; little or no use of PVC; hemp insulation.
> Energy: Passive heating to south and east elevations; floor and wall heating with modern system; low-energy appliances; water heated by solar power.
> Water: Rainwater harvesting.
> Waste: Black- and greywater treated and recycled.
> CO2 emissions: Carbon footprint is being measured with a view to offsetting emissions.

> Conservation & cultural projects: Support for four organizations working for human rights, helping poor countries, ecology movements or underprivileged children. Guests are encouraged to make a donation of 1% of their room cost. Young Asturian horses are suckled on the land.
> Food supplies: All food prepared is certified organic; vegetarian available. Local products are sourced.
> Employment: Family-run; there are no paid employees.
> Ownership: Local family-run commercial enterprise

> Adventure sports
> Dance, music
> Farm and vineyard work
> Food and cookery classes
> Swimming, water sports
> Walking, trekking, hiking
> Yoga, Tai Chi

Can Marti SPAIN

Can Marti, on the Spanish island of Ibiza, is a leading example of sensitive agro-tourism, nestling into a terraced agrarian landscape of almond, carob and olive trees with a woodland backdrop. In this tranquil setting there are slower rhythms. The eco-architecture affords many passive features, such as the ancient thick walls to keep out the summer heat, with solar technology for energy needs. There are several studios and apartments, each decorated in Spanish or North African style and accommodating two to four people. The working farm is organic and there is a shop selling its produce to visitors and locals. The main farmhouse is several hundred years old and has been restored using an ecological approach.

> Materials: Local wood, clay, chalk, natural pigments and eco-paints and other eco-certified materials.
> Energy: Solar energy provides 50% of lighting and 80% of hot-water needs.
> Water: All rainwater is collected and used for irrigation.
> Consumables: Fair Trade products where possible.
> Waste: Waste water is treated in a reed bed; all other waste is recycled.
> CO2 emissions: The owners use a carbon offset scheme, Atmosfair, based in Germany, for any flights they take.

> Conservation & socio-cultural projects: Guests are taught the intricacies of compost-making. 7% of profits are given to support a school and orphanage in Tanzania.
> Food supplies: Organic produce is generated on the farm or bought locally, and Fair Trade tea, coffee and honey are served at breakfast.
> Employment: 100% local.
> Ownership: International commercial enterprise.

> Swimming, water sports
> Walking, trekking, hiking
> Yoga

Quinta do Barrieiro PORTUGAL

This complex of restored old buildings, landscaped grounds, pools and sculptures reveals the deep empathy of the owners, José Manuel Coelho, an architect, and Maria Leal de Costa, a sculptor, for the history and landscape of the locality. Set in the limestone and schist geology of the Serra de São Mamede Natural Park on the eastern border of Portugal, across from Spain's Extremadura region, the location offers peace, solitude and the beauties of nature. Attention to detail is everywhere, the result exuding a quixotic balance between modernity and tradition. The accommodation is self-catering but fresh local bread and breakfast food are provided. An assortment of unique houses, apartments, suites and rooms, each with its distinctive aesthetic character, fits a range of budgets. The farm serves as a mini sculpture park and you can visit Maria's atelier to see works in progress. Nearby Portalegre is a well-preserved old town well worth exploring.

> Certified to Green Key standards, the buildings were restored using sympathetic local materials and traditional skills.
> Materials: Certified resources or eco-label materials where possible.
> Energy: Double glazing to help with thermal temperature control; low-energy lighting.
> Water: Toilets with low-flush system.
> Consumables: Fair Trade and other eco-label products.
> Waste: Composting of organic waste, plus recycling of other materials.

> Conservation & socio-cultural projects: Guests are encouraged to be sensitive to the local environment and are introduced to art projects that refocus on nature.
> Food supplies: Local food supply is encouraged, especially from other farms in a scheme promoting regional food.
> Employment: 100% local.
> Ownership: Local commercial enterprise.

> Swimming, water sports
> Walking, trekking, hiking
> Tours arranged

Constance Le Prince Maurice Hotel MAURITIUS

Situated on the north-east coast of Mauritius, just 35 kilometres (22 miles) from the capital of Port Louis, this hotel resort is often found on the lists of awards for luxury hotels worldwide. There are nearly ninety suites dotted in informal groups around the well-vegetated and landscaped 60-hectare site, which abuts a lagoon; some are by the beach, others within a tropical garden facing the sea or on stilts overlooking the fish reserve in the lagoon. Local vernacular architecture, with extensive use of thatched roofs, blends with modern international style, and each suite has its own balcony or terrace. The restaurants and bars are set around the main pool or on the beachside. Full international five-star spa and terrestrial or aquatic sports facilities are available. The cuisine fittingly reflects the trading history of Mauritius, combining influences from the spice routes of Africa, Asia and Europe.

> The hotel's environmental management system is certified to Green Globe 21 standards.
> Materials: FSC or other certified materials sourced when required.
> Water: Water recycling for irrigation purposes.
> Waste: Grease traps and composting areas; recycling.
> CO_2 emissions: There are some measures in place to reduce the hotel's carbon footprint.

> Conservation & socio-cultural projects: There is a natural fish reserve (Barachois) surrounded by forest in the grounds of the hotel. The hotel engages in environment-consultative meetings with local stakeholders and takes part in environmental contests and projects with schools. Scholarships are offered annually for two local students to study in France or the UK.
> Food supplies: Local food procurement is encouraged.

> Employment: 75–99% local.
> Ownership: National commercial enterprise.

> Dance, music
> Swimming, water sports
> Walking, trekking, hiking
> Conservation work

Aruba Bucuti Beach Resort & Tara Beach Suites DUTCH CARIBBEAN

The resort is on the island of Aruba, part of the Lesser Antilles and the Dutch Caribbean, just off the Venezuelan coast. Comprising the main resort hotel and a separate apartment block, the Tara Beach Suites, this is everything a subtropical luxury resort should be. Decor is modern with cool whiteness and strong splashes of colour. There is a wide range of facilities for enjoying water-based activities, swimming in the pool or lazing in the spa. Cuisine is local and international, served, uniquely, in a replica 17th-century Dutch galleon. Visit the colonial architecture of Oranjestad, see the wild donkeys or just amble along a perfect beach.

> The resort is certified to Green Globe 21 standards, the environmental management standard ISO14001 and quality assurance standard ISO9001.
> Materials: Farmed wood for building and furnishings.
> Energy: Solar panels; electricity use is regularly monitored.
> Water: All monitored; waste water is treated and re-used for the gardens.
> Consumables: Only natural cleaning products.
> Waste: Recycling where possible – packaging, paper, glass.

> CO2 emissions: The resort encourages guests to purchase carbon-offset credits to offset airline emissions. Funds go to renewable energy projects.

> Conservation projects: Sponsor of Turtugaruba project to protect and educate people about sea turtles; sponsor of Animal Rights Aruba; board member of Arikok National Park. Involved in school mentoring programmes and promoting best environmental practice to other resorts.

> Food supplies: Aruba is arid, so there is little local food, but food is sourced regionally. Vegetarian food provided.
> Employment: 50–74% local.
> Ownership: Local commercial enterprise.

> Dance, music
> Swimming, water sports
> Volunteer work
> Walking, trekking, hiking

Hôtel Villas Les Goëlands FRANCE

The coastal town of Saint-Jean-de-Luz is close to the city of Biarritz in the extreme south-west of France near the Spanish border. This part of the French Basque region, also referred to as Gascogne or Gascony, offers the pleasures of the Atlantic coast, the dramatic Pyrenees mountains and a rich history. The hotel sits a couple of hundred metres back from the seafront in a wooded residential area and comprises two adjacent villas of strikingly different styles, one white and timbered, the other solid stone with wooden shutters. The atmosphere is family-friendly and there are some sea-view rooms with balconies. Local excursions can be made on hired electric bicycles.

> Management certified to La Clef Verte (Green Key) criteria.
> Materials: Good thermal insulation installed on all buildings.
> Energy: Rechargers and accumulators instead of batteries; solar collector for hot water; low-energy light bulbs; thermostats on radiators.
> Water: Rainwater harvesting for garden.
> Consumables: Recycled toilet and printing papers; phosphate-free detergents.
> Waste: Waste paper, newspaper, batteries, bulbs, ink cartridges and glass are collected and recycled; cooking oils and fats recovered for safe collection.
> CO_2 emissions: Electric bikes for hire.

> Employment: 100% local.
> Ownership: Local and national family enterprise.

> Cycling, mountain biking
> Swimming

Hotel Pension Hubertus AUSTRIA

Situated about halfway between Innsbruck and Graz, this family-run guesthouse, built in the 1950s, was the first pension in Zell am See, Austria, to be awarded the EU 'flower' eco-label and the Austrian ecotourism label. Rooms are bright and airy, with warm wood detailing. The pension enjoys a setting among some challenging mountains and a local lake, where outdoor pursuits include water sports, hiking in the summer season and a full range of adventure winter sports, as the cable-car lift to the local mountain, the Schmittenhöhe, is close by and leads to 77 kilometres (48 miles) of ski runs from black to blue grade. The pension has an informative website about local attractions and the operators will even book you a sustainable public-transport journey right to your destination – typical of their exceptional attention to detail and service.

> Materials: Mostly natural and local materials.
> Energy: Solar collectors for hot water and wood-pellet boiler for heating; eco-energy from the supplier Ökostrom; double-glazed windows; guests are encouraged to be energy-conscious.
> Water: Low-flow showers and low-flush toilets; guests are encouraged to minimize room linen changes to save water.
> Consumables: low-eco-impact cleaning products; recycled paper.
> Waste: Glass bottles recycled.
> CO$_2$ emissions: Guests are encouraged to use public transport, which is all close by. Every guest arriving by train gets a Clima Protection Certificate offset or Fair Trade gift.

> Food supplies: Local organic food including Salzburger Bio-Frühstück products, yogurts, honey; Fair Trade tea and coffee; the pension is a certified Bio Austria partner for organic products with control number AT-S-01-BIO 0476 V.
> Employment: 100% local.
> Ownership: Family-owned commercial enterprise.

> Adventure sports
> Dance, music
> Swimming, water sports
> Walking, trekking, hiking

The Lighthouse Hotel & Spa SRI LANKA

Sitting on a hilltop by the Indian Ocean, this hotel offers 60 deluxe rooms within a sensitively designed complex of buildings. Geoffrey Bawa, a leading Sri Lankan architect, created a diverse mosaic of spaces that continually contrast and interlink. Protection from the coastal elements combines with colonnades, verandas and stimulating vistas. He also commissioned an amazing bronze sculpture for the main stairwell. Jetwing, the owners, operate an extensive corporate social responsibility policy that has encouraged other operators in Sri Lanka to see its benefits. Numerous tours are offered for river, rainforest, savannah and mangrove wildlife safaris, as well as visits to see leopards and elephants at Yala National Park and to the old fort of Galle.

> Materials: Tiles, timber and other building materials sourced nationally.
> Energy: Solar heating is used in the spa and a full energy-management system is in place, under which unwanted equipment and lighting are switched off; energy-saving light bulbs throughout.
> Water: Water-saving cisterns; rainwater harvesting; guests are encouraged to minimize washing of laundry.
> Consumables: Suppliers are asked to reduce packaging; certified sources such as FSC, eco-labels and Fair Trade, are preferentially selected; all chemicals ending up in waste water are biodegradable; no aerosols are used; only organic fertilizers for the garden and grounds.
> Waste: Waste minimization is encouraged via the hotel's mantra, 'reduce, re-use, recycle'; there is a dedicated sewage treatment plant; some food waste goes to a local piggery.

> Conservation & cultural projects: Support is given through the Tree for Life programme, guests being encouraged to visit the local tree nursery in Hiyare and/ or donate a small amount. The hotel's naturalist works with schools and universities. Victims of the 2005 tsunami disaster have been supported with the Jetwing Tsunami Relief Fund. The hotel initiated the Taxi Service Through the Community scheme, training 45 youths to become local guides and taxi operators.
> Food supplies: Traditional Sri Lankan food, low-calorie options and international cuisine.
> Employment: 100% local.
> Ownership: Local commercial enterprise, Jetwing.

> Adventure sports
> Craft workshops
> Cycling, mountain biking
> Dance, music
> Farm and vineyard work
> Food and cookery classes
> Swimming, water sports
> Volunteer work
> Walking, trekking, hiking
> Wildlife safari

Udayana Eco-Lodge INDONESIA

Set on 30 hectares (74 acres) of bush land on Jimbaran Heights owned by a university, with views of Mount Agung and Jimbaran and Benoa Bays, this is a peaceful lodge-cum-hotel. Although the design is rather plain at first sight, detailing reveals Balinese craftsmanship and features, including traditional *ikat* soft furnishings. Open-air shower rooms are graced with ferns, making for a refreshing experience. Serving local organic food, the restaurant offers great views of Bali or the butterflies chasing around the gardens. Visits to the Ubud craft and cultural village, Balinese dances and nearby temples can easily be made.

> Materials: Fired clay tiles; modern building materials.
> Energy: Solar power for hot water, pumps and lighting; passive design to provide maximum wind cooling combined with shady colonnades, verandas and terraces.
> Water: A rainwater storage system.
> Waste: A biological sewage treatment plant generating irrigation water for the gardens.

> Food supplies: Organic and local produce.
> Employment: Local.
> Ownership: The lodge is professionally managed by INI RADEF, a foundation that encourages low-impact tourism while maintaining local culture.

> Dance, music
> Swimming, water sports

Palace Farm Hostel UK

London tourists requiring a little bit of respite would do well to jump on the train and enjoy a walking or cycling break in the Kent countryside. Palace Farm Hostel is a private hostel offering a range of en-suite rooms for two, four, five, six and eight persons, with a total capacity of 30 beds. The bright, modern conversion is arranged around a courtyard and is sensitive to local vernacular traditions on this working farm – a good example for any farmer wishing to diversify into eco-tourism. Bikes are for hire, complete with a set of maps, and the North Kent Downs Area of Outstanding Natural Beauty (AONB) is right on your doorstep. There are several pubs near by and Leeds Castle is not too distant.

> Certified to the Green Business Tourism Scheme, scoring an overall Gold Standard against 60 criteria. The building was designed with the aim of achieving maximum passive solar gain.
> Materials: Re-use of old farm buildings and reclaimed materials; fencing from local sweet chestnut coppice; outdoor picnic tables are FSC.
> Energy: High-efficiency wood-burning stove; high insulation specification; solar water-heating.
> Water: Ball valves regulate supply.
> Waste: On-site sewage treatment plant saves 120 lorry journeys per year for conventional slurry removal; all possible waste recycled or composted.
> CO_2 emissions: Guests are encouraged to take out the hire bicycles.

> Conservation projects: Collection box for Kent Wildlife Trust is in the hostel.
> Food supplies: The hostel patronizes the local village butcher; produces own fruit, some organic vegetables, free-range eggs; Fair Trade tea and coffee.
> Cultural events: For the last two years the farm has hosted a local wassailing event to celebrate the apple harvest; owner is chair of parish council.
> Employment: Local.
> Ownership: Local commercial enterprise.

> Craft workshops
> Cycling, mountain biking
> Swimming, water sports
> Nature walks

Cardamom House INDIA

Situated on the edge of Kamaraja Lake in the foothills of the Western Ghats in the state of Tamil Nadu, Cardamom House is a hotel, guesthouse and organic farm rolled into one. Bougainvillea, jasmine and frangipani trees scent the property and the deep veranda hints at lazy post-lunch naps. The whole facility has a low footprint, thanks to passive design features and local materials, in combination with solar heating and pumping. This is further enhanced by locally sourced and home-grown produce, along with trips to the local village and other points of interest with Tamil staff, who really know the people. Modest yet connected to its locale, Cardamom, like many eco-destinations, represents the vision and continuing focus of one person dedicated to making a small but tangible difference to the experiences of tourists and locals alike.

> Passive design with deep veranda, cross-wind circulation and evaporation cooling on stone walls ensures the house is naturally cooled.
> Materials: Local handmade bricks, stone.
> Energy: Solar water-collectors for hot water.
> Water: Rainwater harvesting.
> Waste: Plastic, paper, cardboard and metal waste is all recycled locally.

> Conservation & educational projects: Support for a local project, 'Children out of Poverty'.
> Food supplies: An organic farm is currently being developed on 1.4 hectares (3.5 acres) using irrigation by bore well and solar-voltaic pump, shade netting, composting and natural pest control. Produce sourced from the market at Athoor village near by.
> Cultural events: Trips to the village with staff speaking Tamil and English.
> Employment: Staff originate from Athoor village.
> Ownership: Locally owned enterprise.

> Walking, trekking, hiking
> Birdwatching

Chan Chich Lodge BELIZE

This development of twelve thatch-roofed cabanas and a villa is set on a 50,000-hectare (123,500-acre) private nature reserve in north-western Belize, alongside the plaza of an ancient Mayan city discovered after hacking through the jungle in 1985. Work started in 1987 following a survey by the Department of Archaeology to ensure the integrity of the site was preserved. Guests can now relax amid the forest and visit the nearby ruins. Diverse activities are offered including birdwatching, walking, horse riding and tours to other Mayan sites such as La Milpa and Lamanai, the largest site in Belize.

> Materials: Timber and thatch, all locally harvested.
> Energy: Passive cooling to assist ceiling fans.
> Water: Use is controlled.

> Conservation projects: The Wildlife Conservation Society has been based at Gallon Jug Estate, part of the Belize Estates Company that operates Chan Chich Lodge, since 1990. Researchers are active in La Selva Maya, an important Mesoamerican corridor for biological diversity and movement. Work focuses on bats, jaguars and other wildlife.
> Food supplies: Fresh produce grown locally and by employees, when seasonally available, with Belizean and international cuisine
> Employment: 75–99% local. All employees are provided with housing, water and electricity.

> Ownership: Local and nationally owned commercial enterprise.

> Cycling, mountain biking
> Swimming, water sports
> Walking, trekking, hiking
> Bird, archaeology and other tours

Tamarind Tree Hotel DOMINICA

Perched 30 metres (100 feet) up on a cliff-top site, with a spectacular balcony overlooking the Bay of Salisbury and the island's highest peak, Morne Diablotin, the Tamarind Tree is a friendly, small hotel. There are nine double rooms, all simply furnished and leading out on to the communal porch. Drop down the hill to the beach to enjoy snorkelling or diving from the East Carib Dive centre. Enjoy a locally brewed Kubuli beer on the terrace or public restaurant, which serves a big Sunday brunch.

> Green Globe benchmarked, the hotel has a published environmental and social sustainability policy and constantly monitors activities to improve on performance.
> Energy: Solar power and heating.
> Water: Use is minimized.
> Waste: The hotel has adopted the principle 'reduce, recycle, re-use'.

> Conservation projects: Supports ROSTI, an organization promoting turtle conservation work; founder of the Central West Coast Turtle project.
> Food supplies: Locally sourced where possible from farmers, butchers and fishermen.
> Employment: Local guides are encouraged and 75–99% of staff are local.
> Ownership: Local, commercial family business.

> Swimming, water sports
> Walking, trekking, hiking
> Whale watching

Inverness Youth Hostel UK

The bustling town of Inverness is the gateway to the Scottish Highlands, sitting at the northern end of the Great Glen, which bisects the mountainous landscape with its dramatic lochs and navigation canals. This large, 200-bed hostel accommodates the swell of summer tourists and offers family and en-suite rooms as well as dormitories. It is just a few minutes from the town centre, where you can absorb the history, visit the museums, enjoy a night at the theatre or cinema and walk on the bouncy Victorian pedestrian suspension bridge over the river.

> Certified to the Green Business Tourism Scheme, scoring an overall Gold Standard against 60 criteria.
> Materials: FSC wood materials preferred.
> Energy: Efficient combination of lighting, heating, appliances, insulation and renewable energy use; wind and solar power generation.
> Water: Good maintenance of low-consumption and low-flush appliances; rainwater harvesting.
> Consumables: Products made from recycled materials; eco-cleaners.
> Waste: Minimization encouraged by 'eliminate, reduce, re-use, recycle' principles; supplier take-back agreements.

> CO_2 emissions: The hostel aims to minimize visitor car use by promoting local or human-powered transport.

> Conservation projects: All visitors are informed about the hostel's responsible green charter and the importance of working with the local community and using local resources. Corporate social responsibility reporting is a priority.
> Food supplies: Some sourced from Fair Trade.
> Employment: Less than 25% local.

> Ownership: Not-for-profit national enterprise.

> Walking, trekking, hiking
> Wildlife safari

Alila Manggis INDONESIA

Representing a classic blend of contemporary and Balinese architecture, this resort is the embodiment of a luxury escape, set in a coconut grove with warm tropical seas lapping the beach. The *alang alang* thatch roofs mimic a typical local meeting hall, or *wantilan*, and protect two-storey buildings that accommodate 54 rooms, with balcony or private terrace. The setting on the steeply sloping east coast of Bali, with Mount Agung as a backdrop, and the local environs of terraced *padi* fields and villages provide an intimate picture of Balinese spiritual and traditional rhythms. Various walking or cycling tours are available for visitors to explore the countryside at leisure. Manggis is renowned for the quality of its diving and marine biodiversity. For visitors who want to gain a few east Balinese culinary skills and tips, there is a celebrated cooking school at the organic garden on the slopes of Mount Agung, where the ingredients also come from. Aspiring chefs cycle up to the farm, have a restorative tea, visit the permaculture-inspired farm and then knuckle down to learning about the local delicacies. This is a high-class resort with all the usual facilities but offering some down-to-earth surprises.

> Certified to Green Globe 21 standards.
> Materials: Many local, including grasses for the thatch.
> Energy: Various energy-saving initiatives, including reduced use of air- conditioning; water pumps; use of low-energy light bulbs.
> Water: Recycling and treating of waste water on site.
> Consumables: Only biodegradable chemicals used; increasing use of recycled paper.
> CO2 emissions: Promotion of tours on foot or by bike rather than by car gives a better experience of local environment and culture.

> Conservation & socio-cultural projects: Alila collaborates with a local NGO, the Indonesian Development of Education and Permaculture, by sharing seeds, plants and organic husbandry know-how. The organic garden acts as a working farm, demonstrating permaculture and sustainable husbandry practices, as well as producing food for the resort. Support for humanitarian organizations, such as the Foundation for Mother Earth and the East Bali Poverty Project, provides help to local Balinese on financial, health and education issues.
> Food supplies: Alila organic garden provides produce for the hotel and cooking lessons.
> Cultural events: Tours of local temples, water palaces, weavers' homes and traditional villages.
> Employment: Mixed local and international.
> Ownership: International commercial enterprise.

> Food and cookery classes
> Swimming, water sports
> Walking, trekking, hiking
> Diving

Villas Ecotucan MEXICO

Set near one of Mexico's largest freshwater lakes in Yucatán is the small, partner-run Villas Ecotucan. Luxuriant gardens harbour six cottages, built in colourful vernacular style using local labour, each simply but adequately furnished. This is comfortable budget accommodation. Activities are strictly leisurely – a stroll to the nearby town of Bacalar, hiking or biking on jungle trails, lazing on the veranda or kayaking on the lagoon.

> Materials: Natural thatch, stone and other local materials.
> Energy: 100% solar-powered.
> Water: Rainwater harvesting; filtered greywater used for irrigation of gardens.

> Conservation & cultural projects: The buildings occupy just 0.5 hectares (1 acre) of a 60-hectare (150-acre) estate where vegetation is left wild. A shop selling artifacts made by local artisans takes no commission.
> Food supplies: Meals at the lodge and at local restaurants in Bacalar.
> Ownership: Local and international partnership.

> Cycling, mountain biking
> Swimming, water sports
> Walking, trekking, hiking

Villa Sebali INDONESIA

Surrounded by rice terraces, with distant views of Mount Agung and the dramatic landscape of the north island of Bali, Villa Sebali comprises a three-sided courtyard graced by an infinity pool. The luxuriant, organically husbanded garden provides a perfect foil for the Balinese architecture, showing empathy for the site and local culture. Guestrooms are spacious and simply but luxuriously furnished and have access to the garden via terraces or seating areas. Guests can indulge in simple pleasures or engage in learning the Balinese arts of *gamelan*, dancing, crafts and cooking. From biking and elephant rides to yoga, meditation and spiritual activities, there is no dearth of things to do.

> Materials: Designed by a Balinese architect with respect for local materials, including *alang alang* to provide thatch roofing.
> Energy: Solar power and water heating; passive architecture – shading by traditional grass roofing and many trees in the garden, cooling via infinity pool to courtyard, although air-conditioning is available if required.
> Water: Pure well water. Waste water is treated in a natural system and used to water the garden.

> Food supplies: Local organic garden and orchard supplies some needs.
> Cultural events: The house was blessed according to local custom when first opened and receives daily offerings from a lady in nearby Sebali village. A wide range of activities allows guests to enjoy the cultural experiences of Bali.
> Employment: Six full-time local staff.
> Ownership: Expat partnership.

> Craft workshops
> Cycling, mountain biking
> Dance, music
> Food and cookery classes
> Swimming, water sports
> Walking, trekking, hiking
> Yoga, meditation

The Lodge at Chaa Creek BELIZE

Twenty years old, this Belizean resort has a comprehensive environmental and social policy that has underpinned the creation of a unique wildlife reserve. Low-impact sustainable development has involved a number of initiatives – a butterfly-breeding centre, a summer teacher-training programme twinning Belize and New York State, a natural history and activities centre, extensive use of local products and encouragement of local employment. All this is reflected in the architecture of the villa and cottages, on a well-maintained site perfumed with frangipani blossom. Once you get your early-morning call from the toucans, colourful parrots or Howler monkeys, you will be ready for a day's exploring, adventuring in the nearby Maya Mountains or just absorbing the Belizean way of life.

> Materials: Bay leaf palm thatch; hardwoods from sustainably managed forest.
> Energy: Vernacular architectural features encourage passive building design to lower energy needs; low-energy light bulbs with automatic timers; rest of electricity from well-maintained diesel generators; Macal River Camp is 100% solar-powered.
> Consumables: Recycled paper.
> Waste: Policy is to reduce, re-use and recycle; inert waste materials (glass, cans) are re-used for new building works.

> Conservation projects: The lodge is situated on a private 150-hectare (370-acre) nature reserve where there has been extensive encouragement of the black howler monkeys, reafforestation with bay leaf palm, various research projects by New York Botanical Gardens and an archaeology project at Xunatunich by the University of California. Chaa Creek is involved in numerous local community, welfare and educational projects.
> Food supplies: Vegetables from on-site organic farm or local farmers and livestock producers.

> Employment: 100% local, including ten naturalist guides.
> Ownership: Local commercial enterprise.

> Adventure sports
> Craft workshops
> Cycling, mountain biking
> Dance, music
> Farm and vineyard work
> Food and cookery classes
> Swimming, water sports
> Volunteer work
> Walking, trekking, hiking
> Wildlife safari
> Horse riding

Soneva Fushi & Six Senses Spa MALDIVES

The Maldives in the Indian Ocean comprise numerous islands and atolls, but Soneva Fushi offers relative solitude away from the crowd. An island with just 65 residences, it affords luxurious accommodation in ecologically sensitive surroundings. Rooms vary from a basic double to a villa suite, tree house and retreats in the jungle. An attraction for foodies is the organic garden restaurant, situated beside the garden and surrounded by jungle. Herbs, vegetables and fruit are mainly supplied from this garden, fish comes fresh from the sea and some organic meats are used, but the animals are all humanely treated before ending up in the pot. After a lengthy siesta digesting, you'll enjoy an afternoon of snorkelling or diving in clear ocean waters. Tired muscles can be unknotted at the Six Senses Spa, where all animal by-products and plants grown using environmentally destructive practices are avoided.

> Materials: Teak, cedar, pine, acacia, eucalyptus, coconut palm and bamboo are sourced from managed plantations. Some recycled wood is used.
> Energy: Natural ventilation is favoured over air-conditioning and detailed design encourages air circulation. Low-energy light bulbs are used wherever possible.
> Water: Swimming pools are filled with saltwater; groundwater is used to flush toilets; rainwater is collected. Native planting for drought resistance.
> Waste: Guests are asked to take back home all their batteries, spray bottles and plastic waste.
> CO_2 emissions: The resort plans to be carbon-neutral by 2010; working with the Carbon Neutral Company.

> Conservation projects: All laundry revenue is donated to local environmental groups such as EcoCare, protecting shark and turtle populations.
> Food supplies: Herbs, vegetables, fruit from own organic garden; organic and Fair Trade products purchased where possible.
> Cultural events: Six Senses donates 0.5% of revenue to a social and environmental responsibility fund for local and global projects.
> Employment: 75–99% local.
> Ownership: International company.

> Food and cookery classes
> Swimming, water sports

Alila Villas Uluwatu INDONESIA

This design-conscious luxury green residential resort, opened in summer 2008, is the work of Singaporean architects Woha for a local developer, PT Bukit Uluwatu Villa, and is managed by Alila Hotels group in Singapore. This 13.5-hectare (33-acre) retreat will house up to forty detached villas with full hotel and central management facilities set in the local forest savannah vegetation. It is perched on a limestone cliff over 100 metres (328 feet) high, in the southern coastal area of the Bukit Peninsula, just half an hour south of the main airport in Bali. Each villa is distinctly 21st-century modern with Balinese details. Villas are sold to individual investors but Alila lets the one-bed or three-bed villas. The whole resort is to be certified to Green Globe 21 standards, which include a list of criteria ranging from climate-change gaseous emissions, to energy conservation measures, ecosystem management, land-use planning and management, waste and recycling systems.

> Materials: Reclaimed *ulim* wood from local telegraph poles and used railway sleepers; local stone.
> Energy: Heat pumps for heating.
> Water: A range of water-conservation measures, including rainwater harvesting; greywater recycling systems for landscape irrigation; rainwater gardens.

> Conservation projects: Use of local Balinese plants to promote savannah ecosystem development.
> Employment: Mainly local.
> Ownership: Local commercial enterprise.

> Swimming, water sports

Alila Ubud INDONESIA

Alila Ubud is perched above the Ayung River in the centre of the island of Bali, in the steeply terraced rice fields and forests near the village of Panyangan. This boutique hotel resort comprises a discrete arrangement of 56 rooms and 8 villas, built on stilts and all with balconies or private decks, which merge with the surrounding vegetation. Natural materials and local craftsmanship contrast with modern materials and details. An amazing infinity pool allows guests to enjoy the lushness of the surroundings and magnificent views, as well as a mosaic of courtyards, terraces and gardens offering seclusion and intimacy. Explore the dramatic terrain on foot or by mountain bike, or take an organized tour to nearby volcanoes. Here in the cultural heart of Bali you can discover the weavers of the traditional *ikat* cloth and visit the nearby artisan centre of Ubud town.

> Certified to Green Globe 21 standards.
> Materials: Many local, including grasses for the thatch.
> Energy: Various energy-saving initiatives, including reduced use of air-conditioning; water pumps; use of low-energy light bulbs.
> Water: Recycling and treating of waste water on site.
> Consumables: Coconut oil, sea salt and soaps are sourced from local community cooperatives in east Bali.

> Conservation & socio-cultural projects: Involved in numerous local projects with schools and communities to promote best environmental practices.
> Food supplies: 70% sourced from within 50 kilometres (30 miles) of the hotel.
> Cultural events: Alila Experience encourages all guests to get to know Balinese culture through classes or events, including cooking, spiritual and other activities that support local businesses.

> Employment: Mixture of local and international.
> Ownership: International commercial enterprise.

> Cycling, mountain biking
> Swimming, water sports
> Walking, trekking, hiking

Banyan Tree Bintan INDONESIA

The stilted villas and facilities of the resort poke out of the natural forest canopy in this luxury resort hotel, just 55 minutes by high-speed catamaran from the city of Singapore. Each villa enjoys unparalleled views over the South China Sea in the secluded bay of the north-west of Bintan Island in Indonesia. Indulgences abound, from villas with private spa pools to candlelit dinners on the rocky seashore and full-blown sensual and cleansing massages in the main spa. There is a Greg Norman championship golf course, together with a full range of water sports, local food and cookery lessons or leisurely walks to take in the luxuriant vegetation, chattering monkeys and sensory pleasures of the tropical life.

> Most of the buildings literally tread lightly on the land, being elevated on stilts, avoiding disturbance of the steeply vegetated slopes. Similarly, landscaping has been kept to a minimum.
> Materials: Local Balinese-crafted grass roofs and timber features throughout the resort.
> Energy: There is an energy-saving policy and the resort is investing in energy-saving devices for water systems and air-conditioning.
> Consumables: Non-chlorinating agents for swimming-pool and jet-pool treatment.
> Waste: Recycling of waste water by means of a biological treatment facility for irrigating the landscaped areas and golf course. All solid waste is collected and sorted for recycling or composting.
> CO_2 emissions: As part of the Greening Communities initiative, Bintan is included in a ten-year tree-planting programme.

> Conservation projects: Launched in June 2007, Banyan Tree Bintan Conservation Lab employs a full-time environmental naturalist and two wildlife rangers who develop local conservation programmes and encourage community development and local health projects. The lab has links with the National University of Singapore and Victoria Zoo in Australia. There is a project for coral rehabilitation and conservation of the spiny terrapin (an endangered species).
> Food supplies: A small vegetable and herb garden is cultivated and local supplies are encouraged where possible.
> Employment: 75–99% local.
> Ownership: International commercial enterprise.

> Adventure sports
> Food and cookery classes
> Swimming, water sports
> Walking, trekking, hiking
> Conservation work

Verana MEXICO

Situated some 200 kilometres (124 miles) west of the historical city of Guadalajara are the Bay of Banderas and Puerto Vallarta on the Pacific coast of Mexico. Beyond the popular resorts, and accessible only by boat, lies the exclusive resort of Verana. Its most striking feature is its attention to aesthetics, manifest in all the accommodation, from villas to rustic *palapas*, modernist bungalows and a jungle suite. Those who love colour will naturally embrace Verana, enjoying the proximity to jungle and ocean alike. Pamper yourself in the spa and *watsu* (body massage in water) pool, or sign up for a day's whale watching.

> Materials: Local materials for a 'handmade' hotel.
> Consumables: Biodegradable products in spa and rooms.
> Waste: Recycling; waste water treatment.

> Food and cookery classes
> Swimming, water sports
> Walking, trekking, hiking
> Wildlife safari
> Whale watching

> Conservation & cultural projects: The resort pays the salary of a doctor's assistant for the local village hospital.
> Food supplies: Organically and locally grown vegetables and herbs.
> Employment: 75–99% local.
> Ownership: Commercial enterprise, land leased from local community.

Whare Kea Lodge & Chalet NEW ZEALAND

Luxury in nearly 30 hectares (74 acres) of stunning, privately owned farmland and remote wilderness makes this lodge an exclusive and deeply serene experience. The kea parrot, found at high altitudes on New Zealand's South Island, lends its name to the Whare Kea Lodge. The minimal aesthetic and open-glazed windows, by the architect John Mayne, make the most of the astonishing panoramic views. This setting is complemented by the family atmosphere (there is a maximum of 12 guests), superb local food and immediate access to a trekker's paradise. Lake Wanaka offers a blue foreground, with lots of water-based activities, such as swimming and kayaking. To see Mt Aspiring National Park close up, hitch a ride on a helicopter to stay in the Whare Kea Chalet, an Alpine-style building high on the snow slopes. Those concerned with their carbon footprint can engage a professional guide to get there by the slow route. Here the same minimalist and stupendous views greet the guests.

> Lightweight construction.
> Energy: Modelled on traditional farm buildings, good natural lighting.
> Consumables: Only uses biodegradable products.

> Food supplies: Local supply and suppliers encouraged.
> Cultural events: Supported.
> Employment: 75–99% local and local guides as well as employees are encouraged.
> Ownership: International company, a member of Relais & Châteaux.

> Swimming, water sports
> Walking, trekking, hiking
> Spa
> Lake cruises

Hotel Vila Naia BRAZIL

The pristine 15-kilometre (9-mile) beach of Corumbau in southern Bahia sits on the 17th Parallel on the Atlantic coast of Brazil. The boutique hotel, designed by the architect Renato Marques, is empathic with its setting among the *restinga* forest and nut-palm trees. A series of villa suites and bungalows of natural and local materials is linked by a boardwalk to a central square and swimming pool. Attention to detail gives the complex a human scale and traditional techniques have been revived using woods such as *peroba do campo* (*Paratecoma peroba*) and, for the roofs, *aderno* (*Heberdenia excelsa*). Activities include visits to the Mato Grosso reefs and tours inland to the village of Pataxó near the mouth of the Corumbau River.

> Designed to minimize disturbance to the existing vegetation and harmonize with the vernacular architecture of fishermen's huts. Construction and craft work by local people. The hotel is aiming for ISO14001 certification but is already certified to the Brazilian ecotourism scheme.
> Materials: Reclaimed wood; native local woods; non-toxic materials.
> Energy: A wind generator for lighting and solar collector for water heating. Passive cooling by orientation and detailed design of accommodation and facilities.
> Consumables: Prioritizes use of environmentally low-impact products.

> Waste: The hotel tries to minimize waste but also practises recycling, re-use (transporting to the local town) and composting.

> Conservation projects: The owner encouraged the establishment of a 5-hectare (12-acre) nature reserve under the government scheme RPPN, Reserva Particular do Patrimônio Natural. Only native plants are used in the landscaped or garden areas.
> Food supplies: Vegetables, grains, fowl and fish purchased locally. There is an organic vegetable garden at the hotel.
> Cultural events: The owner has cultivated relationships with many local communities and supports the production of handicrafts by the Pataxó Indians.
> Employment: 100% local.
> Ownership: National commercial enterprise.

> Swimming, water sports
> Walking, trekking, hiking
> Conservation work

Hotel de Lençóis BRAZIL

It is hard to reconcile the dramatic landscape of the Chapada Diamantina National Park, Bahia, with one of the 19th and 20th centuries' most productive diamond-mining areas. This is where the city of Lençóis gained its fame and fortune. Now in a secluded and green part of the city sits the Hotel de Lençóis, a combination of the old and new, with fifty apartments furnished in a modern yet local style, in their own 4 hectares of gardens. In the environs of the national park you can enjoy spectacular scenery of cliffs, gorges, caves and three rivers, all criss-crossed with trails and clothed in biodiverse vegetation including amazing bromeliads and orchids. If you are more of a city person, then visit in August for the annual fiesta and extravaganza.

> The hotel is currently in the process of being certified by the Brazilian Institute for Hospitality's Sustainable Tourism Programme.
> Materials: Recycled doors and windows from an antique house were used in a recent remodelling of apartments; preferential use of wood from reafforestation projects with IBAMA certification to ensure preservation of natural forests.
> Energy: Solar heating for water; natural lighting in bathrooms; low-energy light bulbs.
> Water: Recycled water for the gardens.
> Consumables: Use of recycled paper.

> Waste: Organic garbage is composted; selected materials are recycled locally.

> Conservation & socio-cultural projects: Planting of many trees and bushes in the hotel grounds; sponsorship of local not-for-profit organization Grão de Luz; and purchase of their products; other campaigns include Clean the Trails and the substitution of plastic bags with cloth ones.
> Food supplies: Policy to source 50% of food locally.

> Cultural events: Supports local musicians and groups.
> Employment: 100% local.
> Ownership: National commercial enterprise.

> Adventure sports
> Dance, music
> Swimming, water sports
> Walking, trekking, hiking

Banyan Tree Maldives Vabbinfaru MALDIVES

The Maldives, an oceanic archipelago of 1,200 islands, sits plumb in the middle of the tropical waters of the Indian Ocean. Such a grand setting serves to remind us of nature's grandeur and yet highlights the vulnerability of these startling brilliant-white coral islands to the forces of climate change. In the North Malé Atoll, just 25 minutes from the capital, Malé, sits the tiny island of Vabbinfaru. Five exclusive villas, either on the beach or a stone's throw away, provide the kind of cosseted ambience most only dream of. Private wooden decks and walkways lead to thatched retreats surrounded by 360-degree tangy sea breezes. This is a diving paradise, with diverse coral life and over 900 species of fish recorded throughout the Maldives.

> Materials: Local thatched roofs.
> Energy: Design ensures passive cooling of open spaces by sea breezes to reduce the need for air-conditioning.
> Water: A desalination plant and ultraviolet treatment provide for water needs.
> Waste: All waste is made safe by treatment before disposal.
> CO_2 emissions: As part of the Greening Communities initiative, Maldives Vabbinfaru is included in a ten-year tree-planting programme for all Banyan Tree resorts.

> Conservation projects: A specialist marine lab, with five dedicated staff, has been set up to work with national and international scientists to conserve the Maldivian environment. Work focuses on turtle, shark, stingray and coral conservation. Local projects funded via the group's Green Imperative Fund (GIF) include rebuilding after the 2004 tsunami, support for the national Thalassaemia (blood disease) Centre and teacher training. The gallery in the resort supports local craftwork and handiwork.
> Food supplies: Some produce is

grown on site, and reef fish and tuna are from local fishermen.
> Employment: 76–99% local, with local and international dive instructors.
> Ownership: International commercial enterprise.

> Adventure sports
> Dance, music
> Food and cookery classes
> Swimming, water sports
> Wildlife safari
> Conservation work

Sonaisali Island Resort FIJI

Here on Viti Levu, the westernmost of Fuji's two largest islands, sits this resort, on its own self-contained islet, where traditional craftsmanship meets modern architecture and where Fijian culture sets the ambience. There's a good range of accommodation, from 32 beachfront rooms with balcony in a modern block to traditional conical thatched bures with high ceilings, shuttered louvre windows, natural materials and local artifacts. The bures offer family or multiple-occupancy options, some equipped with their own spa bath. The complimentary activities celebrate traditional Fijian culture and even include a language class. Diving facilities are eco-conscious and there are plenty of other water activities to choose from.

> Green Globe 21 certified with a detailed environmental and social- sustainability management strategy that includes the resort, tours and activities.
> Materials: Sourced from local suppliers where possible; local woodcarvers and thatchers are showcased around the resort.
> Energy: Auto-timers and low-energy lighting; monitoring and reduction of gas usage; intelligent load-management of electrical equipment.
> Water: Low-flow showerheads; greywater system.
> Consumables: Biodegradable products used for cleaning.
> Waste: Policy for minimizing solid waste; recycling; waste-water management; composting; recycling programme for old linen, blankets, paper.

> Conservation & socio-cultural projects: Sponsorship of an ecosystem reef conservation project by the Mamanca Environmental Society; guests are introduced to local ecosystems; emphasis on diving with care, including a PADI Aware programme, which includes removal of invasive crown of thorn reef 'weeds'; various beach clean-up campaigns; Korovuto village is supported in a number of projects involving education, jobs and IT skills, and support of local suppliers to encourage 'positive impact'.
> Food supplies: Hydroponic farm on the resort to provide organic vegetables; locally sourced where feasible, especially fresh prawns, crabs and fish from local Korovuto fishermen; minimum fish sizes strictly enforced.
> Cultural events: There is a diverse range of cultural events promoted weekly, from the traditional *meke* dance performed by 25 Korovuto village members to fire-walking and a youth dance troupe.
> Employment: 275 local people are employed.
> Ownership: Commercial enterprise.

> Adventure sports
> Dance, music
> Food and cookery classes
> Swimming, water sports
> Walking, trekking, hiking
> Reef tours

Six Senses Hideaway at Samui THAILAND

Koh Samui, an island of some 500 square kilometres (190 square miles), faces the Gulf of Thailand and hosts this exclusive resort of 66 unique villas, each built in modern style with Thai influence. All the larger villas have a private sun-deck and come with their own private infinity-edge saltwater swimming pools; the smaller Hideaway Villas have plunge bathtubs with panoramic views. There is a spa with a diversity of treatments, including Thai massage using herbs grown in one of three special organic gardens in the grounds. Everything is on your doorstep in this compact island. Visit the local golden Big Buddha, view the mummified body of the monk Loung Pordaeng, who died in mid-meditation in the 1980s, take a look around a fishermen's village, swim with sea lions, trek with elephants or just stroll on the beach. There is good nightlife, too.

> Green Globe 21 benchmark certified in December 2006, with a commitment to environmental and social policies, including management of energy to reduce climate change through the Holistic Environmental Management Programme (HEMP) and assessment of Key Sustainability Indicators (KSIs).
> Energy: Natural ventilation where possible rather than air-conditioning; bio-diesel plant using recycled kitchen waste oils; low-energy lighting; heat exchangers in some air-conditioning units used to heat laundry water; purchase of eco-efficient kitchen appliances and other equipment.
> Water: Waste water and desalination plant; 100% recycling of water.
> Consumables: Refrigerators and air-conditioning units are converted to MK22; only seawater is used for swimming pools.
> Waste: Mantra is 'reduce, re-use, recycle': this applies to aluminium, glass, paper, plastic and organic waste; treated greywater is used for irrigation.
> CO2 emissions: The Carbon Neutral Company has a programme that allows guests to offset their emissions related to air travel and other impacts.

> Conservation projects: Donations of 0.5% of revenue to projects benefiting the local and global communities and environmental projects; planting of King's grass to prevent erosion; planting of mangroves, beach cleaning and other activities in Baan Plai Laem area; herbal gardens include products such as aloe vera for the spa treatments; a wide range of local youth and children's projects is supported; there is a new project to experiment with the production of bio-gas from coconut, leaf waste and sewage.
> Food supplies: Three organic herbal gardens provide herbs, fruit and vegetables; preference for local purchases where possible; policy to source from reputable animal welfare concerns.
> Culture: Guests are offered a complimentary Thai culture class.
> Employment: 75–99% local.
> Ownership: National commercial enterprise.

> Adventure sports
> Craft workshops
> Dance, music
> Food and cookery classes
> Wine tasting
> Swimming, water sports
> Volunteer work
> Walking, trekking, hiking
> Conservation work

Hotel Jardim Atlântico PORTUGAL

This hotel sits in a spectacular location 536 metres (1,760 feet) above the sea on the cliffs of the southern coast of Portugal's Atlantic island of Madeira, near the village of Prazeres. Accommodation includes 61 studios, 27 one-bed and 2 two-bed apartments and 8 bungalows with a good range of common facilities. This is a dramatic natural landscape for walking. Guests can take guided cultural and botanical tours of the local village. In the botanically diverse gardens there's an unusual landscape feature called the 'barefoot walk', comprising a path of rounded stones, providing an ideal complement to the spa treatments to restore body and soul. Holder of an EU 'flower' eco-label for accommodation, the hotel was built on ecological ideals in 1991, including feng shui orientation of the rooms that takes advantage of natural sea breezes.

> Consumables: Use of products containing recycled materials.
> Waste: A biological waste-water treatment plant is on site and reclaimed water is used for irrigation purposes.

> Conservation projects: Situated in a natural green area, the hotel has endeavoured to encourage native planting, including over 400 species as part of the Laurisilva World Heritage site designated by UNESCO since 1999.
> Food supplies: Local, fresh and organic food is obtained where feasible; a good vegetarian menu includes homemade bread and yogurts.
> Employment: 75–99% local.
> Ownership: Family commercial enterprise.

> Adventure sports
> Dance, music
> Farm and vineyard work
> Food and cookery classes
> Swimming, water sports
> Walking, trekking, hiking
> Wildlife safari
> Canyoning
> Conservation work

Tobermory Youth Hostel UK

Now immortalized in a children's TV programme and catchy song, Tobermory has newly acquired fame for its brightly coloured houses. The hostel is on the main street of Tobermory on the island of Mull, just a short ferry ride from the Scottish west-coast town of Oban. The island is geared toward summer tourism, with whale- and dolphin-watching tours, day-trippers visiting the ancient site of Christian pilgrimage on the islet of Iona, pony-trekkers and, of course, walkers enjoying the landscape. There is a good cultural heart to the island, so expect some dancing and a tipple of good malt whisky from the distillery at Ledaig.

> Certified by the Green Business Tourism Scheme, scoring an overall Gold Standard against 60 criteria such as compliance with environmental legislation, improving environmental performance and commitment to social involvement and communication.
> Materials: FSC wood products are encouraged.
> Energy: Efficient combination of lighting, heating, appliances, insulation and renewable-energy use.
> Water: Good maintenance of low-consumption and low-flush appliances; rainwater harvesting.
> Consumables: Products made from recycled materials, eco-cleaners.
> Waste: 'Eliminate, reduce, re-use, recycle' principles are followed; supplier take-back agreements; glass, cardboard, tin and paper recycling.
> CO_2 emissions: The hostel aims to minimize visitor car use by promoting local or human-powered transport.

> Conservation projects: All visitors are informed about the hostel's responsible green charter and the importance of working with the local community and using local resources. Corporate social responsibility reporting is a priority.
> Food supplies: Some sourced from Green City Whole Foods.
> Employment: 25–49% local.
> Ownership: Not-for-profit national enterprise.

> Dance, music
> Walking, trekking, hiking
> Wildlife safari
> Diving

Pousada Picinguaba BRAZIL

Three and a half hours from either Rio de Janiero or São Paulo on the south-eastern coast of Brazil, this seaside hotel, nestled into luxuriant tropical hillsides, is the ideal place to chill out. The hardest decision you are going to face is where to stretch out to enjoy the scenery, what your next delicious meal will be or which cocktail to sip. Local trekking, messing about on the river, sea sports or lazy snorkelling will keep you active. The nearby town of Paraty, 30 kilometres (20 miles) away by bus, is full of quaint colonial houses and restaurants.

> Materials: Colonial-style architecture with attention to first-class materials.
> Energy: There are no TVs or telephones.
> Waste: Recycling is mandatory and encouraged in the local community.

> Swimming, water sports
> Walking, trekking, hiking
> Sailing in a schooner

> Food supplies: Fresh fish straight from the mid-Atlantic Ocean.
> Employment: Local.
> Ownership: Local commercial enterprise.

Guludo Beach Lodge MOZAMBIQUE

Vast, deserted white tropical palm-fringed beaches, lapped by the Indian Ocean. It doesn't get much better than this for a dream tropical idyll. Guludo Beach Lodge is on the northern coast of Mozambique in the Quirimbas National Park. This development represents a new ethical approach aimed at nourishing rather than taking away from the host community, acknowledged at the 2007 Responsible Tourism awards as contributing to reducing poverty. All efforts have been made to work with the vernacular building tradition yet meet the demands of modern travellers. The result is the thatched tented *banda* built on a polewood frame. This is a commodious, open yet shaded space. housing lounge, bedroom and alfresco bathroom. Leisure pursuits abound, including diving, boating in mangrove swamps or visiting faded colonial Portuguese islands.

> British architects Cullum and Nightingale maximized passive cooling and shading by extensive use of local materials and orientation of the individual *bandas* to achieve the most benefit from the sea breezes.
> Materials: Predominantly constructed of locally available, renewable materials.

> Swimming, water sports
> Walking, trekking, hiking
> Wildlife safari
> Diving

> Conservation & socio-cultural projects: British co-founder Amy Carter won the New Statesman Young Social Entrepreneur of the Year 2006 for her work in embracing the local community in the new development. There are many projects including the Milala palm weaving group for women, adult literacy classes, a new village water pump and an anti-malaria campaign.
> Food supplies: Fish, including kingfish and yellow-fin tuna, come straight out of the water; other local food supplies are encouraged.
> Cultural events: Integration with the local community gives many opportunities for cultural exchange.
> Employment: Local.
> Ownership: Commercial enterprise by Bespoke Experience, a Fair Trade tourism company.

Salamander Hideaway BELIZE

This well-managed but laid-back resort near Ambergris Caye in Belize consists of eight cabanas on stilts at varying heights above the lush island vegetation or right on the beach. Travelling by boat from San Pedro, new arrivals are greeted by sun, sand and surf, plus a rich array of leisurely options – wildlife-spotting (everything from turtles to manatees and bats), kayaking, fishing, snorkelling, diving, beachcombing or lazing in the shade.

> Materials: Palm-frond thatch, timber, brick and concrete.
> Energy: 100% energy provided by solar panels and wind generator; sea-breeze-cooled stilt cabanas; no TVs.

> Cultural events: Guests are encouraged to participate in local cultural activities.
> Employment: Local.
> Ownership: Local and international partners in a family enterprise.

> Swimming, water sports

Balamku Inn on the Beach MEXICO

Local palapa grass roofing and ceramic tiles blend with Mexican artworks to provide an authentic aesthetic for this small hotel on the Costa Maya. This sensitivity is also reflected in the light ecological footprint, thanks to a policy of on-site renewable energy supplies and water and waste management. The beach backdrop, organic breakfasts and tours of local Mayan ruins combine with a personalized approach to give each guest a memorable experience.

> Materials: Palapa grass and ceramic tiles; traditional techniques.
> Energy: All solar- and wind-powered. Back-up generator runs on propane but is rarely used.
> Water: Low-flush composting toilets; all blackwater and waste is collected in bins, so nothing is disposed of on the land. Greywater from showers and sinks goes towards man-made wetlands filled with plants.
> Waste: All organic waste and plastics are recycled.

> Conservation projects: The inn is engaged in no specific projects but guests are encouraged to use local guides to gain maximum understanding of the natural environment.
> Food supplies: Guests are encouraged to buy local food.
> Employment: 100% local.
> Ownership: A national company.

> Adventure sports
> Swimming, water sports
> Walking, trekking, hiking
> Archaeology tours

Lyola Pavilions in the Forest AUSTRALIA

North of Brisbane there are two unique, self-contained pavilions nestled in the coastal hills, which literally tread lightly and maximize the sense of place. Designed by GOMANGO architects, the pavilions, called, respectively, 'Hide' and 'Seek', are elevated on stilts and accessed by wooden walkways. The striking feature of the double-bedroomed pavilions is the light, airy and 'close to nature' atmosphere, enhanced by the privacy to enjoy the natural surroundings. This is an idyllic setting for romantics, 'creatives' and bushtrekkers alike.

> Since 2003 the project has been certified by the Advanced label of the Australian Ecotourism Association.
> Materials: Timber, roundwood and finished, galvanized steel with eco-label sourcing where possible.
> Energy: Large sliding glazed panels permit natural ventilation to reduce energy requirements.
> Water: Rainwater is harvested from the roofs.
> Waste: Greywater is treated and used on the gardens; organic waste is composted.

> Conservation projects: The project is recognized by Land for Wildlife and contributions have been made to bush regeneration, wildlife nesting boxes and habitat creation for the endangered Richmond birdwing butterfly over the 22 hectares (54 acres) of the estate.
> Food supplies: Local cheeses and milk supplied.
> Employment: 100% local.
> Ownership: Local not-for-profit enterprise.

> Swimming, water sports
> Walking, trekking, hiking

The Green Hotel INDIA

In the south of the state of Karnataka, and to the south-west of the metropolis of Bangalore, sits the spice and silk town of Mysore. Surrounded by landscaped gardens, this hotel is a restored former palace of a princess, the Chittaranjan Palace, retaining many beautiful features including stained-glass windows and diverse craftwork. There are several stately rooms in the palace, as well as more modest accommodation within the gardens, including some suites. The charming atmosphere is complemented by a locally renowned restaurant. From here you can make excursions to visit the cooling heights of Ooty Hill Station and the game reserves of the Nilgiris range. All profits from the venture go directly to charitable works locally and nationally.

> Materials: Restored building of historic interest; use of local materials and craft skills.
> Energy: Some solar-powered energy; no electrical air-conditioning – shade-trees and cross-flow breezes instead.
> Waste: Recycled or composted.

> Conservation & socio-cultural projects: Profits go to environmental and other charitable projects in India, including local projects to plant 2,000+ trees, reedbed sanitation, landscaping and slum resettlement. Other projects include support for tribal communities in the Nilgiris mountains and tertiary educational grants for students.
> Food supplies: Fresh local ingredients are used for southern and northern Indian dishes in the restaurant.
> Ownership: Operated by a not-for-profit (charitable status) enterprise based in the UK.

> Excursions

Paradise Mountain Lodge COSTA RICA

Also known as Arenal Waterfall Lodge, this is a small ten-roomed lodge set in its own landscaped grounds and 160-hectare (262-acre) private park with a vista that takes in the Arenal and Cerro Chato volcanoes and the San Carlos valley. Accommodation is clean, simple and unimposing and the usual common facilities are provided. The lodge is a good base for families and groups or those wishing to explore the natural surroundings. Tours offer, among other activities, birdwatching, trekking, volcano-climbing or swimming near waterfalls, especially the La Fortuna, all in the beautiful Arenal National Park.

> Built following the environmental impact guidelines from the Environmental Protection Agency of Costa Rica (SETENA). Certification in Sustainable Tourism (CST) for accommodation facilities.
> Water: Current project to recycle water.
> Waste: Recycling and waste management policy for whole private park.

> Conservation projects: Planting of native trees with nutritional value to wildlife. Guests are invited to be involved in Adopt a Tree reafforestation project protecting a water-spring area for the property and local community. Established a group, Hope and Wellness 4 Kids, to help local children and families.
> Employment: 75–99% local; partnership with new local enterprises is being sought.
> Ownership: Local commercial enterprise.

> Adventure sports
> Farm and vineyard work
> Swimming, water sports
> Volunteer work
> Walking, trekking, hiking
> Wildlife safari
> Conservation work

The Summer House NEW ZEALAND

Set in the Bay of Islands and Kerikeri region towards the north-east of the North Island, this boutique bed and breakfast offers a little retreat in its own landscaped flower garden. Ideally situated for an excursion to the amazing Ninety Mile Beach and North Cape, it is also a fine base for visits to local attractions, such as vineyards, the huge kauri trees and Maori lands. There is a self-contained suite overlooking the pond, as well as a double room with orchard views and a romantic room with a 19th-century French bed. Expect gourmet breakfasts and a warm Kiwi welcome.

> Green Globe 21 certified.
> Materials: Hebel aerated blocks for high insulation; *Macrocarpa* and *Pinus* radiate timber.
> Energy: Low-energy house design; solar water-heating; pond pumps have been replaced by lower-energy units.
> Water: Filtered rainwater is used for domestic and potable water.
> Waste: Biological sewage system replaced septic tank; recycling of glass, paper, cardboard and plastic.

> Conservation projects: Birds are encouraged by garden planting, including subtropical pond; restored citrus orchard and extensive plantings in gardens; owner is an active member of several conservation organizations; growing of native plants for conservation projects.
> Food supplies: The house uses local suppliers; organic coffee, tea (Fair Trade) and wine.
> Employment: 100% local.
> Ownership: Family-run enterprise.

> Dance, music
> Walking, trekking, hiking

Covert Cabin FRANCE

Set in oak and chestnut woodland in the Périgord Vert National Park in the Dordogne region of France, this timber-constructed cabin-cum-house is off-the-grid and away from it all. Adjacent to its own lake, with a small boat and floating turf pontoon, it's a place where you'll soon establish a refreshing set of rhythms as you light the evening oil lamps and stoke the wood-burning stove. This is ecotourism in miniature, a gem of a place with low environmental impact.

> Materials: Timber from the surrounding forest, reclaimed materials.
> Energy: Wood-burning stove heats the water; wind-up radio; gas oven, hob and refridgerator; oil lights.
> Water: Raised from the lake by a wind pump, filtered and purified (for drinking).
> Waste: Recycling and composting systems in place.
> CO2 emissions: The cabin has an inherently low footprint.

> Food supplies: Bicycles are available so that visitors can shop locally.
> Employment: No employees; run by owners.
> Ownership: International owners; commercial enterprise.

> Swimming, water sports
> Walking, trekking, hiking

Crescent Moon Cabins DOMINICA

Set in rainforest near the La Croix River in the Morne Trois Pitons National Park, this destination affords an intimate and down-to-earth experience, where you can help make cocoa, roast coffee and juice fresh fruits. There is a strong emphasis on providing creative local cuisine; each meal starts with home-baked bread. Wonderful natural landscapes are in easy reach, including the UNESCO World Heritage Site of the Boiling Lake and Valley of Desolation, a volcanic area with hot springs. Near by is the coastal village of Massacre, mentioned in the novel *Wild Sargasso Sea* by Jean Rhys. A place to absorb the relaxed atmosphere and culture of Dominica.

> Developers 'recycled' the ruins of an old hotel by building on former foundations using the existing land area.
> Materials: Locally hand-harvested timber, handcrafted beds for each cabin.
> Energy: Wind and hydroelectric power.
> Water: Utility water provided by a 'ram pump' from the La Croix River, drinking water from mountainside natural spring.

> Food supplies: Most produce is grown on-site in the garden and greenhouse.
> Employment: 100% local and encouragement to use local guides.
> Ownership: National commercial enterprise.

> Farm and vineyard work
> Swimming, water sports
> Walking, trekking, hiking

Blancaneaux Lodge BELIZE

This lodge forms part of the Francis Ford Coppola trio of resorts in the Caribbean, aimed at the high-end ecotourism market. Good features of passive design (such as dense thatch for cooling), an independent hydroelectric power supply and a 1.2-hectare (3-acre) organic garden all help to reduce the environmental footprint of Blancaneaux Lodge. The luxuries expected of such a resort abound. The difference is that you can indulge in your afternoon doze by the pool with a relatively clear conscience, providing you offset the long-distance flight to reach Belize. A sustainable tourism policy is published, so the resort has to live up to its claims. As in many 'international' resorts, local employment is high, but whether this is generating a long-term sustainable local economy has yet to be seen.

> Vernacular architecture complements sensitive siting and orientation of buildings. The resort operates an environmental policy and will shortly be applying for Green Globe membership.
> Materials: Local bay leaf palm thatch, timbers (sustainable hardwoods, Caribbean pine, bamboo) and ceramic and *saltilla* tiles.
> Energy: Own hydroelectric facility; 98% of the property is naturally ventilated using window shutters, screens and overhead fans.
> Water: Waste water is treated via three-chambered septic tanks and soak-aways.
> Consumables: All swimming and plunge pools are treated with non-chlorine-based treatments or technologies.
> Waste: Solid waste is compacted prior to disposal in a local government landfill. Organic waste is composted on-site.

> Conservation & educational projects: The lodge supports Dr Marcella Kelly's (Virginia Tech) jaguar, puma and ocelot monitoring programme. In response to a local infestation of pine bark beetle, the lodge intends to start planting a pine tree for each guest or couple. The resort also helps to sponsor children's education, supports local football teams and gives financial support to health clinics.
> Food supplies: More than 80% of products eaten are grown organically on the property's garden or purchased locally.
> Employment: 98% of the 200 or so staff at the three properties are hired and trained locally.
> Ownership: Belize-registered commercial company paying corporate tax in Belize.

> Adventure sports
> Swimming, water sports
> Volunteer work
> Walking, trekking, hiking

Banjos Bushland Retreat AUSTRALIA

If you are visiting Sydney, you could do well to take a two-hour excursion north to stay in one of three five-star (AAAT-rated) luxury lodges in the bush of the Hunter region. The self-catering lodges, with two, three or four bedrooms, each have their own deck, glorious views and myriad wild creatures on the doorstep, from typical Australian mammals such as possums, wombats, kangaroos and wallabies to parrots, wrens and eagles. Ideal for couples, small groups or families, this child-friendly place offers plenty to do on its 400-hectare (990-acre) reserve, including bushwalking on nature trails, swimming, 'giant chess' and tennis. Off-site activities include wine tours and golf. For many, the greatest pleasure is just being in the bush.

> Advanced ecotourism certificate from the Australian Ecotourism Association.
> Materials: Natural or certified materials used where possible.
> Energy: Ceiling fans cool the central high-ceilinged lounges; airy decks contribute to good ventilation and lower energy demand; electrical key tags ensure everything is automatically switched off on exit.
> Water: Estate and all lodges have their own water tanks.
> Consumables: The swimming pool holds seawater, not chlorinated water.

> Waste: Greywater is recycled for garden use. Guests are encouraged to recycle where possible.

> Conservation & socio-cultural projects: The retreat raises funds for local carnivals, fairs and schools.
> Food supplies: The lodges are self-catering, but information is available on local sources and businesses.
> Employment: Managed by local owners.
> Ownership: Privately owned and managed enterprise.

> Swimming, water sports
> Walking, trekking, hiking
> Nine-hole golf
> Tennis
> Children's activities

Friday's Place INDIA

Establishing eco-accommodation can have a beneficial trickle-down effect on the locality. Friday's Place has done just that for Poovar Island, on a backwater of the Neyyar River on the border of Kerala and Tamil Nadu, southern India. This is a quiet, private escape with just three hand-crafted teak and mahogany cabins, where guests are sure to unwind. Take a slow boat along the canals, stroll down to the sea just a kilometre away or head for the wonderful temples of Trivandram and its sprawling Chalai bazaar.

> Materials: Local materials are favoured, such as palm thatch.
> Energy: Solar electric system; bio-electric sewage plant.
> Waste: Recycling and composting.

> Conservation & cultural projects: Donations are made to the local temple and mosque and two local children are sponsored annually to attend an English-medium school.
> Food supplies: Local fish and vegetable market.
> Employment: 100% local.
> Ownership: An international and local partnership; not-for-profit enterprise.

> Farm and vineyard work
> Food and cookery classes
> Swimming, water sports
> Walking, trekking, hiking
> Birdwatching

Hotell Kubija ESTONIA

Near the Russian border is the Estonian city of Võru, set in wooded countryside, and nestling into the forest is this 56-bed hotel, with nine designated 'eco-rooms' and a spa. Furnishings are done in a simple Scandinavian aesthetic and the eco-rooms are decorated with warm colours. A traditional restaurant displays examples of regional craftsmanship and textiles and serves local foods. A unique feature of the hotel is its Pintmann Sleep Centre, where specialists investigate and treat sleep disorders. The Pintmann Grupp also operates a traditional group of farm buildings, Haanjamehe, just ten minutes away, which has been converted into a peaceful rural refuge.

> Certified to Green Key eco-label standards.
> Materials: Natural materials are predominantly used in the spa, such as clay, clay-plaster walls and wooden floors.
> Energy, water & waste: Policies are in place to conserve energy, reduce water consumption, reduce waste and maximize recycling.

> Food supplies: The hotel restaurant prides itself on serving local and regional food.
> Employment: 100% local.
> Ownership: A local and national cooperative enterprise.

> Adventure sports
> Dance, music
> Swimming, water sports
> Walking, trekking, hiking

Ammende Villa ESTONIA

The Baltic states are becoming a more popular destination for European and international travellers, and no wonder, as the historical and cultural heritage of these countries has much to offer. This lovely Art Nouveau villa has been tastefully renovated but retains many original features, such as the solid oak stairway. It now serves as a high-quality hotel and restaurant set in its own landscaped grounds near the famous Blue Flag (a European environmental standard) beach of Pärnu, on the Gulf of Riga. There is a choice of 17 rooms, common features being the elegant proportions, original early 19th-century decor and solid wood furniture, all creating a mildly regal ambience. A successful blend of seaside resorts of yesteryear with all the modern comforts of today.

> This hotel is certified to the Green Key eco-label.
> Energy: Targets set to reduce energy consumption for heating and power.
> Water: The hotel maintains an active water-conservation policy.
> Consumables: Biodegradable and environmentally safe cleaning products.

> Food supplies: Local supply chains are favoured and as much local food sourced as possible.
> Cultural events: The town of Pärnu offers a theatre, concert hall and other cultural venues.
> Employment: 75–99% local.
> Ownership: National commercial enterprise.

> Adventure sports
> Craft workshops
> Dance, music
> Food and cookery classes
> Swimming, water sports
> Walking, trekking, hiking
> Conservation work

Le Hameau du Sentier des Sources FRANCE

This is a new hamlet built from 1990 onwards using traditional Périgord stone, materials and workmanship of such excellence that it is difficult to believe these are new buildings. Accommodation comprises gîtes, garden studio flats and chalets that sleep from two or three people up to ten or twelve. With views over the Dordogne valley and surrounded by oak, holly and pine forest, this idyll provides a romantic, rustic, French retreat with modern comforts. Here is a place to experience the French seasons, especially the autumn, when bounty from the gardens, including figs, mixes with the woodland fare of walnuts, chestnuts and boletus (or porcini) mushrooms.

> Conforms to La Clef Verte (Green Key) standards.
> Materials: Salvaged natural local stone, hemp, cork, aerated lime, terracotta.
> Energy: One of the *gîtes* produces hot water with solar panels; the rest have open fires or wood-burning stoves; low-energy light bulbs.
> Water: One of the *gîtes* has rainwater collection.
> Consumables: Use of low- and no-impact cleaning products.
> Waste: Recycling or composting of garbage.

> Food supplies: Guests have access to herb and vegetable gardens.
> Employment: All local.
> Ownership: Local commercial enterprise.

> Adventure sports
> Craft workshops
> Swimming, water sports
> Walking, trekking, hiking

Matuka Lodge NEW ZEALAND

Aoraki/Mt Cook National Park is a UNESCO World Heritage Site on the South Island of New Zealand. Just 40 minutes' drive from the foothills of the 3,754-metre (12,300-foot) summit of Mt Cook and its stunning mountain cousins sits Makuta Lodge. This is a luxurious homestay bed and breakfast with well-appointed bedrooms overlooking a trout lake in which the nearby mountains of the Mackenzie High Country are reflected. Gourmet cooking and the personal attention of the owners offer a homely approach. Just on your doorstep is a variety of activities for adrenaline junkies, sightseers or nature-lovers. The high country is pure and simple.

> Benchmarked to Green Globe 21 standards.
> Energy: Orientation of the building takes advantage of passive solar heating; the pond permits passive summer cooling; insulation ameliorates internal temperatures; low-energy lighting system.
> Water: Dual-flush toilets.
> Consumables: All cleaning and personal hygiene products are made of natural ingredients.
> Waste: All composted or recycled.

> Conservation projects: Hundreds of trees have been planted on the property. The local town of Twizel is home to the world's most endangered wading bird, the black stilt, for which there is a breeding programme.
> Food supplies: Local suppliers are used where possible.
> Employment: 100% local.
> Ownership: Local commercial enterprise.

> Walking, trekking, hiking

Pousada Pouso da Marujo BRAZIL

The surfing beach of Mole in the southern state of Santa Catarina is a good reason to head for Florianópolis. Ideal for those on a budget, this *pousada* is a cosy, small hotel complex with five self-catering apartments for up to four or five people and three suites for two to three. The surrounding garden and pool offer privacy and a place to relax. If the surf is not up, or is a little on the big side (Mole is for the experienced only), then head to the amazing dunes of Joaquina Beach for a spot of sand surfing. Other activities in the area include walking, trekking, sailing and whale watching. Book early for the New Year and carnival breaks.

> Currently certified to the Brazilian sustainable tourism scheme, PCTS.
> Energy: Low-energy lighting; solar hot-water heating.
> Consumables: Biodegradable soap.
> Waste: Rubbish is separated and recycled.
> CO_2 emissions: The hotel uses an ethanol-powered car.

> Conservation projects: The lodge contributes to the Saving the Turtle project and keeping the local lagoon and beaches clean; it also supports local handicrafts.
> Food supplies: Local seasonal fish.
> Employment: 100% local.
> Ownership: International family-run commercial enterprise.

> Swimming, water sports
> Volunteer work
> Walking, trekking, hiking
> Surfing, diving
> Conservation work

Pousada Vila Tamarindo Eco-lodge BRAZIL

The island of Santa Catarina sits just off the city of Florianópolis, a beachside city with a Costa del Sol skyline, some 500 kilometres (310 miles) south of São Paulo. Set in rather more idyllic surroundings just 200 metres (650 feet) from the beach, the *pousada* offers apartment-style accommodation of various kinds. Fresh, pastel-coloured suites, in basic but contemporary style, sleep three or four people and afford views of either the ocean or the landscaped garden. Two separate apartments, some way from the main block, offer a little more luxury, with hammocks, private verandas and bathrooms with jacuzzis or Japanese-style bathtubs. Home-baked bread, homemade jam and other local ingredients are served at breakfast. Forays further afield into the Atlantic Forest, the cooler nearby mountains of Serra Catarinense, the State Park of Serra do Tabuleiro and more than a hundred beaches of Florianópolis offer a rich choice for all.

> This hotel is certified under the PCTS scheme and is working towards ABNT NBR 15401: 2006 Brazilian Sustainable Management Hotel System.
> Materials: Sourced from certified resources or eco-labels where possible.
> Energy: Rooms are oriented north–south with high ceilings to maximize passive ventilation and daylight.
> Water: Recycled for garden irrigation.
> Waste: There are facilities for recycling waste in the buildings.
> CO_2 emissions: The 0.35 hectares (¾ acre) of vegetation surrounding the *pousada* helps neutralize some CO_2 emissions.

> Conservation & socio-cultural projects: Dunes vegetation receives protection and staff guard against deforestation and fire damage to natural vegetation. The lodge supports Arte Suave and Casa Canemba projects for children and young people from the local community.

> Food supplies: Local food supply is encouraged.
> Employment: Mixed local, national and international.
> Ownership: National and international commercial enterprise.

> Adventure sports
> Swimming, water sports
> Walking, trekking, hiking

Hotel Kürschner AUSTRIA

Set in its own landscaped gardens and adjacent to forest, this family-run hotel reflects an authentic Austrian vernacular tradition, from the building to the menu and the health spa. It lies close to the southern border with Italy, near Kötschach. Sunflowers and hay meadows proliferate in summer, while deep snow and winter sports activities prevail in the winter season. A consistent all-year-round feature is the extensive health programme, including the local speciality of a 'hay bath' plus the usual sauna, mudbath and herbal treatments. It offers an insight into the Austrian way of food and pleasure.

> Certified to the EU 'flower' eco-label for tourist accommodation.
> Materials: Built in 1740, the hotel has been continuously restored using natural local materials – timber without varnish and stone.
> Energy: Wood-chip district heating with heat recycling; eco-electricity sources.
> Consumables: Natural ingredients are used for spa treatments including hay, wine, alpine flowers and herbs.

> Conservation projects: The hotel supports a nature activity park at Museen and uses own hay meadow for spa treatments.
> Food supplies: Fair Trade coffee, chocolate, some fruit; special diets catered for in the health spa; basic foods sourced from local suppliers.
> Cultural events: The hotel works with the local tourism council of Kötschach.
> Employment: 75–99% local, including mountain guides and porters.
> Ownership: International commercial enterprise.

> Adventure sports
> Dance, music
> Swimming, water sports
> Conservation
> Walking, trekking, hiking
> Kayaking
> Wine tasting

Hotel Balance SWITZERLAND

If you want to choose somewhere to get snowed up in the Swiss Alps, then Hotel Balance could be the perfect place. Built in 1899 out of local stone and timber on sound local vernacular principles, the building has been adapted to provide apartments and individual rooms. On more clement summer days, the solar-heated natural swimming pool permits a panoramic view of 4,000-metre (13,100-foot) high mountain peaks. Macrobiotic and vegetarian food is the order of the day, with aromatic herbs from the garden. Various body- and mind-calming activities are offered – from the cuisine to shiatsu healing, Ayurvedic massage and meditation. Clearly this is Hotel Balance by name and by nature.

> The hotel is certified under the OE-PLUS scheme and has received five stars (ibexes), the maximum award. It is also part of the Bio-hotel scheme.
> Materials: Traditional late 19th-century construction in local vernacular.
> Energy: Solar energy, warm pump.
> Water: Special potable water from a natural spring source, Les Granges. There is a natural bio-pool for swimming.
> CO2 emissions: There is a policy to reduce emissions wherever possible.

> Conservation projects: A local alternative energy project, Green Valley. is supported.
> Food supplies: Organic macrobiotic and vegetarian food is sourced locally where possible.
> Employment: 75–99% local.
> Ownership: Local family business.

> Swimming, water sports
> Walking, trekking, hiking

Aviemore Youth Hostel UK

The 94-bed Aviemore Hostel, part of the network of Scottish Youth Hostels Association, sits in the wide valley to the north of the central massif of the Cairngorm range in the Grampian mountains of Scotland. Ben Macdui mountain, rising to 1,310 metres (4,300 feet), dominates the southern horizon and provides some fantastic walking and trekking terrain. It's a modern building, with a wide range of facilities, just five minutes from the town centre. Summer activities include strolling or mountain biking in the ancient Caledonian woodland in the foothills, but the opportunities are even better in winter, with access to the ski lifts for snowboarding and skiing. This is a good family destination.

> Certified to the Green Business Tourism Scheme, scoring an overall Gold Standard against 60 criteria.
> Materials: FSC wood products are encouraged.
> Energy: Efficient combination of lighting, heating, appliances, insulation and renewable energy use – new boilers installed.
> Water: Good maintenance of low-consumption and low-flush appliances; rainwater harvesting.
> Consumables: Products made from recycled materials, eco-cleaners.

> Conservation projects: All visitors are informed about the hostel's responsible green charter and the importance of

> Waste: Minimization is encouraged by 'eliminate, reduce, re-use, recycle' principles; supplier take-back agreements and glass recycling.
> CO_2 emissions: Aim is to minimize visitor car use by promoting local or human-powered transport.

working with the local community and using local resources. Corporate social responsibility reporting is a priority.
> Employment: 25–49% local.
> Ownership: Not-for-profit national enterprise.

> Adventure sports
> Walking, trekking, hiking

Penzion Jelen CZECH REPUBLIC

Set in the beautiful Dyje River valley near the Czech–Austrian border, this lovingly restored 1920s Art Deco villa, in the Czech town of Vranov nad Dyjí, has a total of 24 bedrooms accommodated in two- or four-bed apartments or suites, each with own kitchenette. Set in its own spacious gardens with views of the impressive local baroque and neo-classical Vranov castle, this hotel is a good place from which to explore the town and its environs. Nearby Podyjí National Park, with its unique, steep, wooded river canyon, offers numerous outdoor activities. Here you can indulge in simple summer pursuits such as fishing, cycling, swimming and walking, along with tours to ancient castles, neo-gothic wonders and strange museums, including one with a collection of stuffed dogs.

> The hotel is certified to European Eco-label standards.
> Materials: Wooden floors and many original architectural features.
> Energy: Energy-efficient equipment and automatic switching-off mechanisms; gas heating system is regularly maintained to minimize greenhouse gas emissions.
> Water: Water-saving taps, showers and toilets for rooms; water-efficient dishwashers and washing machines.
> Consumables: Products with eco-labels are favoured.
> Waste: All waste is separated and safely disposed of.

> Conservation & socio-cultural projects: Guests are encouraged to visit nearby Podyjí National Park and observe conservation codes. The pension gave financial and material aid to the local community after flooding.
> Food supplies: Local food suppliers.
> Cultural events: Local events and traditions are strongly supported.
> Employment: 100% local.
> Ownership: Local commercial enterprise.

> Cycling, mountain biking
> Farm and vineyard work
> Swimming, water sports
> Volunteer work
> Walking, trekking, hiking
> Conservation work

Primrose Valley Hotel UK

This smart Edwardian seaside villa, in the historic fishing village of St Ives, was the first hotel in Cornwall to be accredited with the Green Tourism Business Scheme (GTBS) award. A sustainability ethos underpins all aspects of this ten-bedroom hotel, from the refurbishment of the building to the extensive support of local food producers for the menu and the owner's involvement in local sustainable tourism projects. Rooms mix period and Scandinavian furniture with neutral, earthy colours and bright highlights. Porthmeor beach and the Tate St Ives art gallery are just a couple of minutes away and the influence of famous St Ives artists – Barbara Hepworth, Ben Nicholson, Patrick Heron, Bernard Leach – lives on in other town galleries. Here culture buffs mingle with surfers and deckchair tourists. Check the hotel website to find 50 things to do without a car. Local is beautiful.

> The hotel aims to be responsibly accountable for the social, environmental and economic impacts of the business, to spread the message and to introduce guests to the positive effects of a sustainable approach. GTBS certified.
> Materials: Re-used and local Cornish granite for new retaining walls; internal granite, brick and slate features restored; FSC certified timber for recycling shed.
> Energy: Most public areas use LED or low-energy compact fluorescent bulbs; mains electricity sourced from Ecotricity, a green supplier; hot water from a Bosch Worcester Greenstar High-flow 440 efficient condensing boiler.
> Water: All toilets fitted with small 6-litre cisterns and most are dual-flush; water is metered and usage monitored to prevent wastage; guests encouraged to minimize towel laundry.
> Consumables: Shopping done with re-usable jute bags; low-impact cleaning products; all marketing and PR material is printed locally using recycled stock and vegetable inks.
> Waste: 'Reduce, recycle and re-use policy': all paper, cardboard, newspapers, bottles, tin cans and more are recycled and packaging is minimized.

> Conservation & socio-cultural projects: Guests are requested to pay a nominal surcharge per room per night as a contribution to the Marine Conservation Society. The hotel is a corporate sponsor of the Cornwall Wildlife Trust. Staff are actively encouraged to learn about sustainable tourism. The hotel is an ambassador for CoaST (Cornwall Sustainable Tourism Project).
> Food supplies: The hotel actively promotes Cornish food producers and the Seafood Cornwall Initiative, and returns packaging to meat and fish suppliers. Fish are purchased according to the ethical guidelines of the Marine Stewardship Council. Tea, coffee and sugar are Fair Trade.
> Employment: 100% local.
> Ownership: Local commercial enterprise.

> Swimming, water sports
> Walking, trekking, hiking

Casa Melo Alvim PORTUGAL

Just 60 kilometres (35 miles) north of the famous Portuguese port of Porto (Oporto) sits the equally historic town of Viana de Castelo on the Lima River. The 16th-century Casa Melo Alvim, built in 1509, is the oldest manor house in the town, with an illustrious history featuring royal treasurers, navigators and adventurers. Each room is done in a different style, with influences including Manueline, Chão, baroque, rococo and Romantic, sensitively restored to modern levels of comfort without losing the historical ambience. Additionally, there are two rooms in distinctive contemporary style. Aside from the architectural attractions, the hotel offers an extensive wine cellar, local food and a fine location from which to explore the area including the Lima valley. With a packed picnic from the hotel kitchen, you can take excursions following rural trails, ancient and modern, where you'll see terraced fields, the curious corn straw *meda*s ('measures'), ox-carts and other features of rural life long lost from much of mainland Europe.

> Certified by the EU eco-label and Green Key schemes.
> Materials: organic Hempel paints for decoration; Natura Pura natural textile products for bed linen and Media Strom mattresses
> Energy & water: Policies and equipment to reduce consumption.
> Consumables: Ecolab household and sanitary cleaners; Renovagreen recycled toilet paper.
> Waste: Reduction, re-use and recycling where possible.

> Conservation & socio-cultural projects: Some support given to social institutions with special needs and to the restoration of the Melo Alvim family chapel in the town church.
> Food supplies: The restaurant prefers to choose food and wine from the Lima valley and beyond, with its own Portuguese wine cellar for wine tastings and social gatherings.
> Cultural events: A guided walk through the historical town of Viana do Castelo is offered.
> Employment: 75–99% local.
> Ownership: Local family-run enterprise.

> Craft workshops
> Dance, music
> Food and cookery classes
> Swimming, water sports
> Walking, trekking, hiking
> Horse riding, carting, golf

L'Orri de Planès FRANCE

Set high on the French side of the eastern Pyrenees, near the long-distance trail GR-10, is a beautifully converted stone farmhouse with enormous solar panel roof, the Orri, and an adjacent building, the Réfugi. There are eight bedrooms in the Orri, accommodating 28 people, and dormitory-style accommodation for up to 12 and four single beds in a lovely loft space in the Réfugi. The interiors are decorated in a modern aesthetic using stone, wood and warm colours. The many facilities include a solar-heated swimming pool. Near by you can discover rural life in the village of Planès, visit the 11th-century Romanesque church or stretch your legs in the mountains.

> The latest eco-tech systems are incorporated, thanks to a holistic approach to the restoration of buildings. A strong ethos of sustainability informs day-to-day operations. Certified by the Green Key (La Clef Verte) eco-label.
> Energy: High-quality insulation materials significantly reduce heat loss; there is a combined solar collector array and gas for space and water heating; a solar photovoltaic array produces electricity for appliances and lighting; other energy comes from Enercoop, a renewable-energy supplier; buildings use one-third of a typical traditional building. Guests are encouraged to make their contribution to energy and water conservation too.
> Water: Flow reducers on all showers.
> Consumables: Low environmental-impact cleaning products.
> Waste: The policy is to reduce, recycle and compost where possible.

> Conservation & socio-cultural projects: The lodge works closely with local suppliers, farmers and the tourism industry.
> Food supplies: Local and organic foods, including cheese made in the village.
> Employment: 100% local.
> Ownership: Local commercial enterprise.

> Adventure sports
> Craft workshops
> Swimming, water sports
> Walking, trekking, hiking

Ratagan Youth Hostel UK

The famous Eilean Donan castle, whose history is a reminder of the times when defending your clan's territory was a prerequisite for survival, is just 13 kilometres (8 miles) down the lochside from the Hostel at Ratagan. This superb location affords stunning views of the Scottish Highlands on the approach route to the Isle of Skye. The 40-bed hostel has some family rooms. It is an ideal place from which to make a leisurely exploration of the indented coastline by walking, cycling or paddling your canoe, before heading out to Skye or the dramatic but exposed Western Isles.

> Certified to the Green Business Tourism Scheme, scoring an overall Gold Standard against 60 criteria.
> Materials: FSC wood products are encouraged.
> Energy: Efficient combination of lighting, heating, appliances, insulation and renewable-energy use.
> Water: Good maintenance of low-consumption and low-flush appliances; rainwater harvesting.
> Consumables: Products made from recycled materials, eco-cleaners.
> Waste: 'Eliminate, reduce, re-use, recycle' principles ensure waste reduction; supplier take-back agreements; composting.

> CO_2 emissions: The hostel aims to minimize visitor car use by promoting local or human-powered transport.

> Conservation projects: All visitors are informed about the hostel's responsible green charter and the importance of working with the local community and using local resources. Corporate social responsibility reporting is a priority.
> Food supplies: Some sourced from Fair Trade.
> Employment: 25–49% local.

> Ownership: Not-for-profit national enterprise.

> Cycling, mountain biking
> Walking, trekking, hiking

BioHotel at Lunik Park GERMANY

This relatively newly built hotel in the countryside outside Berlin has set its sights on providing a good range of organic food and having an integrated energy policy to drive down its carbon footprint. The whole establishment is smart and clean. Bedrooms are decorated with muted or warm colours. There is a sauna, and massage and other health treatments are available. Leisurely strolling around the locality offers a fresh perspective of the city and its environs.

> A member of Viabono, a German association that has a strict system of vetting the environmental and social performance of accommodation, based on a set of published criteria.
> Materials: The building is only ten years old, but when refurbishment is needed attention is paid to sourcing low-impact and safe materials.
> Energy: Energy sourced from renewable, green supplier, giving an effective 85% reduction of carbon footprint.

> Conservation & socio-cultural projects: The hotel supports the Deutsche Waldjugend, associations of young people who look after the forest. Next door to the hotel is a project called Naturschutzturm Berliner Nordrand, which encourages young Berliners to visit a former watchtower on the Berlin Wall that now forms part of a local nature area.
> Food supplies: Most products sourced from organic farms and suppliers conforming to the Bioland Ökologischer Landbau, the leading German organic farmers' association.
> Employment: 100% local.
> Ownership: Local and national commercial cooperative enterprise.

> Swimming, water sports
> Walking, trekking, hiking
> Wildlife safari

Dunstanburgh Castle Hotel UK

Not far from Lindisfarne Castle and Holy Island on the Northumberland coast sits the coastal village of Embleton, where you will encounter the homely comforts of Dunstanburgh Castle Hotel, a family-run establishment with 18 traditionally decorated bedrooms, three cottage suites in converted stone buildings within the gardens and two restaurants. It is an ideal location for coastal walkers, for cyclists, as the Sustrans national cycleway runs through the village, for nature-lovers, who will be especially drawn to the nearby nature reserve of Farne Islands and the sands of Embleton Links, for golfers, with 15 courses within easy reach, and for those with an interest in historic buildings. Indeed, Embleton is known as the 'castle capital' of the north: there are six castles within half an hour of the hotel, including Alnwick Castle which featured as 'Hogwarts' in the first two Harry Potter films.

> The hotel comprises a series of restored traditional buildings and its environmental management system is certified under the Green Tourism Business Scheme (GTBS).
> Energy & water: Both are closely monitored to keep use to a minimum; zero-carbon mains electricity supplier.
> Waste: All waste is sorted and recycled, including glass, paper, plastic, cans; cooking oil is collected and turned into bio-fuel by a local company.

> Conservation projects: Extensive hedge planting with native species, introduction of wildflowers, bird nesting boxes and feeders. The hotel set up and supports the Alnwick branch of Friends of the Earth.
> Food supplies: Fair Trade tea and coffee and purchasing from the local butcher, baker and fish merchant.
> Employment: 75–99% local.
> Ownership: Local commercial enterprise.

> Cycling, mountain biking
> Walking, trekking, hiking
> Golf

Sankt Helene DENMARK

This diverse complex of 25 holiday apartments, 40 family rooms, 28 cabins and a campsite sits in the Danish countryside of North Zeeland within easy reach of the sea. Certified to Green Key standards since 1997, it is a relaxed destination for family holidays or weekend getaways. Accommodation is basic with the clean lines of the Scandinavian aesthetic. The quirky triangular-roofed cabins are fun, economical and have that real holiday atmosphere. Central facilities include a large restaurant. All kinds of sports activities and ball games can be found on the site, but a bicycle and a route map give you freedom to enjoy visiting local castles, museums, nature trails (there's a Nature Team for the children), the vast forest of Tisvilde Hegin or miles of clean, white, sandy Blue Flag beaches. According to folklore, the nearby Helene Kilde Spring has restorative properties, especially if visited on Sankt Hans, or Midsummer's Eve, in June.

> Certified to Green Key ecotourism label
> Materials: Old buildings feature traditional thatch and timber and brick walls.
> Energy: Solar energy for hot-water heating; low-energy lighting.
> Water: Low-flow equipment to conserve water.

> Conservation and socio-cultural projects: The resort sponsors several local community projects. The Nature Team produces a monthly nature bulletin, field kits and a quiz trail, and generally encourages children to explore the natural environment.
> Cultural events: Visitors are encouraged to explore and attend local events.
> Employment: 75–99% local.
> Ownership: Local not-for-profit enterprise.

> Cycling, mountain biking
> Swimming , water sports
> Walking, trekking, hiking
> Games and sports

Rufflets Country House Hotel UK

This turreted mansion house on the outskirts of the famous golfing town of St Andrews is full of character. Designed in the 1920s by a local architect, Donald Mills, for the widow of a successful jute-trading baron from Dundee, it was converted into a hotel in the 1950s. A substantial 4-hectare (10-acre) garden embraces the hotel and two self-catering lodges and is managed for guests and local wildlife in equal measure. Indulge yourself in the selection of a hundred malt whiskies or dine in the acclaimed Garden Restaurant on food from the kitchen garden and regional Scottish fare. With over six golf courses close by, this is nirvana for enthusiasts. The Fife peninsula offers fantastic walking and biking along the coastal path.

> The hotel publishes a detailed environmental policy as part of its Green Tourism UK Gold Award.
> Energy: Policy to improve energy efficiency via radiator thermostats, insulation, energy-saving light bulbs, external lights on movement-sensitive timers, house-staff vigilance and reduced laundry washing.
> Water: New banqueting suite is equipped with rainwater harvesting system to supply on-site laundry; greywater is treated and used for toilets and the garden.
> Consumables: Ecolab cleaning agents.
> Waste: Policy to reduce wastage and increase recycling of glass and paper; safe removal of cooking oils.
> CO_2 emissions: This is a carbon-neutral business offsetting 273,000 kilograms of CO_2 annually (audited data from the Carbon Neutral Company) by investing in reafforestation in south-west Scotland, an energy-efficiency scheme in Jamaica and a wind-farm energy project in New Zealand.

> Conservation & cultural projects: The gardens are a project in themselves, having extensive formal, vegetable, flower and 'wild' sections improved with native planting. The hotel is involved with diverse projects to support the local community and increase people's skills with personal development training.
> Food supplies: Where possible local suppliers provide herbs and vegetables to complement those grown in the garden.
> Cultural events: Annual *ceilidh* dance.
> Employment: 25–49% local.
> Ownership: Local commercial enterprise.

> Annual Scottish *ceilidh* dinner
> Golf
> General leisure pursuits

YHA Ninebanks UK

Along the valley of the River Tyne is the market town of Hexham and some 20 kilometres (12 miles) to the south-west, in the peaceful valley of Mohope Burn in the North Pennines Area of Outstanding Natural Beauty (AONB), sits the Ninebanks youth hostel. This converted 17th-century leadminer's cottage has been extended to create a 26-bed hostel. The local landscape is rich in natural and industrial history, including the Killhope lead-mining centre, and is best explored on foot or by bicycle. The diverse geology of the area has been recognized with a UNESCO European Geopark designation and is reflected in the striking landforms in the region.

> Certified to the Green Business Tourism Scheme, scoring an overall Gold Standard.
> Materials: The hostel buys secondhand furniture and equipment, where possible and appropriate, as well as ethically sourced wood.
> Energy: Solar hot water and solar photovoltaic panels; high levels of insulation; a log burner uses scrap wood from a local estate.
> Water: Spring water is UV-filtered.
> Consumables: Recycled goods are purchased where possible; Ecover cleaning products used.
> Waste: All sorted, composted, or recycled.
> CO_2 emissions: The hostel aims to minimize visitor car use by promoting local or human-powered transport. There is a C2C (Sea to Sea) cycle route near by.

> Conservation projects: The hostel supports the British Trust for Conservation Volunteers (BTCV) and provides accommodation for working holidays for volunteers.
> Food supplies: Where possible, food is Fair Trade or purchased from a local wholefood cooperative.
> Employment: Local part-time warden.
> Ownership: National enterprise with charity status.

> Cycling, mountain biking
> Walking, trekking, hiking
> Industrial archaeology

YHA Alfriston UK

This robust 16th-century listed building, part flint house and part Tudor, sits in its own large garden in the quiet Cuckmere valley near the village of Alfriston in East Sussex. This 68-bed hostel with four twin-bedded rooms is an ideal centre from which to ramble or cycle over the South Downs exploring the rich local history, from Norman to medieval times. The National Cycle Network 2 is near by and it is just 5 kilometres (3 miles) to the coast and the stunning Seven Sisters cliffs. Here is the rural idyll of England's green and pleasant land.

> Certified to the Green Business Tourism Scheme, scoring an overall Gold Standard against 60 criteria. The guidelines from the association Hospitable Climates are also followed.
> Materials: The hostel uses only FSC timber and purchases secondhand or refurbished goods.
> Energy: Green electricity supplier; low-energy lighting.
> Water: Rainwater harvesting for toilets.
> Waste: Recycling of packaging for consumable goods; recycling of equipment and textiles where possible.
> CO2 emissions: The Youth Hostels Association (YHA) aims to minimize visitor car use by promoting local or human-powered transport.

> Conservation projects: The YHA works with the British Trust for Conservation Volunteers (BTCV) and provides accommodation for working holidays for volunteers at certain hostels.
> Food supplies: Fair Trade tea, coffee and hot chocolate.
> Cultural events: Alfriston Hostel works with the local village community.
> Employment: 100% live-in staff, 25–49% local origin.
> Ownership: National enterprise with charitable status.

> Cycling, mountain biking
> Swimming, water sports
> Walking, trekking, hiking

Aislabeck Eco-lodges UK

A new breed of eco-lodge is stirring in the green countryside of the UK. The lodge at Aislabeck in the Swale valley of the Yorkshire Dales set the standards that other aspiring eco-preneurs will have to aim for. Nestled in 21 hectares (52 acres) of meadow and woodland, the ten lodges are designed to blend with the landscape, utilize the best green technology and provide a sense of space and luxury. This is achieved by a design principle of 'nature meets e-glazing' combined with renewable energy sources (local and national grid electricity), natural filtered spring water, rainwater harvesting and other measures. Operated by Natural Retreats, Aislabeck could be the 'greenprint' for a zero-carbon footprint development, treading sensitively and embracing the distinctive landscape, habitat and locality. Being in a national park has no doubt helped in the creation of the lodges, but such standards should be applied to any landscape: planners take note.

> Materials: Timber-framed from sustainable woodlands; insulation from recycled paper; evergreen sedum turf roof.
> Energy: Solar heating; wood-burning stoves; e-glazed high-insulation windows.
> Water: Natural spring water for drinking and showers.
> Consumables: Eco cleaning and bathroom products.
> CO2 emissions: Zero-carbon footprint rating for the site.

> Conservation projects: The company gives a percentage of its annual profits to the Yorkshire Wildlife Trust and a guaranteed annual minimum payment. It is also a member of the Woodland Trust and allows a local sheep sanctuary to graze its sheep rent-free on the Aislabeck pastures.
> Food supplies: Food hampers containing local products are given to guests on arrival. The company has also sponsored a town shopping and eating guide, which promotes local facilities.

> Employment: Local.
> Ownership: Natural Retreats is a UK company.

> Adventure sports
> Craft workshops
> Swimming, water sports

Agriturismo Colle Regnano ITALY

Italy is the leading country in Europe in developing its agro-tourism industry. Colle Regnano is perhaps typical of the quality of accommodation and experiences that agro-tourism can offer. Situated some 40 kilometres (25 miles) from the Adriatic Sea, in the Marche of Italy, these restored farm buildings nestle into the agrarian landscape of the Macerata hills. Simply decorated and appointed with natural materials, the three rooms and five self-catering apartments can sleep 25 people. There is a wonderful rural vista just outside the door and plenty of opportunity to explore the farm and its environs. You can watch demonstrations of traditional bread-making in the old furnace or attend classes in handicrafts, ceramics and painting. Near by are the Monti Sibillini National Park and sporting facilities in the thermal spa town of Tolentino.

> Certified by AIAB, the authority for Legambiente Turismo, the Italian eco-label. Colle Regnano is a 17th-century farmhouse and outbuildings restored using natural materials with reference to bio-building techniques and the cultural and architectural heritage.
> Materials: A lot of natural wood has been used without chemical treatment or adhesive, together with tiles and stone.
> Energy: Renewable energy sources, energy conservation including passive architectural features such as a *solaio* (a ventilated loft).
> Waste: Recycling policy.

> Food supplies: Products from the farm are used, including wine, oil, jams and salami; Fair Trade for some goods.
> Cultural events: Excursions to see the art of local cities and rural way of life.
> Employment: 100% local; use of local guides is encouraged.
> Ownership: International agricultural enterprise.

> Craft workshops
> Farm and vineyard work
> Food and cookery classes
> Swimming, water sports
> Conservation work
> Walking, trekking, hiking

The Second Paradise Retreat CANADA

Just an hour's drive from Halifax in Nova Scotia, on Canada's Atlantic shore, lies the town of Lunenburg, an 18th-century colonial town now designated as a UNESCO World Heritage Site. Another ten minutes away is The Second Paradise Retreat, a superb getaway with four self-contained guesthouses and a complete farmhouse, all with stunning views of the sea. The landscaped gardens run down to the pristine shore and old boathouse where you can hire kayaks and rowing boats to explore the indented coastline. Screw up your eyes and you can almost glimpse the bygone days when the pioneers lived simple, uncluttered lives.

> Certified by the Canadian Audubon Green Leaf™ Eco-rating Program, with four out of five 'leaves'.
> Materials: Vernacular materials predominate, especially timber from farmland, local plaster and low-VOC paints.
> Energy: Very efficient Kachelofen wood-burning stoves heat two of the cottages and the farmhouse; the other two cottages are heated with propane; low-energy light bulbs and motion sensors used for night lighting.
> Water: Natural springs feed two wells that supply all water needs; showers only, no baths.

> Consumables: Anti-allergenic and environmentally safe detergents and cleaning agents, all eco-certified.
> Waste: Glass, metal, plastic and paper are recycled and organic waste is composted.

> Conservation projects: The gardens and pastures are tended using organic methods only; the retreat is a member of two coastal conservation projects, including one at nearby Mahone Islands.
> Food supplies: Guests are encouraged to buy at local farmers' markets.

> Cultural events: The retreat supports the local folk music scene.
> Employment: 100% local.
> Ownership: Local commercial enterprise.

> Craft workshops
> Dance, music
> Swimming, water sports
> Volunteer work
> Walking, trekking, hiking

Ecocabin UK

Reconnecting to nature needs relearning. Ecocabin, in the hills of Shropshire, UK, is a small establishment that facilitates that process. Basic but comfortable, utilitarian yet charming, this larger-than-average hut states its position simply, and uses natural materials honestly and modestly. Nourishment from local spring water, organic milk and food are enhanced by the song of curlews and buzzards, and wildflowers on your doorstep.

> Materials: Built with homegrown wood, wool insulation, reeds, lime and clay.
> Energy: Heated with a wood-pellet stove; solar panels; electricity from a renewable-energy supplier.
> Water: Local spring water.
> Consumables: Chemical-free decor, cleaning and maintenance
> Waste: Most household waste is sorted, then recycled or composted.

> Conservation projects: There is a wildflower meadow outside the front door, planted with native species only. Ecocabin works closely with Shropshire Hills Area of Outstanding Natural Beauty. Discounts offered to car-free visitors.
> Food supplies: The hut provides a 'buy local' shopping service.

> Craft workshops
> Walking, trekking, hiking

Hunas Falls Hotel SRI LANKA

About 1,000 metres (3,280 feet) up in the montane cloud forest, near the town of Kandy, sits the tranquil resort of Hunas Falls, a waterfall forming a dramatic backdrop to the restaurant and lake. The climate supports such diverse vegetation as bamboo, fern and avocado, and a medicinal-spice, vegetable and herb garden. Local guides will take you on mountain walks. A relatively large complex houses rooms that mix modern, traditional and minimalist styles and afford a certain level of relaxing luxury.

> Energy: Staff implement an energy conservation policy, for example, by switching off unnecessary lights and air-conditioning; all equipment is kept at high levels of efficiency.
> Water: The hotel conserves and manages water; treated water from the sewage plant is used to irrigate the garden and golf course.
> Consumables: Chemical pollution is prevented; environmentally friendly products are used; shampoo distributed in ceramic bottles; flowers instead of air fresheners; no aerosols; biodegradable chemicals used for pest control.
> Waste: Plastic packaging reduced; coconut shells used for barbecues; other waste separated for collection and recycling; organic waste is composted.

> Conservation projects: Seedlings of indigenous trees are grown in the hotel's nursery for a programme to reafforest 1.4 hectares (3 acres) of denuded hillsides near by. Guests may buy a tree for planting. Wedelia, an invasive weed, is gradually being replaced with native species. The Hotel donates to a ward at Wattegama hospital.
> Food supplies: There are several gardens with over 70 species of medicinal plants, 30 spices, 30 vegetables and 30 herbs.
> Cultural events: Tours of local tea factories, villages.
> Employment: 100% local.
> Ownership: Local commercial enterprise.

> Dance, music
> Farm and vineyard work
> Food and cookery classes
> Swimming, water sports
> Volunteer work
> Walking, trekking, hiking
> Wildlife safari

Diamond Beach Village KENYA

Situated on the island of Manda, with sister island Lamu close by, is Diamond Beach Village, an exceptionally relaxed environment where boat and donkey are the only forms of transport. About six hours north of Mombasa, Kenya's main port, the resort offers a range of accommodation including a tree house and six *bandas* (traditional huts) for two to six people. Leisure comes easy here. Stroll the beaches, watch the *dhows* glide past or visit Lamu, the oldest town in East Africa, which hosts a market and a Swahili museum and is great for seafood feasts. Enjoy traditional food after a hard day's snorkelling, windsurfing or fishing.

> Materials: All *bandas* (huts) are made from local timber in a traditional style with coconut-palm thatched roof, woven star-palm floors and walls.
> Energy: Solar and paraffin lamps are used after the evening generator is closed down.
> Water: Greywater is used for garden irrigation.
> Waste: Plastic bags are not used, the woven local bags being preferred; all biodegradable materials are composted.

> Conservation & community projects: Guests are encouraged to visit the local turtle project. Member of the Lamu Safi group to keep local beaches clean.
> Food supplies: The resort buys fish and some farm produce, including jams and wild honey, from local sources.
> Employment: 100% local.
> Ownership: International commercial enterprise.

> Adventure sports
> Craft workshops
> Dance, music
> Food and cookery classes
> Swimming, water sports
> Walking, trekking, hiking

Ocotal Beach Resort COSTA RICA

With extensive views over the Papagayo Gulf on Costa Rica's northern Pacific coast, this four-star resort offers all the usual facilities, with excellent diving and sports fishing for all kinds of fish, from rays, jacks, whale sharks, giant mantas, sea turtles and dolphins to scary sharks such as the bull and white-tip.

> Certified to CST, the Costa Rican sustainable tourism standard, with a rating of three out of five 'leaves'.
> Energy: The resort tries to use natural ventilation and illumination where possible; low-energy lighting.
> Consumables: All cleaning products are selected for their low environmental impact.
> Waste: A complete water-treatment plant ensures greywater is used for irrigation; organic waste is composted; bulk purchases reduce consumption of packaging.

> Conservation & socio-cultural projects: The resort's dive shop received an environmental award in 2006 for its efforts towards aquatic conservation.
> Cultural events: Guests are alerted to events in Coco Town.
> Employment: 80% Costa Rican staff.
> Ownership: International commercial enterprise.

> Adventure sports
> Swimming, water sports
> Walking, trekking, hiking
> Conservation work

Le Relais du Bastidou FRANCE

In the middle of the Gascony countryside in south-west France, this Logis de France establishment offers a taste of rural French life, yet is just a couple of hours from the bustling cities of Toulouse and Bordeaux. The accommodation comprises eight bedrooms, each with its own lounge and en-suite shower, and many featuring stone walls and massive wooden-beamed ceilings, offset with French country-style furnishings. The galleried restaurant specializes in local cuisine and celebrates the Slow Food movement. A sauna room and hot tub as well as other facilities are all contained in a friendly gaggle of buildings. This is a good touring base in the centre of a thriving cultural region, yet within easy reach of the Pyrenees mountains and the Spanish border.

> Certified to the Green Key (La Clef Verte) scheme and by the Association Française d'Ecotourisme.
> Materials: Traditional materials used to restore existing buildings.
> Energy: Wood-burning stoves; thermostats on radiators.
> Water: Low-flush toilets.
> Waste: Waste is sorted for disposal or recycling; waste-water treatment plant.

> Food supplies: The hotel supports the Slow Food movement and 90% of the products for the hotel and restaurant are of local origin, encouraging suppliers from the region.
> Employment: 100% local.
> Ownership: National and international commercial enterprise.

> Cycling, mountain biking
> Farm and vineyard work
> Swimming, water sports
> Walking, trekking, hiking
> Fishing

Hotel Mocking Bird Hill JAMAICA

Situated on a hilltop just ten minutes from Port Antonio, this eco-boutique hotel is surrounded by 2.5 hectares (6 acres) of tropical greenery and offers stunning panoramic views towards the Blue Mountains and Caribbean Sea. Comprising ten white, cosily decorated rooms and an independent villa for rental, this is a small retreat where you can just hang out in the hammock on your balcony, engage in a wide variety of sports, tours and community-based projects or indulge yourself in the renowned Mille Fleurs restaurant. The restaurant has been nurtured by the owners, Shireen Aga and Barbara Walker, and has recently been boosted by the addition of chef Elmar Rench. Here you can have your palette titillated by a mélange of Caribbean flavours – jerk, prawns, mangoes, peanuts and coconut – all based on local ingredients. The hotel is forging new ideas in carbon-offset schemes.

> The original choice of site, building layout and day-to-day operations arising out of an integrated environmental management system all represent a conscious effort to minimize environmental impacts.
> Materials: Re-use of materials on site, especially for landscaping.
> Energy: Existing site buildings in traditional Caribbean style include passive cooling features such as covered balconies, louvred windows and the use of cross-wind ventilation; low-energy and minimal night-time lighting; solar LEDs; solar water-heating, solar panels with accumulator batteries to reduce reliance on generator.
> Water: Rainwater is harvested and treated; low-flow toilets and water savers on taps; drinking water supplied in re-usable containers; garden designed to fit local rainfall patterns.
> Consumables: Re-usable and recyclable products used in all departments; local sourcing where possible.
> Waste: Most materials recycled, re-used, composted or supplied as feedstock to local farm; anaerobic waste-water treatment plant.

> CO_2 emissions: All vehicle movements associated with the hotel are kept to a minimum. The hotel works with the Sustainable Tourism Initiative and Myclimate programme. Carbon offsets are offered to support the Jamaican Conservation and Development Trust.

> Conservation & socio-cultural projects: The gardens are organically managed to attract local fauna, including the hummingbirds and the endemic Jamaican owl; the hotel participates in events organized by the Portland Environmental Protection Association. It also works closely with the community, encouraging local businesses, an AIDS charity and an educational programme, ENOUGH, and promotes sustainable tourism.
> Food supplies: Locally sourced seafood, meat and vegetables for the creation of Jamaican, Caribbean and European fusion food. Breads, pasta and ice-creams are always made in the hotel. Suppliers include Tamarind Hill Farm,

the College of Agriculture, Port Antonio, Long Road Cooperative (Annotto Bay), Miss Cherry fishing village and Tom Finnegan.
> Cultural events: Tours to the village of Charles Town to meet the local Maroon community and experience local music, dance and food.
> Employment: Of the 20 staff, 18 are local.
> Ownership: National, commercial enterprise.

> Food and cookery classes
> Swimming, water sports
> Volunteer work
> Walking, trekking, hiking
> Community-based tourism
> Yoga, life coaching

Meliá Bali Villas & Spa Resort INDONESIA

This tropical idyll is set in ten hectares of gardens bordering the white sands of Nusa Dua beach lapped by the Indian Ocean on the southern coast of Bali. This self-contained resort, with a vast range of facilities, offers hotel-style rooms as well as ten luxurious private villas. Balinese decor, furniture and craftsmanship predominate in the common areas, but merge with modern styling in the accommodation areas. Each palatial, palm-shaded, thatch-roofed villa boasts marble floors and teak furnishings and its own private swimming pool. The hotel rooms are also full of natural materials such as wood and rattan in a warm palate of colours. The activity list is enormous, but then the spa might just tempt guests to take it easy.

> Green Globe 21 certified, Gold status, with constant improvements in environmental performance over the last five years following the guidelines produced by the Sol Meliá group's environmental protection manual.
> Energy: Regular monitoring; liquid petroleum gas is used for kitchen operations; efficient washers, driers and ironing machines have been installed.
> Water: Guests are encouraged to think about water conservation; efficient new machinery and maintenance help conserve water resources; bulk water coolers are provided for staff, rather than bottled water.
> Consumables: Recycled paper is used for printing; salt filtration, not chlorine, for swimming pools; biodegradable or low-phosphate laundry detergents.
> Waste: Treated greywater, processed using a biodegradable system, is used to irrigate the landscaped grounds; office paper is re-used; plastic bottles and containers are collected and returned to the manufacturer; old linen is re-used for dusters.

> Conservation & socio-cultural projects: The resort gives financial assistance to tumour surgery; sponsors various local employment programmes and a school for children with physical and mental disabilities; joined the community campaign Clean-Up-The-World, an environmental awareness campaign; and assists a poverty alleviation project in Karangasem.
> Food supplies: The Nursery Corner is a dedicated organic garden, the produce of which is used for vegetarian dishes; buys food locally where possible.
> Cultural events: A Balinese *gamelan* orchestra accompanies dancers for a traditional nightly show.
> Employment: 75–99% local.
> Ownership: Local commercial enterprise.

> Adventure sports
> Craft workshops
> Dance, music
> Food and cookery classes
> Swimming, water sports
> Volunteer work
> Walking, trekking, hiking
> Conservation work

Quinta do Rio Touro PORTUGAL

Between Lisbon and Cabo de Roca, Portugal's westernmost tip, near the historic UNESCO World Heritage Site of Sintra, is a welcoming guesthouse, sitting in its own valley with its subtropical microclimate. Quinta do Rio Touro is a certified organic farm providing bed and breakfast in the main house plus a separate guesthouse nestled in its own sweet spot 100 metres away. Traditional Portuguese hospitality, lots of facilities, including a library, and the tranquillity of the location will help visitors slow down. Visits to the prehistoric remains at Sintra, the sacred hill and the old historical centre are a must, but you can also enjoy just wandering among the lime trees and orange groves or along the nearby coastal paths.

> The complex comprises several traditional buildings restored over the last decade.
> Water: Accessed from the Touro River in the valley.

> Conservation projects: The organic farm sits within the Sintra-Cascais Natural Park, so the management of the land takes due account of ecological needs.
> Food supplies: Organic food from the farm plus local suppliers.

> Employment: Managed by local owner.
> Ownership: Owner-operated commercial enterprise.

> Cycling, mountain biking
> Swimming, water sports
> Walking, trekking, hiking
> Historical visits

Ard na Breatha NORTHERN IRELAND

Situated in Donegal in north-west Ireland, Ard na Breatha is a six-bedroomed guesthouse with restaurant attached. It is well placed for touring the northern half of the Emerald Isle, the nearby Blue Stack mountains providing stunning views over Donegal Bay as well as distant County Tyrone and County Fermanagh in Northern Ireland. Rooms are decorated in creams and warm colours in country style, with pine floors, rugs, pine furniture and wrought-iron bed-heads. The restaurant is light and airy, with a wood-fired stove, and the organic menu takes produce from the farm that surrounds the accommodation. Outdoor pursuits abound: hill-walking, horse riding and a number of golf courses are nearby.

> Certified to the European Eco-label standard.
> Materials: The hotel chooses FSC and other certified materials.
> Energy: Low-energy light bulbs; guests encouraged to turn off lights.
> Water: Reduced water-flow toilets; rainwater collected for garden use.
> Waste: All waste is re-used, recycled or composted.
> CO_2 emissions: Visitors are provided with information on public transport and bicycle hire to encourage lower-impact modes of transport in the area.

> Conservation & socio-cultural projects: The farm is organic and free from all chemical use; local wildlife is encouraged. The guesthouse supports local charities and supply chains.
> Food supplies: All the produce used in the restaurant is local and organic.
> Employment: 100% local.
> Ownership: Local commercial enterprise.

> Food and cookery classes
> Swimming, water sports
> Volunteer work
> Walking, trekking, hiking
> Horse riding
> Golf

Baden Youth Hostel SWITZERLAND

This modern bright hostel is a former 19th-century stable building on the banks of the Limmat River in the thermal spa resort of Baden, equidistant between Basel and Zurich. There are a few two- or four-bed rooms, the remainder being in dormitory style, with well-designed public spaces and a terrace. Next door is the town's well-equipped sports arena and the Véloland Schweiz cycle route Mittelland Route 5 runs near by. So this is a good base for those with active pursuits in mind. Baden Youth Hostel is the first hostel in Switzerland to be awarded the EU 'flower' eco-label for tourist accommodation.

> Energy: Wood-pellet-fired heating system; general energy conservation measures.
> CO2 emissions: The hostel has a partnership with Myclimate and guests are invited to offset the emissions associated with their stay.

> Conservation projects: Monies from the CO2 offset scheme go to ecological projects in Switzerland and abroad; the Hostel supports and has partnerships with WWF.
> Food supplies: The Hostel buys in food daily from local stores.
> Cultural events: Local events and traditions are supported.
> Employment: 75–99% local.
> Ownership: Local and national not-for-profit enterprise.

> Cycling, mountain biking
> Swimming, water sports
> Walking, trekking, hiking

Songjiang Hotel CHINA

The world-renowned design firm, W. S. Atkins, the British company with a track record of eco-tech architectural projects, has won an international design competition for a massive new commercial hotel complex near Shanghai. The 400-bed resort has comprehensive corporate facilities, including conferencing and banqueting rooms, many restaurants, cafés and more. Situated in a disused, water-filled quarry, the location affords unique possibilities for water sports, an underground aquarium and extreme sports including rock climbing and bungi jumping. Natural waterfalls on the quarry face will be embraced by a central atrium, which is to act as a green lung for the complex. This kind of development manifests the same ethos as carbon-neutral eco-city in the planning, Dongtan, to be built for the Shanghai Industrial Investment Corporate (SIIC) on an island in the mouth of the Yangtze River – this one by consulting engineers Arup. Could these developments be the first trickles in a flood of joint British–Chinese ventures that will sweep in an eco-renaissance in the hotel and tourism industry? We will know shortly... .

> Energy: Naturally lit atrium reduces need for artificial lighting and provides ventilation in the core of the building; green roofing controls diurnal temperature range; geothermal heating system.

> Employment: Lots of construction and operational phase jobs for local Shanghai people.
> Ownership: Simao is the client.

> Adventure sports
> Swimming, water sports

Per Aquum Eco-Resort TANZANIA

The resort market is just beginning to wake up to the threat of climate change and the opportunities that exist in the luxury end of the eco-tourism market. The Per Aquum group has a number of resorts and spas in the Maldives, Sri Lanka and Dubai, that regularly feature in the *Condé Nast Traveller* lists catering for the elite traveller. The group's latest development in Nungwi, on the island of Zanzibar, just off the mainland coast, is billed as the world's first zero-carbon five-star resort. London architects Hywel Evans Architecture & Design were given the challenging task of making this brief a reality. Due to be completed in 2008, the eco-resort is entirely powered by solar collectors and wind turbines, predominantly utilizes local materials and includes an array of features designed to minimize environmental impacts. For example, villa walls are shaped to accelerate the cooling effect of sea breezes that pass over natural water infinity pools just in front of each of the 35 villas. Perhaps the biggest question-mark remains over its location, which involves long-distance air travel by its customers and hence copious emissions of climate-changing gases. However, this is an unresolved dilemma affecting all international tourism. Depending on the planned lifetime of the resort, it can only be hoped that the predicted Indian Ocean sea-level rises have also been factored in to the design!

> It remains to be seen whether the developers and architects will go for any kind of building regulation certification, environmental management system or eco-tourism certification. On the face of it, this resort seems to exceed expectations set by many of these certifying authorities.
> Materials: Local reinforced-earth walls, renewable timber and reclaimed stone.
> Energy: Autonomous resort using only solar and wind energy generated on-site, including a solar-powered restaurant. Waste from the planned farm and kitchen will be used to power a bio-mass generator. Even the guests will generate energy when using the gym equipment.
> Water: Rainwater harvesting and seawater desalination.
> Waste: Bio-mass waste used for electricity generation.

> CO_2 emissions: The anticipated 100 staff will all be given bicycles, and electric cars (charged with renewable energy) will be used to pick up guests from the airport. Guests will have their flights carbon-offset at a (non-opt-out?) charge.

> Conservation & socio-cultural projects: None known to date.
> Food supplies: The resort will have its own farm.
> Employment: The intention is to build and staff the hotel with local people.
> Ownership: Commercial international enterprise.

> Swimming, water sports
> Walking, trekking, hiking

culture

These destinations offer everything from self-improvement activities to volunteer work and agro-tourism, where visitors can experience the traditions, music, food and spirituality of indigenous cultures. This provides a rich contrast to the globalized culture in which most of us live. These are earthy, colourful destinations that imbue deeper understanding of diverse socio-cultural values.

Black Sheep Inn ECUADOR

High in the Ecuadorean Andes, the Black Sheep Inn proves that significant socio-cultural benefits can flow to a whole village, Chugchilán, from a small tourism enterprise. The holistic permaculture philosophy, ensuring low-impact buildings and day-to-day operations, is mirrored by local pragmatism, the encouragement of new village services and genuine respect for the cultural value of the people and location. This seems to have resulted in a rare win–win situation, where the facility has comfortably grown alongside and with the residents of the village. For a spectacular Andean location and a window on a living culture, the inn is a real find for the low-footprint adventurous traveller. This might be one of the few places in the world where people are known to take photos of spectacular views from the windows of the composting toilet.

> Materials: Natural and renewable resources such as adobe, straw and eucalyptus beams; hand-digging on the site.
> Energy: Low-energy light bulbs throughout; solar-powered water pump for irrigation of gardens. On average one US citizen consumes in a year 10,656 kWh of electricity; BSI uses less than half that amount of energy for the whole facility.
> Water: Rainwater is harvested and used for washing and irrigating the gardens; toilets are of the dry composting type.
> Consumables: Bulk purchasing to minimize packaging.
> Waste: All rooms have three baskets for waste separation.

> Conservation & community projects: The Black Sheep Inn has actively encouraged conservation on the Iliniza Ecological Reserve. Native guides, trained in guiding ethics, natural history, first aid and local routes, are provided. Local people are encouraged to continue to build out of adobe and preserve their cultural architectural heritage. Since 1995, when BSI opened, the village of Chugchilán has preserved its cultural charm and now has several small community businesses that also profit from sustainable ecotourism: these include horse-riding tours, a women's knitting cooperative, two locally owned hostels, native guides, a transport cooperative, a public library/computer learning centre and a recycling centre. Other benefits to the community from the influx of tourists include employment, a telephone service, a new health clinic, pavement in the plaza, a doubling of bus routes and a police station. BSI contributes directly to these improvements with library and school books, phone lines, water tanks and tubing, IT and sports equipment, electrical installations, public address systems and teachers' salaries.
> Food supplies: Most food products are

bought locally and some are grown on site.
> Cultural events: There is an Andean folkloric musical instrument lending library and a group of elementary school students perform a traditional dance presentation at the inn once a week.
> Employment: 75–99% local.
> Ownership: Local enterprise, non-national owners.

> Craft workshops
> Swimming, water sports
> Walking, trekking, hiking
> Horse riding

Apani Dhani Eco-lodge INDIA

In the region of Rajasthan, in north-east India, Apani Dhani provides a modest but robust model for aspiring eco-accommodation entrepreneurs throughout the subcontinent. Various different buildings, constructed using traditional craft techniques and decorated with regional handicrafts, surround an intimate courtyard. Pampas thatch huts are cheek-by-jowl with larger brick buildings, surmounted by photovoltaic and solar collector panels. This truly family-run eco-lodge offers workshops from craft (basket- and seat-making, tie-dye) to music, cookery and learning Hindi. See the 19th-century wall paintings on the *havelis* (urban mansions) in nearby Shekhawati, but most of all just absorb the pace of Indian life.

> Materials: Local materials traditionally worked – pampas grass for thatch, sundried clay bricks for interior walls, fired bricks for exterior.
> Energy: Photovoltaic panels for electricity; solar collector and geyser for heating water.
> Water: Rainwater collected into underground tanks and used for organic agriculture. Guests encouraged to wash by pouring water over the body, to conserve water. A reverse osmosis filter is used for potable water in the dining room.
> Waste: Food served on single-use leaf plates, which are composted. All waste composted or recycled.

> Conservation & educational projects: 5% of turnover on room rent supports a local school for disabled children, Asha ka Jharna, and a reafforestation programme.
> Food supplies: Only local vegetarian food, much from the surrounding land, is cooked; vegan can be provided.
> Cultural events: Workshops run by local artisans, *tabla* playing and learning Hindi. Local guides take visitors to Shekhawati, supported by a not-for-profit organization, The Friends of Shekhawati.
> Employment: 100% local.
> Ownership: Family-owned and -run enterprise.

> Craft workshops
> Food and cookery classes
> Volunteer work
> Walking, trekking, hiking

Balenbouche Estate ST LUCIA

Since 1965, the Lawaetz family, originally from St Croix, has owned and managed Balenbouche Estate, a former sugar plantation. Balenbouche was one of the first properties in St Lucia to promote an authentic, sustainable form of tourism. The development and beautification of the property have become the life's work of Uta Lawaetz and her two daughters, who have amassed a sizable collection of Amerindian and colonial artifacts with a view to developing an interpretation centre for visitors. Historical references permeate the buildings and remnants of industrial agriculture, providing an 'otherworldly' point of reference that sits comfortably with the sensitively modern, low environmental-impact facilities. The local organic food is reputed to be among the best on the island. Activities are diverse: birdwatching, hiking, yoga, diving, windsurfing, a field school and research into local history and culture.

> Materials: Natural, salvaged and recycled materials, especially wood.
> Energy: Solar water heating, gas cooking; no TVs, air-conditioning or microwaves.
> Water: Rain and river water is collected.
> Consumables: Visitors encouraged to use natural insect repellent and mosquito nets instead of sprays.
> Waste: Composting.

> Conservation projects: Member of the St Lucia Heritage Tourism Association, which encourages members to implement an effective environmental management system; also involved in a local watershed project.
> Food supplies: Organic garden and local food, with vegetarian and vegan options; homemade local cuisine.
> Cultural events: Member of Choiseul Association for Tourism, Craft and Heritage (site owners and artisans).
> Employment: Local.

> Ownership: Family-owned commercial enterprise.

> Craft workshops
> Dance, music
> Farm work
> Food and cookery classes
> Swimming, water sports
> Volunteer work
> Walking, trekking, hiking

Chalalán Ecolodge BOLIVIA

On the shore of Chalalán lagoon in the heart of the Madidi National Park in the Bolivian Amazon rainforest, Chalalán Ecolodge was built using local techniques and materials to maximize contact with the environment. Featuring over 4,739 plant species, 1,370 vertebrates and 867 tropical birds, Madidi is a biodiversity hotspot. It is also home to the people of San José de Uchupiamonas and a rich archaeological heritage (Inca, Mollo and pre-Columbian peoples). Unusually, it is the local village residents who own and run the lodge, cooperating with several local tour operators. Numbers at the lodge are restricted to 28 at any one time. Tours last from four to six days.

> Materials: These are renewable, breathable buildings, with walls of Copa palm, roofs woven with Asai palm leaves and floors of local hardwood.
> Water: Rainwater harvesting.

> Conservation & cultural projects: Part of the income from the lodge is set aside for local community development.
> Food supplies: Mainly local cuisine.
> Cultural events: As the lodge is run by the local community, guests are exposed to a distinct way of life. Most travel is by river boat.
> Employment: 37 employees, all local.
> Ownership: The local village community of 110 families, which owns the land and lodge and operates the company, is represented by a TCO (Tierra Comunitaria de Origen).

> Craft workshops
> Dance, music
> Swimming, water sports
> Walking, trekking, hiking
> Wildlife safari
> Birdwatching

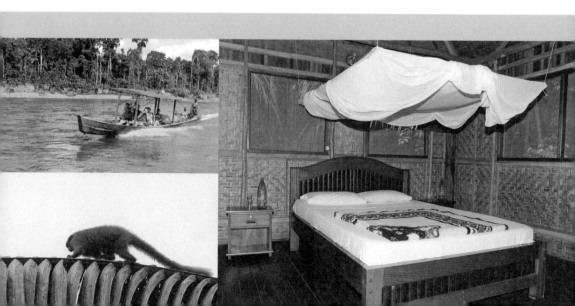

Dar Raha MOROCCO

The mud architecture of northern Morocco is an unusual attraction of this restored traditional and ancient house in the valley of the Dra. Many rooms open to a central courtyard; some have a private terrace and all are elegantly yet simply furnished and decorated, with passive cooling afforded by the artisan construction. Sip your tea in a *salon de thé* while you watch the bustle of the *kasbah* below or gaze at the local mountain range, Zagora, 791 metres (2,595 feet) high. Enjoy the authentic, home-baked and traditional food cooked in tajines. Take a trek on foot or by camel to see the impressive local archaeology, from an 11th-century citadel to an 18th-century fortified village, or *ksar*, Amezrou. The architecture is *pisé* (rammed earth), designed to reduce the discomfort of the hot desert climate.

> Materials: Traditional and local; mud bricks, artisan detailing.
> Energy: Passive architecture.
> Water: Minimal consumption encouraged by raising cultural awareness.
> Waste: Recycling system.
> CO2 emissions: Journeys by camel and trekking on foot are favoured over 4WDs and quads.

> Conservation projects: Projects are concerned mainly with preserving the local pisé architecture, which is threatened by modern building practices.
> Food supplies: All food is local, as are most other supplies.
> Employment: 75–99% local.
> Ownership: International enterprise.

> Dance, music
> Volunteer work
> Walking, trekking, hiking
> Archaeology tours

Kasbah du Toubkal MOROCCO

This destination is a mould-breaking and successful joint venture between Berber and European partners, offering semi-luxurious or basic accommodation, serious trekking or leisurely cultural trips, remoteness yet comfort. Set in the spectacular but traditionally managed Azzaden valley, the facility is a former restored caïd's palace in the village of Id Issa, overlooked by the snow-capped, 4,170-metre (13,675-foot) peak of Jbel Toubkal, North Africa's highest mountain. Though popular with Condé Nast travellers and corporate managers, these amazing buildings attract more modest eco-adventurers too, and reflect the genuine intent of the partners to create something that will sustain the local economy without transforming it. There is a separate remote mountain trekking lodge, high up in the Atlas mountains.

> Architecture is in the local vernacular style (which was beginning to die out) and the government, apparently seeing its benefits, has taken the architecture of the Kasbah du Toubkal as a blueprint for the High Atlas area.
> Materials: Stone, bricks.
> Energy: Passive architecture encourages night-time cooling; solar power is used for some water heating; candles in the evening replace electricity; all firewood comes from sustainable sources.
> Water: Spring water is fed by gravity and filtered.
> Waste: Rubbish is recycled or incinerated.
> CO_2 emissions: Monthly management flights to Morocco are carbon-offset.

> Conservation & community projects: An environmental management system was developed with input from Friends of the Earth and Green Globe, which jointly fund annual tree planting in the area. The destination has a tourist code that encourages the protection of biodiversity, but its biggest influence comes from engagement with the authorities to protect and promote the Toubkal National Park. Since 1998, a self-imposed tourist tax of 5% has been levied to fund the Association Bassin Imlil, a local NGO that provides a 4WD ambulance service for locals and tourists (there are now two ambulances in different valleys with poor road access), the rubbish clearance system, a *hammam* (public baths) for the village and a boarding house for children to extend their education beyond primary level. Other economic activity is also encouraged and start-up capital was given to the region's first trout farm.
> Food supplies: Mainly local. Excess food is distributed to local communities.
> Cultural events: Kasbah du Toubkal periodically holds open days for up to 700 villagers and their children. The traditional circle dance is performed in the large open space of the garden.

> Employment: Qualified local mountain guides from Imlil are trained in wildlife conservation as part of their government-run training course. Over 95% of all employees are from the local Berber community. In-house training has allowed many to join the workforce and language skills are being encouraged. Employees with eye problems are taken to Marrakech for spectacles.
> Ownership: A socially responsible commercial enterprise with local and international owners.

> Adventure sports
> Dance, music
> Volunteer work
> Walking, trekking, hiking

Gecko Villa THAILAND

In the rural heartlands of north-east Thailand, on the Isaan plateau, sits a three-bedroomed getaway on 20 hectares (49 acres) of gardens, orchards, woodlands, pastures and paddy fields. Three villages are near by, but here there is private seclusion and the rhythms are of Thai country life. Visitors rent the whole villa and can engage with Thai cooking lessons, volunteer work or cultural tours, including rice harvesting, marriage ceremonies and music festivals. This is a far cry from the tourist hotspots of Phuket, Chiang Mai and Pattaya.

> Materials: Local 'Pradoo' wood, harder and stronger than teak.
> Energy: Raised roof, under-house ventilation and veranda assist passive cooling; electricity is metered and guests are encouraged to minimize air-conditioner use; energy-saving fittings are used.
> Water: Rainwater is harvested; the swimming pool contains saltwater and is not chlorine-treated.
> Waste: Recycled wherever possible; local community is encouraged to recycle and not litter.

> Conservation & socio-cultural projects: Projects focus on reafforestation. More than 3 hectares (7 acres) of mature woodland adjoining the property have been acquired to protect from felling and conversion to rice paddy; a similar area is being converted from paddy to woodland. Gecko Villa's existence has maintained family structure in the community by reducing migration to the big cities.
> Food supplies: Own organic fruit, vegetable and herb gardens, plus local rice. Visitors can obtain protein from traditional sources such as insects, snails and frogs if they wish! Banana leaves are used as food wrappers.
> Cultural events: Local guides show guests traditional hunting and food-

gathering techniques; the hotel supports local handicraft activities.
> Employment: 100% local. Village families are stakeholders rather than employees; income from the establishment goes directly to them.
> Ownership: Local and national enterprise.

> Dance, music
> Farm work
> Food and cookery classes
> Swimming, water sports
> Volunteer work
> Conservation work
> Wetland visits

Milia Mountain Retreat GREECE

This is an old Cretan village lovingly restored since 1991 by people passionate about the place, its culture, traditions and environment. Set in 120 hectares (296 acres) of tranquil mountain forest and bush at 500 metres (1,640 feet) in altitude, in the province of Kissamos, this really is a peaceful retreat from the rush of modern life. There are 13 guesthouses and rooms, each with its own distinct atmosphere. Honest materials, chestnut wood and stone, are offset by locally restored furniture. All rooms have fireplaces or wood-burning stoves for the winter and a balcony, terrace or garden. Local organic food emphasizes the *genius loci*, with specialities such as rabbit with *mizithra* (an unpasteurized soft cheese), pork with orange cooked in a wood stove and vegetarian dishes. 18 kilometres of treks around Milia ensure a healthy appetite for the active.

> Materials: All old houses were renovated using local natural materials and restored old furniture.
> Energy: All energy is solar and natural gas supplies the kitchens.
> Water: Comes from a private natural spring; water-saving systems are installed.
> Waste: The waste management system uses greywater for gardens.
> CO2 emissions: Food is local, local transport is minimized, energy is renewable and guests are encouraged to minimize energy use.

> Conservation & socio-cultural projects: Hunting is prohibited on Milia itself; 2,000 carob trees were planted ten years ago; cereal is cultivated to feed wild birds; Milia supports a programme by the Natural History Museum of Crete to protect an endangered vulture, *Gypaetus barbatus*. The gradual development of Milia has brought life back to adjacent villages.
> Food supplies: Only local food, 70% of it coming from own production. Vegetarian food is available.
> Cultural events: An old festival,

held on 8 May, has been revived at the St George Chapel.
> Employment: 25–49% local; a self-employed cooperative.
> Ownership: Local cooperative enterprise.

> Farm work
> Food and cookery classes
> Conservation
> Mountain biking
> Walking, trekking, hiking

Kapawi Ecolodge & Reserve ECUADOR

This lodge complex sits on the Pastaza River in the territory of the Achuar, the indigenous people of this part of the Amazon basin in south-east Ecuador, 80 to 150 kilometres (50 to 95 miles) east of the Andes. The lodge, comprising 19 double or triple rooms with private balconies, has been developed for the benefit of the Achuar people, who number 5,000 individuals in 64 communities, in order to ensure a viable future for the forest, with its 530 species of birds and 10,000 different plants. Here you can wonder at the luxuriant world of the rainforest lining the riverbanks, enjoy exciting new tastes, learn local crafts and explore the distinctive Achuar culture.

> Materials: The lodge is based on a native Achuar design concept with predominantly traditional materials – bamboo, palm thatch, lianas, timber.
> Energy: Lighting is by 6V or 12V low-energy systems powered by a hybrid system of solar energy and a diesel generator; showers are solar-heated.
> Water: River water is taken through sand and ceramic filters, ozone-treated and returned to the river after use following suitable treatment.
> Consumables: All soaps and detergents are biodegradable.
> Waste: Sewage is treated in a three-step system; plastic, glass and metal are packed and transported back to urban areas for recycling; biodegradable waste is composted.

> Conservation and cultural projects: The lodge itself represents a unique experiment, providing up to 60% of the income of the Achuar, including direct employment and handicraft income. It is the largest community-based ecotourism project in Ecuador.
> Food supplies: Manioc, plantain, papayas, fish, lemons and seasonal fruits are supplied locally; other vegetables come from organic farms.
> Cultural events: Guests are given a briefing about Achuar culture and ethics before visiting a local village to learn about a very different way of life.
> Employment: 50–74% local.
> Ownership: National commercial enterprise with community cooperation.

> Dance, music
> Swimming, water sports
> Volunteer work
> Walking, trekking, hiking

Ruboni Community Camp UGANDA

Ruboni Community Camp is in Nyakalengija village at the foothills of the Rwenzori Mountains National Park in Uganda. The camp is a member of the Uganda Community Tourism Association, which promotes tourism that offers real economic benefits to local communities. Accommodation varies from tents to *bandas* (local huts) and homestays. Guided cultural and nature walks are provided by local people, including a visit to a traditional healer and medicinal garden. There are handicraft demonstrations and many opportunities to connect with the daily rhythms and cultural ways of the community.

> Materials: Tin roofs covered by papyrus reed.
> Energy: Solar power.
> Water: Gravity spring-fed water.
> Waste: Dry composting toilets.

> Conservation & community projects: 20 hectares (50 acres) of natural forest are set aside for conservation; seeds are collected for indigenous planting. Natural barriers prevent soil erosion. The local community is trained about conservation issues and sustainable resource use. Tourism supports craft production and the community.
> Food supplies: Organic and local farming is supported.
> Cultural events: Special evening events and daytime cultural tours are organized.
> Employment: 100% local.
> Ownership: Local community-owned and run enterprise.

> Craft workshops
> Dance, music
> Food and cookery classes
> Swimming, water sports
> Volunteer work
> Walking, trekking, hiking
> Wildlife safari

Tahuayo Lodge PERU

Situated in a rainforest reserve, the Reserva Comunal de Tamshiyacu Tahuayo (RCTT), the thatch-roofed buildings sit on stilts in a clearing by the side of the Tahuayo River. This incredibly diverse reserve, a four-hour riverboat trip from Iquitos, hosts the highest recorded density of primate species in the world, and is managed in collaboration with the local Ribereños people. Thanks to this intimate access to such biodiversity, the lodge offers a host of wildlife experiences, from excursions to see medicinal plants to night-time wildlife trips and river canoeing. The accommodation is built from local renewable materials to a design that fits the setting.

> Materials: Locally sourced thatch, timber.
> Energy: Passive ventilation and cooling.

> Conservation & cultural projects: Amazonia Expeditions works with the government and Rainforest Conservation Fund managing the RCTT with local Ribereños people. Dolores Arevalo Beaver, an owner of Amazonia Expeditions, founded an NGO called Angels of the Amazon, which cares for the educational and health needs of the Ribereños community while maintaining their self-sufficient culture.

> Food supplies: This is a full-board-only lodge using local and national suppliers.
> Employment: Mainly local.
> Ownership: National commercial enterprise.

> Adventure sports
> Swimming, water sports
> Walking, trekking, hiking
> Zip-line
> Birdwatching

Momopeho Rainforest Home Hacienda ECUADOR

If you want to discover life down on the farm in the Ecuadorean jungle, Momopeho offers a real insight into the rhythm and reality of daily life on a smallholding, where activities range from early-morning milking to cutting back hearts of palm and bananas, making local cheese and regional culinary recipes, learning handicrafts and riding horses. This family-run hacienda offers comfortable but basic accommodation. The rooms are on a sharing basis and meals are communal, but the camaraderie is part of the deal. The emphasis is on participation.

> Materials: Low embodied-energy (EE) and local materials including timber.
> Energy: Low-energy lighting and use of rechargeable batteries.
> Water: General conservation practices for guests and owners.
> CO2 emissions: The owners are smallholders who look after hectares of trees and productive land for mixed farming.

> Conservation & community projects: The hacienda supports various local projects for water conservation, recycling and protection of the fauna. It helped to consolidate a local milk-supply group, Ganaderos Asociados del Nor Occidente.
> Food supplies: Mainly local or from own production.
> Employment: 100% local; family and local workers and guides.
> Ownership: Local family enterprise.

> Craft workshops
> Dance, music
> Farm work
> Food and cookery classes
> Swimming, water sports
> Walking, trekking, hiking

Il Duchesco ITALY

If you want to learn about the Tuscan way of life and appreciate organic wines, jams, cheeses, hams and breads of the locality and region, then Il Duchesco is the place to visit. The accommodation on this working farm and vineyard is down to earth, furnished in traditional style. Each room has an independent entrance and access to communal kitchen facilities. A daily breakfast buffet of organic products from the farm and surrounding countryside celebrates a living Maremmana culture. At the organic certified winery you can see the wines, grapeseed oil and a natural therapeutic cosmetic range made from Ciliegiolo wine. Courses for visitors are available, including local cookery, wine tasting and pottery. Nature-lovers will enjoy the mountains and wildlife of the Parco Naturale della Maremma.

> Certified to Tuscan and Lombardy region eco-label standards, this was the first farm in Europe to receive the EU 'flower' eco-label.
> Energy: Part supplied by wind power, part by solar panels (for hot water); there has been a 38% reduction in use of propane gas and 45% electricity reduction between 2004 and 2007.
> Water: 31% reduction in use of drinking water.
> Consumables: Organic and eco-label biodegradable products.
> Waste: Reduction of packaging.
> CO2 emissions: Electric bikes can be rented on request to reduce car use; carbon-offset contributions are made to the zero-impact programme of LifeGate.

> Conservation & socio-cultural projects: Il Duchesco contributes to several local groups that promote educational, creative and environmental activities, including the Circuito delle Bio-Fattorie Didattiche. The Wine for Life project allows guests to enjoy a vintage glass of wine, from which a percentage of the proceeds goes to an AIDS project in Mozambique.
> Food supplies: Full organic breakfast buffet.
> Cultural events: The hotel supports local Maremmana cuisine, products and events.
> Employment: 75–99% local.
> Ownership: Local commercial enterprise.

> Cycling, mountain biking
> Farm work
> Food and cookery classes
> Walking, trekking, hiking
> Birdwatching

Enigmata Treehouse Lodge PHILIPPINES

Camiguin Island is just north of the larger island of Mindanao in the south of the Philippines archipelago. The accommodation comprises the lofty Eagle's Nest Suite for four people and rooms on terra firma, eclectically decorated by the local art collective, the Enigmata Creative Circle, which operates the lodge. A brilliant assortment of natural and found materials generates a series of quirky but humane spaces. You'll find sculptures competing with 'stained-glass' walls, twisted wooden beams dancing with the plants, mosaics and more. Open air is everywhere. A number of self-healing activities are available, from putting yourself on a green diet to generating new artwork, dancing, taking the Labyrinth walk or 'moon-bathing' on the nearby beach.

> The tree houses are supported by free-standing pillars to reduce stress on the acacia trees.
> Materials: Timber and recycled materials predominate.
> Energy: Rooms are naturally ventilated; all clothes and linen are sundried; use of electricity is minimized.
> Water: From a mountain spring.
> Waste: The policy is to reduce, recycle, re-use and resell, and to refuse plastic.
> CO_2 emissions: There is a tree-planting programme and a new initiative to impose a local carbon tax on visitors.

> Conservation & socio-cultural projects: Enigmata Creative Circle Inc. is a collective of multidisciplinary artists that holds 'Earth Camps' annually for the local children and women teachers and has a project called GAME to encourage multimedia eco-education via the creative arts.
> Food supplies: Emphasis is on a fresh green diet using home-grown organic food, Fair Trade products.
> Cultural events: The Lodge is embedded in local cultural activities.
> Employment: 100% local.

> Ownership: Local and national not-for-profit enterprise.

> Adventure sports
> Craft workshops
> Dance, music
> Food and cookery classes
> Swimming, water sports
> Volunteer work
> Walking, trekking, hiking
> Conservation work

Fazenda Santa Marina BRAZIL

This early 19th-century farmhouse deep in the state of Minas Gerais, in the region of Estrada Real, exudes colonial charm and is surrounded by a large Atlantic rainforest reserve interspersed with meadows and streams. Up to 20 people can be accommodated at any one time in the main farmhouse, a separate guest house or chalet in the grounds. Fazenda Santa Marina offers an intimate insight into a Brazilian way of life, a culinary tradition and slow rhythms. Activities include horse riding, fishing on the farm's lake, swimming in the pool or in nearby waterfalls, cycling or picnicking with a hamper of best local food. Rural sophistication for the discerning.

> The farm is registered with the Brazilian Ministry of Tourism, PCTS Sustainable Tourism Certification Programme, encouraging local and collective supply-chain management to promote responsible practices.
> Energy: Solar energy is used and there is a policy to reduce consumption.
> Water: A policy is in place to reduce consumption and manage water quality.
> Waste: Preference is given to biodegradable and re-usable materials; plastics are recycled.

> Conservation projects: The farm has just been registered as an eco-corridor linking existing areas of woodland for improved habitat for a primate called *bugio*, a type of brown howler monkey.
> Food supplies: Vegetables, fruit, herbs and flowers are cultivated on the farm, from which also come eggs, milk, cheese, honey, curdled milk and conserves, plus *mineiro* confectionery made in copper pans on a wood stove.
> Employment: 100% local.
> Ownership: National and international commercial cooperative enterprise.

> Adventure sports
> Craft workshops
> Farm work
> Food and cookery classes
> Swimming, water sports
> Volunteer work
> Walking, trekking, hiking
> Conservation work

Banyan Tree Ringha CHINA

Just getting to Banyan Tree Ringha is an adventure. Set in the heart of the dramatic mountainous terrain of Tibet, 3,200 metres (10,500 feet) above sea level in the aptly named Shangri-La County, Diquing Tibetan Autonomous Prefecture, Yunnan, this complex of individual two-storey lodges, built in the traditional Tibetan farmhouse style, is empathic with the rich cultural heritage of the region. Aside from the intensity of the surrounding landscape, the interiors are sure to stimulate the senses, with authentic artifacts, blazing fires and handcrafted wooden bathtubs that reflect a sensitivity to the locale. Most of the buildings at the resort are made from old Tibetan farmhouses bought from local families and then resited and reconstructed, using local labour and needing no new timber, so the income accrued to the benefit of local people.

> Materials: Local recycled stone, timber.
> Energy: Natural lighting where possible, low-energy light bulbs and automatic switching.
> Water: Sourced from snow melt 2 kilometres away.
> Waste: Monthly rubbish collection at the resort and neighbouring village.
> CO_2 emissions: As part of the Greening Communities initiative, Ringha is included in a ten-year tree-planting programme.

> Conservation & socio-cultural projects: All guests are encouraged to contribute a nominal amount per night to the Green Imperative Fund (GIF) set up by Banyan Tree Hotels & Resorts. The GIF backs environmental action and community-based projects around each resort. At Ringha this means sharing knowledge about waste management techniques and supplying an incinerator for the village of Geino, a water pump for farmland and solar heating panels for 14 families. The resort has also supported local AIDS orphans and educational outreach projects.
> Food supplies: As many supplies and materials are purchased from the local market as possible.
> Cultural events: A local Tibetan cultural show is arranged for guests.
> Employment: 75–99% local; eight local guides speak fluent English, Chinese, Tibetan and Hindi.
> Ownership: International commercial enterprise.

> Dance, music
> Volunteer work
> Walking, trekking, hiking
> Conservation work

Landhotel Urstromtal GERMANY

It makes a refreshing change to have access to a major city, in this case Berlin, without being stressed out by urban life. This restored traditional 18th-country farmhouse is in the small village of Kemnitz, in the natural forest reserve of Nuthe-Nieplitz, providing excellent walking, cycling, birdwatching and other country pursuits. Six rooms cleverly combine original antique features with subtle decor and modern comforts, and there is a sauna to ease those tired muscles. Both Berlin and Potsdam are just 40 minutes away. Also within reach are the historic castles of Brandenburg and the Cistercian monastery of Zinna.

> Member of the Viabono scheme focused on improving environmental management.
> Materials: Restoration of the building used only ecological materials.
> Water: Greywater is treated by plants.

> Conservation projects: The hotel supports the Nuthe-Nieplitz Nature Park and landscaped gardens.
> Food supplies: Local food supply is encouraged.
> Employment: Operated by local owners.
> Ownership: Commercial enterprise.

> Cycling, mountain biking
> Walking, trekking, hiking
> City sightseeing

Larsbo Gård SWEDEN

Sweden, land of the lakes, is also the land of the forest and lots of it surrounds the traditional farm smallholding of Larsbo Gård. This family-run bed and breakfast is a working smallholding that breeds Gute sheep, keeps two workhorses for tending the hay meadows and pastures and has its own vegetable garden. Summer, autumn and winter offer such varied pursuits as canoeing on the lakes, hand-scything the hay, mushrooming in the woods, jig-fishing for char and, just like Santa, running through crisp snow in a horse-drawn sleigh. Here there are some timeless rhythms.

> Certified to Green Key standards.
> Energy: A wood-fired boiler in the basement heats 4,000 litres (1,057 gallons) of water for heating and hot water. Any wood used is sourced from sustainably managed forests.
> Water: Water is sourced from a well on-site; taps are fitted with reduced-flow heads.
> Waste: All organic waste is composted, and plastic, metal, glass and other materials are recycled.

> Conservation & socio-cultural projects: The hotel helps with protection of the freshwater pearl mussel and with the restoration of farm meadows by grazing the land with sheep and horses to increase biodiversity. It is also a member of several community organizations and the regional tourist board.
> Food supplies: Local food supply is encouraged.
> Employment: 100% local.
> Ownership: Local commercial cooperative enterprise.

> Dance, music
> Farm work
> Food and cookery classes
> Swimming, water sports
> Walking, trekking, hiking
> Wildlife safari
> Conservation work

Pousada Vila Serrano BRAZIL

In the centre of the north-eastern state of Bahia sits the Chapada Diamantina National Park. Famed for its 19th- and early 20th-century mining history, this region is fast becoming a popular area for hiking and ecological tours. Lençóis, a pretty, old colonial Portuguese town near the border of the park, is a good base from which to explore the landscape, amazing waterfalls and caves of the region. Visit between November and February if you want frisky, full rivers to swim in, or August to November for the best orchids. This *pousada*, sitting in a forested area just a few minutes from the centre of the town, sensitively replicates the colonial architecture to create an oasis of calm, the gardens attracting their own myriad birds, butterflies and occasional inquisitive monkeys. The 11 rooms are simply but elegantly furnished, with bright bedspreads, clay-tiled floors and local artworks on the walls. Much of the food for the buffet breakfast originates from the garden or from local markets. Here is a cosy, secluded guesthouse to retire to after strenuous forays into the park or walks around the town.

> Certified by the Brazilian sustainable tourism scheme, PCTS.
> Materials: The *pousada* was built in the traditional Portuguese colonial style of Lençóis by local craftspeople, artisans and labourers. For example, the doors and windows were made by carpentry students from the Liceu de Arte. Bricks were made from compressed earth admixed with a very small quantity of cement made *in situ*. Timber came from managed eucalyptus plantations in reafforestation areas, in order not to use native forest timbers. Walls were treated with lime and natural dye colours, allowing them to breathe.
> Energy: Showers are heated with solar power.
> Water: Laundry system uses minimal water.
> Consumables: Low-impact detergents.
> Waste: Plastic, glass and aluminium cans are recycled and organic waste is composted.
> CO2 emissions: There are plans to buy an ethanol-powered car.

> Conservation & socio-cultural projects: The villa supports the local environmental NGO, the Grupo Ambientalista de Lençóis, on various conservation projects, as well as two local community NGOs and sporting events.
> Food supplies: Some fruit and herbs are grown in the garden. Cheese and yogurt are made from local milk. Organic products are purchased from the local market.
> Employment: 100% local, including guides.
> Ownership: Local commercial enterprise.

> Adventure sports
> Swimming, water sports
> Walking, trekking, hiking

Malealea Lodge & Pony Trek Centre LESOTHO

Nestled in the aptly named Valley of Paradise, Malealea Lodge & Pony Trek Centre is a small complex of five *rondavels* (traditionally constructed stone and thatch huts), farmhouse- and lodge rooms in the breathtaking landscape of the Lesotho highlands. The lodge acts as a focal point for a variety of horse-trekking and hiking tours through the heartland of the Basotho, with stays in village accommodation. Trekking across a land without fences, wading through rivers and embracing the dramatic scenery forge an intimate relationship with the place and its people. For the less energetic, 4WD off-road options can be taken. Either way, here is an opportunity to avoid the usual barriers between tourist and local. In the environs of Malealea you can get close up – meet a *sangoma* (a traditional herbalist), hear local music, see Bushman paintings or just drink in the scenery.

> Materials: Local stone, thatch for the rondavels.
> Energy: Staying in village accommodation while trekking means that energy (gas for cooking) is in limited supply, so careful usage is practised.
> Water: as above.
> CO2 emissions: Trekking by horse is an inherently low-carbon travel option.

> Conservation & community projects: Guests are encouraged to plant trees in the village. The Malealea Development Trust collects funds from hiking trails for a number of community projects – adult education, health education and facilities, skills development, craftwork, heritage and conservation work.
> Food supplies: Vegetables from local farmers when available.
> Cultural events: Pony trekking through the countryside and villages of the Basotho people, including accommodation in native villages.

> Employment: 100% local, including guides.
> Ownership: Local commercial enterprise.

> Dance, music
> Volunteer workshops
> Walking, hiking
> Pony trekking

Desert Lodge EGYPT

Situated on the top of a cliff, Desert Lodge overlooks the historic mud-brick village of Al Qasr, dating from the 12th century – the time of Salahuddin Ayyubi – with distant views of dunes in the Sahara desert. The village's heritage is protected under the governorate of the Dakhla oasis. This care of the built environment manifests itself in the lodge's empathy with the unique landscape. The lodge itself is of traditional construction, with 35 large palace-like rooms, each one measuring more than 35 square metres (375 square feet). There are terraces, a cafeteria, a dining room and tents for tea and Arabic coffee. Elsewhere in the complex there are craft workshops, a hot mineral spring for swimming, a library and an internet café. Take a day tour to explore the wonders of the desert and fascinating archaeology from the time of the Pharaohs onwards, or go on a guided walk or a camel trek.

> Materials: Locally produced bricks, mud, palm reed.
> Energy: Solar power for hot water.
> Water: Tap water is filtered and given to guests in re-usable glass bottles.
> Consumables: Environmentally friendly cleaning products.
> Waste: Waste is reduced and separated.
> CO_2 emissions: The only heating comes from gas in winter and hot-water bottles!

> Conservation & education projects: 3% of revenue goes to local environment and schools projects.
> Food supplies: Some come from the resort's own organic farm and the rest (80–90%) from local sources; some items from Fair Trade suppliers in Cairo.
> Cultural events: The resort encourages tourists to take lessons in language, guiding and cooking.
> Employment: Use of local guides, porters and camel drivers is encouraged; hotel staff about 95% local.
> Ownership: National (80%) and international (20%) commercial enterprise.

> Craft workshops
> Swimming, water sports
> Walking, trekking, hiking
> Wildlife safari

Albergue das Laranjeiras BRAZIL

The rich colonial history and architecture of Brazil are embodied in the state of Bahia. This hostel sits in the district of Pelourinho, a World Heritage Cultural site in the city of Salvador. Accommodation ranges from double rooms (with or without bathrooms) to dormitories, some with balconies facing the elegant street. This is the place to sample everything from Portuguese language to capoeira or Afro dance classes. Time your visit right and you can join in one of the many carnivals that light up the city's streets.

> Certified by the Brazilian ecotourism authority for the hostel's environmental policy.
> Energy: A responsible energy-consumption policy is implemented.
> Consumables: Use of recycled and recyclable paper and Fair Trade goods.
> Waste: Oil and tin cans are recycled.

> Food supplies: Local supplies are sourced.
> Cultural events: The hostel supports local carnivals, for example the Santa Bárbara, São João, Yemanjá, Bonfim and Candomblé festivals.
> Employment: 100% local.
> Ownership: Local commercial enterprise.

> Conservation projects: The hostel is involved with the preservation of buildings in the historical centre; donates bed linen and mattresses to a nursery and homeless people; donates food to the Christmas party of a disabled children's charity.

> Dance, music
> Food and cookery classes
> Swimming, water sports
> Dance, music classes

Toilogt Ger Camp MONGOLIA

Mongolia stretches across the landmass of Central Asia – mountains, desert, steppe – landscapes largely unknown to the international travel market, so it is fantastic that new *ger* (traditional tent) camps are now opening up. Toilogt sits on a thin isthmus on the north-western shore of Hovsgol Lake, in the north of the country, surrounded by trees and forested mountains. The 20 *gers* are heated by a wood stove, with the comfort of a wooden floor, solar lighting and thick sheep's-wool felt walls. There are some wooden cabins and a central lodge providing all the facilities you will need and serving robust Mongolian food. The folk tradition of *hoomi* throat-singing is alive and well, providing entertainment and a taste of a little-known culture. Wildlife is varied and exotic, including elk, reindeer, ibex, roe and musk deer and predators such as the red wolf. Lake pleasures include kayaking, boat trips and strolling by the waterside.

> Materials: Traditional techniques and materials for the lodge and *gers* (cedar poles, felt, horse-mane twine).
> Energy: Solar-powered lighting.

> Food supplies: Lamb, beef and vegetables from local herders and farmers.
> Cultural events: *Hoomi* throat-singing.
> Employment: 100% local.
> Ownership: Mongolian-owned and managed commercial enterprise.

> Swimming, water sports
> Walking, trekking, hiking
> Wildlife safari

Three Camel Lodge MONGOLIA

45 felt *gers* (traditional nomadic tents) cluster around a lodge near an ancient volcanic outcrop in the Gobi desert, Mongolia. These gers are constructed using traditional materials and techniques, but scaled up to accommodate up to four guests, and are solar-powered. The stone and wooden lodge is crafted, without even one nail, according to Mongolian Buddhist principles. The steppe environs offer a wide range of activities in stunning landscapes, from camel trekking to visits to sites of palaeontological interest, interactions with the nomadic way of life or encounters with wild sheep, gazelles and eagles.

> Materials: Vernacular and traditional techniques, using stone, Siberian larch poles and felt fabric.
> Energy: Solar and wind power.

> Conservation & cultural projects: A fundamental aspect of Nomadic Expeditions' policy is the careful balancing of the natural evolution of an existing culture with the genuine benefits of modernization. To this end, a cooperative agreement exists with the Mongolian authorities for sensitive cultural and environmental development. The lodge supports a campaign to stop illegal removal of dinosaur fossils from palaeontological sites.
> Food supplies: Fresh from local farmers for traditional Mongolian fare.
> Cultural events: Guests are encouraged to mix with the locals and nomads who water their livestock near by. The lodge helps fund the Thousand Camel Festival, with a view to helping protect the Bactrian camel population.
> Employment: 50–74% local.
> Ownership: Local commercial enterprise. The founder of Nomadic Expeditions, set up in 1990, Jalsa Urubshurow, is a Mongolian-American.

> Dance, music
> Walking, trekking, hiking
> Horse and camel riding

Chiiori JAPAN

On the island of Shikoku, in Tokushima prefecture, lie the steeply wooded slopes and valleys of an area known as Iya Gorges. This hard-to-reach location is often referred to as 'the Tibet of Japan'. The main buildings are 300 years old and of solid traditional Iya farmhouse construction, with large beams, wooden floors with inset open hearths for cooking, and thatched roofs. The latter is the subject of a renewal programme and the not-for-profit Chiiori Trust has scheduled working holidays in 2008 and 2009 for thatching activities and revitalization of the organic farm. The essence of this destination is the opportunity to learn about the distinctive qualities of the area by embracing a simple way of living while contributing to the restoration of a unique building. Meals are cooked communally and use home-grown or local ingredients selected by the guests. Payment is by donation.

> Chiiori is a member of the Japan Eco-lodge Association.
> Materials: Natural thatch, bamboo, wood.
> Energy: Heated primarily by firewood; some utilities provided by propane, kerosene and local electricity supply company.
> Water: From a natural reservoir.
> Waste: Recycling and composting of waste.

> Food supplies: Home-grown or locally produced food is cooked communally.
> Cultural events: Visitors are encouraged to go to local events in the Iya valley area.
> Employment: Chiiori has no full-time employees, as the house is run by volunteers and part-time staff; less than 25% local staff.
> Ownership: Not-for-profit enterprise; owned by Alex Kerr, a permanent resident of Kyoto.

> Craft workshops
> Food and cookery classes
> Volunteer work
> Walking, trekking, hiking
> Building restoration work

Wenhai Ecolodge CHINA

Whereas China's rampant economic growth is rapidly changing the face of its metropolitan and urban areas, the pace of development in the countryside follows more ancient rhythms. 1000 kilometres (to the west of Guangzhou (formerly Canton) sits the mountainous province of Yunnan. This community-run ecolodge, high in a valley at 3,000 metres (9,840 feet), is situated on Wenhai Lake near the Jade Dragon Snow Mountain and the remote villages of the Yi region. It is a strenuous trek by foot or on horseback to reach the lodge. 12 comfortable rooms have access to shared bathroom facilities, and there are several communal spaces including a small library. Vegetarian meals (unless otherwise requested) are prepared by local cooks in traditional Naxi style. This is a fantastic place to experience Chinese culture and the dramatic landscapes towards the borders of India and Tibet.

> The lodge is converted from a traditional Naxi courtyard house.
> Materials: Extensive use of vernacular materials, timber and tiles.
> Energy: Solar panels for hot water; bio-gas for cooking; a small hydro-generator to provide electricity.
> Consumables: Locally sourced.

> Conservation & socio-cultural projects: Courses are provided to local people to enhance their understanding of environmental issues, including responsible hunting and forest management. 10% of the income from the lodge is shared with local people or goes to local conservation projects.
> Food supplies: Main food supplies are local and a greenhouse provides guests with fresh vegetables.
> Employment: 100% local, including conservation guides.
> Ownership: Local cooperative enterprise comprising 56 households.

> Adventure sports
> Dance, music
> Farm work
> Volunteer work
> Walking, trekking, hiking
> Wildlife safari
> Conservation work

Yogamagic Canvas EcoTel INDIA

Here is a hybrid concept that exudes considerable charm and atmosphere. Seven spacious, luxurious Rajasthani hunting tents are set on the fringe of a paddy field just a short distance from the golden beaches of Goa. This romantic setting is imbued with holistic purpose, as soul, body and mind are tempted with activities embracing Ayurvedic massage, yoga and meditation. The handcrafted tents are decorated with the seven colours of the chakras (energy centres), have private verandas and are very well-appointed. Alternatively, take the Mahrani Suite in the nearby house, suitable for a couple or family, to experience a little colonial splendour. Bathe in the evening in steaming hot water from urns or take a warm solar shower. Pamper yourself on delicious Goan vegetarian food and wholesome drinks, such as lassi, juice, wheat grass and aloe vera.

> Materials: Locally sourced materials, including mud, clay, sand, stone, bamboo, jute, coconut and betel wood, rice grass, palm leaves and cow dung; Rajasthani tents made by traditional techniques.
> Energy: Traditional materials allow passive cooling; photovoltaic panels for lighting tents and pathways. Experiments are underway to grow *Jatropha* plants for bio-diesel.
> Water: Drawn from several clean wells and purified by reverse osmosis.
> Waste: Bathrooms in tents have eco-toilets that separate liquids (urine and greywater feeds banana plants) and solids (degraded off-site with 'effective micro-organisms', a cocktail of 80 strains of microbes). All glass, metal and plastic waste is collected by a local charity for recycling.

> Conservation & community projects: Guests are made aware of local conservation projects to protect mangroves and associated wildlife. An organic approach to horticultural care of the landscape around the lodge includes revival of a 5,000-year-old practice called *rishi-krishi*. Contributions are made to local religious and social institutions.
> Food supplies: Dry goods purchased locally; fresh foods from local markets; milk from the buffalo herd wandering around the lodge; vegan, vegetarian and occasionally fresh fish.
> Employment: 75–99% local.
> Ownership: Local enterprise.

> Adventure sports
> Craft workshops
> Cycling, mountain biking
> Dance, music
> Farm work
> Food and cookery classes
> Swimming, water sports
> Volunteer work
> Walking, trekking, hiking
> Wildlife safari

PART THREE

Eco-products

A great range of products is illustrated in this section, grouped in three categories: products that assist our personal mobility; products that provide personal protection and express our identity; and products that are essential equipment for comfortable and safe enjoyment of travel, adventure or holiday activities. Designed to a high standard of ergonomics and safety, many embed a responsible ethical approach in their manufacturing or use. The products here are well-made, durable and lightweight.

Energy requirements are an important consideration and, of course, have a direct impact on the CO_2 footprint during the production (the 'embodied energy' of materials and production), use and end-of-life phases of the product. Certain products rely on the input of human power, rather than external energy sources. These range from hand-held wind-up devices for providing light or energy for a mobile phone to bicycles of every shape and size for personal mobility. Mobility products include those operating on solar power, electrical battery power, conventional fossil fuels and alternative emerging fuels.

The products demonstrate the many and various ways of designing and manufacturing that try to use resources efficiently, encourage recycling, re-use materials and understand the importance of 'cradle-to-cradle' lifecycle thinking.

Key to symbols

 Manufacturer/designer/supplier

 Materials

 Eco-design features

mobility

Human-powered mobility options are inherently low-energy options.
Walking, that essential bipedal characteristic of the human species,
remains one of the most eco-efficient ways of being mobile. It also
provides us with an understanding of our locality and sense of being
that no other form of mobility can consistently match. In the words of
Common Ground, 'Slow down. Wisdom comes through walking, talking
and listening.'[1] We can't walk everywhere, but there are all sorts of human-
powered machines that can get us around faster, including an extraordinary
range of bicycles for everyday and specialist use: from folding bicycles to
recumbent aerodynamic speedsters, from urban commuter to mountain
bike, and from personal to family transport. A recent trend is the emergence
of more options for battery-powered electric vehicles, from the gyroscopically
balanced Segway to electric motorbikes, scooters, mopeds, cars and
commercial delivery vehicles. Provided that batteries are recharged from
renewable energy sources, carbon emissions are zero, but there are other
benefits too – little or no government road tax, lower insurance premiums
and avoidance of urban 'congestion charges' or taxes.

   The reality of climate change, coupled with significant shifts in
legislation and regulation in the European Union, is forcing car
manufacturers supplying Europe to get serious about reducing the CO_2
footprint of all cars in their range.

[1] S. Clifford and A. King (2006), *England in Particular*, p. xv.

> BICYCLE

Brompton

Brompton have been designing and handmaking these durable, reliable and functional folding bicycles for over 30 years. Today there are three model types: the M3 all-rounder with a distinctive 'U'-shaped handlebar; the P6 long ride bike with 6-speed gears; and the straight-handlebar lightweight S2 with 1- or 2-speed system. Each of these models comes in a standard or lightweight option and there are various gear systems (1, 2-derailleur, 3-hub, 6-hub x derailleur) to suit your needs. They weigh from 9 to 12.5 kg (20–28 lb), and all fold into an easy-to-carry package

within 10–20 seconds. This is a product that is built to last for a lifetime and many of the Bromptons from previous decades are still serving their owners well. It is the benchmark for folding bikes.

 Brompton, UK

 various synthetic materials, metals, rubbers

 lightweight, flexible, portable bicycle for human-powered commuting and leisure

---

> BICYCLE

A-bike

The ultimate folding bike or just a curiosity? Brands like Brompton, Moulton and Strida already have avid fans, but the 5.6-kg (12-lb) A-bike goes micro with its amazing folded size of 67 x 30 x 16 cm (26 x 12 x 6 in.). Ten seconds later, it opens to 100 x 70 x 43 cm (39 x 28 x 17 in.). The main components are made of aircraft-grade aluminium and glass-reinforced polymer, giving a maximum weight tolerance of 85 kg (187 lb). The 15-cm (6-in.) diameter pneumatic tyres are set at

90 psi, helping cushion the worst road or footpath surface undulations.

 Designed by Sir Clive Sinclair and Alex Kalogroulis, Sinclair Research; distributed by Mayhem UK, UK

 Glass-reinforced polymer composite, aluminium, rubber, various synthetics

 lightweight, portable, comfortable bike

> BICYCLE

Airnimal Chameleon Ultra

Airnimal produce a range of folding bikes to serve everyone from serious road racers, triathletes, long-distance cyclists and off-roaders to daily commuters. The Ultra weighs in at just 9.1 kg (20 lb) and has a robust frame with elastomer damping and a sealed pivot system. It is fitted with a 20-speed Shimano Ultegra STI gear set, carbon-fibre forks and Velocity Aerohead 28h rims. Like all Airnimal bikes, it can be

folded into a soft bag, a hard Delsey case or a carry-on bag plus wheel bag, giving a number of options for travel on public transport.

 Airnimal, UK

 7005 aluminium tubing, carbon fibre, elastomer and other materials

 lightweight, multipurpose bike

> BICYCLE
Biomega MN range

Biomega have a reputation for creating fresh designs that catch the eye and deliver the performance, such as their recent development of a folding, full-size bicycle, the Boston. However, one of their classic designs is the MN range, to which the illustrious designer Marc Newson contributed. The simplicity of the monocoque frame imbues a sturdiness and sense of purpose absent in other bikes. There are various versions of the bike with different disc brakes and gearing systems. The MN Extravaganza features a 14-speed Rohloff hub, the MN Relampago a single-speed hub with Joytech, and the MN Guernica, a Shimano 7-speed internal hub. Tough, reliable and guaranteed to give a long service life, this bike is a statement.

 Biomega, Denmark

 super-formed aluminium, alloys, various metals and other materials

 strong chassis, durable, high-quality, contemporary design

> BICYCLE
Ellsworth Ride

'Look, no gears', or so it appears, but jump on the Ride and you'll know why it carries that name. Lurking in the rear hub is the NuVinci gearless continuous variable planetary (CVP) drive designed by Don Miller. That means as you put more effort into the pedals, the drive system responds to give the best power ratio. It is all about the contact area of the rotating balls in the drum, apparently. High-tech design features elsewhere, in the strong elliptical ultra-lightweight aluminium frame, aluminium or carbon-fibre forks and, on a 500 limited edition, a quiet belt drive rather than noisy, greasy chain.

 Tony Ellsworth (bike), Don Miller (NuVinci CVP); Ellsworth and Fallbrook Technologies (NuVinci), USA

 aluminium, carbon fibre, various

 efficient continuous drive system, durable specification, high-quality components

> BICYCLE
Waldmeister

High-tech meets craft-tech in this eye-catching design. A high-strength, handcrafted, wooden laminate frame with 100 thin layers of locally sourced hardwoods, the Waldmeister ('forest master') by Marcus Wallmeyer offers a good ride. The frame is fitted with high-quality durable components, including Xentis Kappa carbon 66-cm (26-in.) carbon fibre wheels, Avid Juicy Carbon brakes, a Brooks leather and titanium saddle, and a Chris King single-speed cog. You can even decide on the finish of the frame: birch, cherry, walnut, birds-eye maple or the 'standard' copper beech. A life-long product that you will cherish, Waldmeister is a definitive statement about the bicycle in your life.

 Waldmeister, Germany

 wood, metal, carbon fibre, titanium, leather and more

 durable, simple, renewable and high-quality synthetic materials

> BICYCLE

Locust

There are many folding bikes but none quite like the Locust. The full-sized wheels are accommodated in the central circular frame when in the folded position. To facilitate the rear wheel folding movement, crankshaft to wheel drive is by belt, not chain. Gearing is in the rear wheel hub, selected with GripShift changer. Saddle and handlebars are quick-release. A modified version of this concept, designed by Josef Cadek, is in the pipeline.

 Ing. Josef Cadek, Czech Republic

 not specified

 multifunctional commuter/ leisure bike

Kangaroo

There is a long tradition in Denmark of providing safe cycling paths to encourage more journeys by bicycle. This is reflected in the wide range of multi-use bicycles for carrying passengers or large loads. The Kangaroo offers an aerodynamic front cabin in impact-resistant polyethylene that ensures comfort and safety for the child occupants. It is easily manoeuvred thanks to the three-point steering system and low-level frame. Handlebars are adjustable to permit mum and dad maximum comfort.

Independent suspension provides a great ride, enabling the use of high-pressure tyres, and results in good road-holding for the front wheels. Weighing in at just 39 kg (86 lb) for the family model, this is a robust genuine option for city and country travel.

 A. Winther A/S, Denmark

 various synthetics, aluminium 7005 framing, polyethylene cabin

 human-powered family transport

> BICYCLE

Go-one

Since 1991 the German manufacturer Beyss Leichtfahrzeuge has crafted lightweight and recumbent bicycles. Go-one represents an all-weather recumbent with monoque chassis, ventilation inlets, clear anti-glare de-fogging windshield, ergonomic seat, two 50-cm (20-in.) aluminium-rimmed wheels for the front and one 91-cm (36-in.) wheel for the rear fitted with Vredestein tyres, and front/rear suspension shocks. Everything is detailed for comfort and safety, with a GripShift gear changer permitting full use of the 27 gears (nine-speed Shimano with three-ring crank), integral lighting equipment fed from a 12v battery and T-bar steering column. There's an electric-assist motor option being tested using a 350W BionX hub motor with 36v lithium

battery, these items adding over 7 kg (15 lb) to the kerb weight of 30 kg (66 lb). Speeds above 30 km/h (19 mph) are achievable but, more importantly, long distances can be covered in relative comfort.

 Designer Michael Goretzky (part of the design team for the DaimlerChrysler SMART car) for Beyss Leichtfahrzeuge, Germany, and distributed by Go-one LLC, USA and Canada

 carbon fibre, acrylic, polycarbonate, alloys, other metals and synthetics

 lightweight human-powered vehicle (HPV)

> BICYCLE

Cycloc

Encouraging commuters to get on their bikes has to be made easy, and that includes where you store it. Cycloc is a simple solution that can fit to any hallway or utility room wall. Available in four colours in durable recycled plastic, the design also enables storage of bicycle paraphernalia ready for your daily commute. To ensure further security,

a typical wire or chain lock can be looped through the Cycloc and the bike frame.

 Cycloc, UK

 100% post-industrial recycled plastic

 recycled material, mono-material, durable

> BICYCLE

Trek Lime

The underlying premise for this everyday bike is that it be easy, fun, practical and customizable. Trek seemed to have worked hard to achieve this with his/hers frames, six-colour-scheme 'lime peels' to customize the silver frame, three-speed automatic electronic rear hub gear powered by a generator in the front wheel, back-pedal braking and a handy bit of stowage under the seat.

Someone's trying to make cycling easy again... Let's hope it boosts the number of journeys taken by bike. In a recent UK survey it was just 2%. Get on your bike.

 Trek Bicycle Corporation, USA

 various metals, polymers, rubber

 simple, durable, usable

> SCOOTER
Segway i2/i2 Commuter

It is five years since the bizarre sight of the curious Segway Personal Transporter (PT) was seen pounding the pavements in US cities. This hasn't made it any easier for certain dignitaries to master the skills, but it has meant that the original version has mutated into the refined i2/i2 Commuter – including LeanSteer (tilts left and right) Frame, Tool-Less release (allows you to pack it away into tiny spaces), LED rear light, better comfort mats for long journeys, handlebar bag and more features.

At just 47.7 kg (105 lb), with two Saphion lithium-ion battery packs, you've got a range of up to 38 km (24 miles). Now, there's a good range for a commuter.

 Segway, USA

 various anodized metals, plastic, rubber, electronics, lithium-ion batteries

 equivalent of 166 km/L (450 mpg)

> SCOOTER
Piaggio MP3

Built on a high-strength tubular steel chassis, the two front wheels and suspension operate as a parallelogram and cantilever system, ensuring brilliant stability without reducing cornering ability. Four-stroke engine options are offered in 125 cc or 250 cc capacity with an economical fuel consumption of 25 km/L (59 mpg) and 23 km/L (54 mpg). Weighing in at about 200 kg (441 lb), it looks as if it needs a bit of muscle to

manoeuvre, but is surprisingly easy to fling through corners or drive around town. The two front wheels permit better road contact and safer braking. This is an elegant, functional trike.

 Piaggio/Vespa, Italy

 various

 eco-efficient, improved ergonomics and safety

> SCOOTER
Sakura S207

This lightweight scooter-cum-moped with a 200W rear-hub motor weighs just 39 kg (86 lb), including the lead-acid battery. On a full charge, requiring eight hours plugged into the electricity supply, it has a range of 30 km (19 miles). Not as sophisticated as its bigger cousin, the Sakura S50, this model is basic, low-cost and rather sedate, yet still offers the potential comfort of zero emissions.

 Sakura Battery Company, UK

 various synthetics, 36v SLA lead-acid battery, alloys

 zero emissions and carbon-neutral if sourced from renewable energy

> SCOOTER
ZiPee e-bike

For a very competitive price, it is possible to equip yourself with a ZiPee electric or 'e-bike', safety helmet, poncho and small courier box. Going zero-emissions has never been so easy. Speeds of 19 to 24 km/h (12–15 mph) allow a 40-km (25-mile) range after a 5–6-hour recharge of the battery using normal 240v, 13 amp mains supply sockets. It is classed as an electric bike, so there's no road tax, no congestion charge and the possibility of saving over a tonne of CO2 per annum

for short-distance commuting. A bicycle is still cheaper, but the ZiPee offers a viable option to people with disabilities or those who don't perceive cycling as 'cool'.

 ZiPee, UK – a social enterprise

 various synthetics, battery

 zero-emissions, low-speed commuter bike

> SCOOTER
E-max

This rugged, tough, Italian-designed and German-engineered electric scooter/moped is powered by a 4 kW rear-wheel motor supplied by maintenance-free silicone batteries. Fully charged after three hours, the E-max delivers a top speed of 50 km/h (31 mph) and a range of 88–96 km (55–60 miles), thanks to its battery and motor combination. This makes the E-max a more flexible daily transport option than some of the smaller electric scooters or bicycles. Running

costs are low and it avoids road tax and congestion or other city 'pollution' taxes.

 Baroni Electric Vehicles, UK

 various synthetics, sealed silicone batteries

 zero emissions and carbon-neutral using renewable energy supply

---

> SCOOTER
Sakura S50

This elegant, streamlined scooter is quiet and smooth, thanks to its brushless hub motor and two-speed automatic transmission. The 1.5 kW motor enables a top speed of 50 km/h (31 mph), with a range of 30 km (19 miles), or lower speeds, with a range of up to 65 km (40 miles). You'll need eight hours overnight to recharge the 48v 5-amp lead-acid batteries, which add to the overall weight of 110 kg (243 lb). This is

not a high-performance electric scooter but it is claimed to do 1,000 km (621 miles) at the nominal cost of recharging the battery, so it helps both the pocket and the planet.

 Sakura Battery Company, UK

 various synthetics, battery, high-efficiency brushless motor

 zero emissions and carbon-neutral if charged by renewable energy supply

> SCOOTER

Vectrix Electrical MAXI-Scooter

In recent years the reduction of air pollution by the application of congestion charges and other fiscal measures by city and municipal authorities has encouraged a resurgence of interest in electrical vehicles. They are fun, fast and flexible. The 20 kW battery enables rapid acceleration of 0–80 km/h (0–50 mph) in 6.8 seconds, with a top speed of 99 km/h (62 mph) and a range of 109 km (68 miles) on a single charge taking two hours. Electric scooters have come of age, so it is a 'no-brainer' if you want to have freedom of movement without surcharge costs in today's conurbations.

 Vectrix Corporation, USA (UK, Europe and Australia)

 various synthetics, nickel metal hydride battery

 zero emissions and carbon-neutral, if renewable electrical energy used for battery charging

> MOTORBIKE

Brammo Enertia

The performance of electric motorcycles is continuously improving, as the Enertia demonstrates with its 80-km/h (50-mph) top speed, 72-km (45-mile) range and just three hours to a full recharge of the six lithium phosphate batteries. The manufacturers claim its overall 'fuel' efficiency is between four and seven times better than a conventional petrol-engined motorcycle. This is achieved by an ultra-light, stiff, carbon-fibre monocoque chassis, housing the 3.1-kWh battery pack on the main diagonal member, a high-output DC 'pancake'-type motor, a battery management system and a direct drivetrain from the motor shaft to the rear wheel. Weighing in at a trim 125 kg (275 lbs) the Enertia looks the part for an urban commuter too.

 Brammo Motorsports, USA

 carbon-fibre chassis, steel tubing, lithium phosphate batteries, various synthetics and metals

 electric motorcycle (zero emissions when recharging from renewable electricity supplies)

> SCOOTER

Ape Web

In 1948 the Italian manufacturers Piaggio first merged the front end of a Vespa scooter with a rear twin wheel axle and pick-up body to create a vehicle concept that is still in demand over 60 years later. In its current incarnation the range includes pick-ups and panel vans. The most modern is the Ape Web, a one-person carrier with rolled steel flatbed behind the cab, which still utilizes a single-cylinder, two-stroke, 50 cc petrol engine, giving a generous 'no load' consumption of 35 km/L (82 mpg) and very modest top speed. Payloads of up to 185 kg (408 lb) make this an ideal commuter-cum-DIY weekender vehicle, albeit for local journeys.

 Piaggio Ape, Italy

 steel, various metals and synthetics

 lightweight, economical fuel consumption, multi-use vehicle

> CAR
Mega MultiTruck II

Aixam-Mega have been making vehicles in France for over 30 years, preferring locally made components. The company's latest version of its popular Mega truck, offering multifunctional options (open sides, panel van, tipper), is claimed to be nearly 100% recyclable, thereby meeting the European Union End-of-Life Vehicles Directive, which came into force in 2008. Equipped with a 4 kW DC electric motor, powered by lead-acid batteries, the truck has a top speed of 50 km/h (31 mph) and can take payloads of up to 435 kg (959 lb).

Recharge takes 5–8 hours from 'empty', the eight-battery version giving a range of 40–55 km (25–34 miles) and the 12-battery providing 65–95 km (40–59 miles).

 Aixam-Mega Group, France, via Nice Car Company, UK

 recyclable metals and synthetics, lead-acid batteries

 zero emissions (renewable energy recharging), electric multipurpose vehicle

> CAR
Sakura Maranello4

This Italian origin micro-electric car is a zero-emissions option aimed at city commuters wishing to avoid 'congestion' and other taxes applied to polluting vehicles. It is a genuine competitor to the more established G-Wiz brand by the Reva Electric Car Company. A DC motor is powered by eight gelled-lead batteries delivering 4 kW, giving a top speed of 50 km/h (31 mph) and a range of 70 km (44 miles). This modest performance is

ideal for short journeys at low speeds but is not suitable for general family use.

 EFFIDI Automotive Group, Italy, and Sakura Battery Company, UK

 various synthetics, stainless steel chassis, gelled-lead batteries, DC motor

 zero emissions and carbon-neutral if charged by renewable energy supply

> CAR
Smart Electric Vehicle

Zytek is a specialist UK company that is converting Smart cars into Smart Electric Vehicles. Mainly aimed at fleet users, the car has a typical range of 80–160 km (50–100 miles) per charge depending on driving style and traffic conditions. The 60-kg (133-lb) motor/inverter unit is electronically limited to 120 km/h (75 mph) but delivers a useful 55 kW of power from a bank of liquid sodium nickel chloride ZEBRA® batteries. Recharge time is 3.5 hours and at current electricity costs equates to around 125 km/L (294 mpg) of fossil fuel. Source

your electricity from a renewable supplier and this is a zero-emissions car. Add the savings of avoiding the London congestion charge and it looks a fairly safe financial punt for the future.

 Smart (from DaimlerChrysler, Germany) with Zytek Group, UK

 various synthetics, stainless steel chassis, gelled-lead batteries, DC motor

 zero emissions and carbon-neutral if charged by renewable energy supply

> CAR

CLEVER

CLEVER (Compact Low Emission Vehicle for Urban Transport) is a prototype, metre-wide micro-car for driver and passenger developed by nine European partners. It is 50 cm (20 in.) narrower than a typical micro-car, enabling more efficient fuel usage and parking advantages. Its most dramatic features are the tilting chassis, strengthened safety frame and power transmission to control stability. The engine runs on compressed natural gas, emits one third of the CO_2 omissions of a contemporary car, consumes 38 km/L (89 mpg) and a top speed of 97 km/h (60 mph).

 University of Bath and Cooper-Avon Tyres, UK; Technical University of Berlin, BMW, WEH Gas Technology and Takata, Germany; Institut français du petrôle, France; ARC-LKR and Institute of Transport Studies, Austria.

 aluminium frame, rubber tyres, various synthetics

 reduced materials, low emissions, functional

> CAR

Tata Nano

'The People's Car' was launched to great acclaim in January 2008 in India by Tata Motors, as an affordable car for the rising middle classes, 3.1 m (10 ft) long and 1.5 m (5 ft) wide, powered by a 623 cc, 33 PS, multi-point fuel-injection petrol engine delivering a maximum speed of 105 km/h (65 mph). We can hope that it will replace some of the more polluting vehicles of India's roads.

 Tata Motors, India

 various synthetic materials, metals, polymers

 low weight, low speed, low emissions, small family car

> CAR

City Car concept

Several overlapping concepts are at the core of this design – an exoskeleton protecting the passenger cabin and connecting independently controllable robotic wheels (which each house an electric motor), drive-by-wire rather than traditional steering system, a lightweight passenger compartment with programmable surface displays and 360-degree turning. Stacks of these electric cars will be located at transport nodes for recharging and sharing.

 Design is a collaboration between MIT Media Lab, Smart Cities, General Motors and Frank O. Gehry. MIT design team: William Lark, Phil Llang, Raul-David Poblano, Axel Kilian, Peter Schmidt, Franco Vairani, Mitch Joachim, Ryan Chin, Susan Seitinger, Marcel Botha

 various, including wheel robots, wafer-thin programmable displays (interior and exterior) and more

 potentially zero-energy if energy sourced from renewables, lightweight

> CAR
Microcab

John Jostins, the entrepreneur behind the Microcab range, sees a small, multi-use, zero-emissions vehicle as an urban taxi, people or freight carrier. Though the recipient of many industry awards, including the Environmental and Sustainable Technology journal's Vehicle Innovation Award in 2005, Microcab remains a micro-business. The latest version, the Microcab H4, a hydrogen-powered, ultra-light 450 kg (992 lb), city taxi should attract the investors and the punters. An electric drive is powered by hydrogen fuel combustion. On a full tank there is a range of 160 km (99 miles), a top speed of 64 km/h (40 mph), an efficient LED lighting system and the option to park in tight spaces. There are light van and pickup options for urban delivery companies too.

 Microcab Industries with Coventry University, Intelligent Energy, Delta Motorsport and RDM, UK

 various

 lightweight, eco-efficient, flexible load/people carrier with zero emissions

> CAR
ECO2 range

European legislation, including the End-of-Life Vehicles Regulations 2003 and 2005, has made all manufacturers supplying Europe take greater responsibility for their vehicles. Renault's ECO2 range includes four models that meet specific requirements – they are made at factories conforming to ISO14001, an environmental management system standard; conform to CO_2 emissions of less than or equal to 140 g CO_2/km; vehicles are 95% recoverable at end-of-life and at least 5% of plastics used in new vehicles are recyclates. Models approved to ECO2 standards include the Renault Clio 1.2 TCE 100, Modus 1.2 TCE 100, Mégane Hatch and Sport Hatch and Scénic, the latter two both using the DCi86/106. Best CO_2 footprint in the Renault range is the Mégane at 120 g CO_2/km.

 Renault, France

 various

 design and manufacture demonstrate lifecycle thinking

> CAR
Seat Ibiza Ecomotive

Launched at the 2007 Frankfurt car show, the 1.4 TDI 80 hp diesel-engine Seat Ibiza Ecomotive was the most environmentally low-impact Spanish car. Emissions are 99 g CO_2/km, well below the European Union's proposed benchmark of 120 g CO_2/km, and low enough to exempt the driver from a revised London congestion charge and UK vehicle excise duty. The standard Seat Ibiza has an improved electronic control unit (ECU), an efficient particulate matter filter, a low drag coefficient of 0.3, Dunlop low resistance, SP10 A 165/70 R14 tyres and a reduction of 22 kg (46 lb) weight by removing central locking and electric windows and replacing the spare tyre with a puncture repair kit.

 Seat, Spain

 various synthetic materials, metals, polymers

 the most eco-efficient small diesel-engine car in Europe?

> CAR

VW Polo BlueMotion

BlueMotion is Volkswagen's most efficient and economical car range. With its efficient 80 hp 1.4-litre, three-cylinder, TDI engine with electronically controlled, high-pressure direct injection, it achieves over 30 km/L (71 mpg) and a low carbon footprint at 102 g CO_2/km. One 45-L (12-gallon) tank of fuel will take you 1,120 km (696 miles), or the equivalent distance of London to the south of France. Such fuel economy is the result of smoother airflows with bumper and grille re-design, 'Jerez' lightweight alloy wheels and 165/70 tyres.

 Volkswagen, Germany

 various synthetic materials, metals, polymers

 highly efficient, high-pressure, direct-injection diesel engine

> CAR

Hybrid X Concept

Unveiled at the 2007 Geneva Motor Show, Hybrid X Concept demonstrates how Toyota wish to build on the success of their electric/petrol hybrid systems, notably the Hybrid Synergy Drive launched in 1997 for the Toyota Prius. Zero emissions are Toyota's short-term goal, especially for the European market. The Hybrid X is a four-door, four-seat, open-space concept with some nice touches – lightweight injected-foam technology seating, swivelling rear seats, drive-by-wire steering pad with a central screen and a touch screen for controlling ambient settings.

 Toyota ED2 design unit, France; Toyota, Japan

 various

 eco-efficient hybrid power system

> CAR

Toyota Prius

More than 750,000 hybrid Toyota Prius's have been bought worldwide since 1997, making it the best-selling hybrid to date. Now in its second generation and still the lowest-emissions family-sized car, at just 104 g CO_2/km, it offers good fuel economy, 28 km/L (66 mpg) and spacious accommodation. T Spirit models even offer Intelligent Park Assist, Bluetooth telephone interface and DVD map/GPS navigation system. Its real success relies on the 'hybrid synergy drive', with an onboard computer managing the switch between petrol and electrical power.

A high-performance nickel hydride battery receives power from a generator and captures regenerative energy from braking. Power from the petrol engine is split to drive the road wheels or the generator, as needed. The high torque of the electric motor makes for an excellent standing start, ideal driving at moderate speeds and extra power under acceleration.

 Toyota, Japan

 various

 eco-efficient hybrid power system

> CAR
Alé

'Lad-mag' editors seem fixated on acceleration, especially on how many seconds it takes from a standing start to reach 100 km/h (62 mph). This strange but appealing prototype, the Alé, has the kind of statistic that grabs the attention of grown men, 0–100 km/h (0–62 mph) in 5 seconds. A less showy statistic is its frugal 39 km/L (91 mpg), and all this from a 180 hp turbocharged 1,500 cc engine. How is this achieved? George Parker, its innovator, says it uses advanced fuel vapour technology running on an air:fuel ratio of 20:1 (most engines run at 14.7:1) to get much more

out of ordinary petrol. This efficiency gain is favourably reinforced by having a lightweight fibreglass composite body on a tube chassis weighing in at just 640 kg (1,411 lb), three-wheeled stability with driven/steering wheels at the front and trailing wheel at rear, and superb aerodynamics.

 FuelVapor Technologies, USA

 fibreglass composite, various

 eco-efficient fuel technology

> CAR
Tesla Roadster

California pursues ambitious legislation to reduce car pollution and reliance on fossil fuels. So it is no surprise that Tesla Motors, based in the state, have a long waiting list for one of the world's fastest production electric sports cars. Blistering acceleration, 0–100 km/h (0–62 mph) in 4 seconds, is combined with eco-efficient power consumption to give 57 km/L (134 mpg) equivalent and a range of over 320 km (199 miles) on one charge. This is partly achieved by an on-board power electronics module, which continuously balances the electric motor torque requirements with charging the lithium-ion battery pack and reclaiming energy by regenerative braking.

 Tesla Motors, USA

 various, including lithium-ion batteries

 zero emissions if charged via renewable-energy supplier

> BOAT

Solar Sailor

Hybrid cars are a familiar sight on our roads. The Solar Sailor has an eco-smart combination of conventional and solar-powered drives featuring on catamarans, trimarans, houseboats and a concept proposal for solar-assisted cargo vessels. The 600-passenger trimaran ferry has a conventional drive centre hull but outer hulls are driven by electric motors powered by the solar 'wing' that can be rotated to capture sunlight with its photovoltaic arrays or act as a sail. Under sun/ wind-power combination alone the vessel can make 11 km/h (6 knots). Diesel engines burning low-sulphur diesel fuel can achieve 13–26 km/h (7–14 knots). Operational in Sydney Harbour, the Solar Sailor is also due to appear in New York.

 Solar Sailor Holdings, Australia

 eco-efficient hybrid propulsion systems

 fibreglass, plastic, photovoltaic panels, metals, synthetics

> BOAT

Sun 21

Sun 21 is a Type C 60 catamaran that is totally solar-powered. Built by the Swiss company MW-Line, which manufacturers a range of public ferries and utility boats, this version was specially equipped to sail from Basel, Switzerland, to New York, USA. The 12,964-km (7,000-nautical mile) sea crossing occurred at an average speed of 9 km/h (5 knots), the 14-m (46-ft)-long vessel being driven by its twin 8 kW electric motors powered by two 5 kW photovoltaic modules. Solar electricity is stored in a bank of 48 volt DC 520 Ah lead accumulation batteries located in each hull. Twelve metric tonnes of boat and a crew of six people made the first transatlantic crossing by solar-powered boat and arrived in New York City on 8 May 2007. Financing for the project was provided by the association Transatlantic 21, who are now planning a circumnavigation of the world with a hybrid solar/hydrogen-powered boat. The experience gained on such projects provides tangible proof that we are only just beginning to realize the potential of harnessing solar energy for our mobile world.

 MW-Line, Switzerland backed by the association Transatlantic 21, Switzerland

 photovoltaic arrays, high-strength composites and alloys

 100% renewable power

> TRAIN

GE Evolution Hybrid locomotive

In May 2007 General Electric unveiled the world's first hybrid freight train locomotive, the Evolution Hybrid. As for any locomotive, the traction motor is electric, whereas the diesel engine acts as a generator. Typically this 4,400-hp locomotive, weighing 188 metric tonnes, dissipates huge amounts of energy during braking, estimated to be enough to power 160 households for a year. The hybrid system, designed by Ecoimagination, GE's leading R&D section, takes advantage of reclamation techniques to capture and store energy dissipated during dynamic braking, a term describing the phase when the traction electric motors become alternators, for example when decelerating or maintaining speeds on downhill sections. Reclaimed energy is stored in sodium nickel chloride (NaNiCl2) batteries and this is managed by an electronic system to provide supplemental power to the traction motor. It is anticipated that this hybrid system will cut fuel consumption by up to 15%, with a subsequent significant reduction in CO_2 footprint. GE estimate that, if every locomotive in North America was as efficient as this hybrid, railways could save up to millions per annum in fuel costs. Now there's a reason to hybridize.

 General Electric, USA

 sodium nickel chloride batteries, various

 improved fuel efficiency

personal

Comfortable, functional, stylish clothes and footwear can contribute significantly to the enjoyment of everyday, business or holiday travel and a typical tourist day. The range of casual and performance clothing shown here indicates that the sport and travel apparel industry is rapidly forging ahead of the typical high-street fashion retailers in terms of their eco- and ethics-conscious manufacturing processes. Supply-chain sourcing of biological, renewable and organic materials ensures these personal products are from the land and can be returned back to nature or recycled. Developments in the technology of recycling synthetic yarns and textiles have encouraged single- and multi-layer fabrics of recycled polyester, polyethers, PET (polyethylene terephalates) and other plastics. There's a diverse range of footwear, from easily recycled mono-materials to re-used, recycled and natural materials.

Do pack the essential personal garments and reliable footwear, but leave a little space in your baggage for local purchases too. Not only does attire made by skilled craftspeople at your destination retain local distinctiveness but also buying local means you can actually help improve their lives by injecting money directly into the local economy.

> OUTERWEAR/TOP

Eco-Blue Ski Jacket

Several years ago Sympatex Technology introduced a synthetic membrane utilizing recycled polyester from PET bottles. Recently this company has bonded this membrane, without using solvents, with an outer and inner fabric of polyether copolymer that is also recyclable. The new laminate is called Ecocycle-SL and has been employed in the design of the Eco-Blue Ski Jacket, winner of the recently introduced ispo European Ski Awards for winter 2007/2008. This is a highly breathable membrane that doesn't contain fluorcarbons and isocyanide derivatives that have a negative environmental impact. The jackets are manufactured in Turkey by Barco Tekstil Company, an environmentally aware producer that is currently building a new eco-factory.

 Sympatex Technology, Germany

 Sympatex® recyclable laminate, Ecocycle-SL

 90% recycled content, totally recyclable at end-of-life

> OUTERWEAR/TOP

Storm Track

A young company located in Cornwall, the surfing mecca of the UK, is forging a new business model for ethical outdoor wear. Finisterre have eschewed the easy option of manufacturing in the Far East and, instead, have established a Columbian production line managed by nuns as part of a 15-year-old social enterprise and regeneration project. The biomimetic waterproof layers of the Storm Track jacket do not use solvents, lamination or heat-sealing technologies. Labelled as a 'multi-activity' jacket, the shell is woven polyester and the lining specially knitted polyester that boasts excellent wicking properties. Designs are evolved by taking an intensive look at the Product Life Cycle to identify where the worse environmental impacts are likely. These 'costs' are offset by donations to Surfers Against Sewage and the Marine Conservation Society. Here's a blueprint for future ethical clothing manufacturers.

 Finisterre, UK

 Nikwax Analogy Fabric, 100% recyclable polyester

 durability, ethical manufacturing facility, life-cycle thinking (LCT)

> OUTERWEAR/TOP

Dos Caras

Travel requires adaptability to climate, culture and spontaneous events. The Dos Caras ('two faces') jacket helps you deal with such circumstances as it can be transformed into a day/night bag or vice versa, with easy movements to zip, pull a ribbon, fold and fix. Whether worn as a jacket or converted into a bag, one separate compartment constantly keeps all those personal items secure – an essential ingredient to relaxing in unfamiliar places.

 Alice Kaiserswerth, Germany

 gortex, nylon, zips

 multifunctional

> OUTERWEAR/TOP

Patagonia Eco Rain shell

The key feature of this waterproof jacket is its use of a two-layer system of 100% recycled polyester with H2No® waterproof/breathable barrier with Deluge® DWR (durable water repellent) finish. Even the internal polyester mesh lining is 100% recycled polyester, proving this is indeed a 'second time around product' aiming at a 'cradle-to-

cradle' approach and helping minimize material and energy use during its manufacture.

 Patagonia, USA

 recycled polyester

low environmental-impact textiles, 'cradle-to-cradle' thinking

---

> OUTERWEAR/TOP

Patagonia Synchilla® Jacket IV

Patagonia have forged the way for the use of recycled synthetic fibres in their clothing range for nearly two decades. This lightweight men's jacket uses 225-g (8-oz) fleece made from 85% recycled polyester and 100% recycled double-faced polyester. It is warm, wind-resistant and durable. At its end-of-life

it can be returned to the Common Threads Recycling Program for further recycling.

   Patagonia, USA

recycled polyester

low environmental-impact textiles, 'cradle-to-cradle' thinking

---

> OUTERWEAR/TOP

Howies NBL Light

As every outdoor adventurer knows, suitable base layers make the difference between comfort and misery. This 100% ultra-fine merino wool layer is lightweight, wicks naturally and is ribbed for breath-ability, all combining to provide improved tactility and reduce odour build-up. Merino is sourced from New Zealand from an accreditation programme called Zque™ merino that comes from 'free

range' sheep cared for by the highest animal welfare and every aspect of the production system is traceable and utilizes sustainable practices.

   Howies, UK

certified merino wool

certified, ethically sourced fibres

> OUTERWEAR/TOP

Skoody 3-in-1

Keeping the clothes wardrobe to a minimum is a challenge for most travellers, so this multifunctional garment that transforms from a scarf into a hooded rain jacket, then can be reversed into an anorak, is invaluable. Designed by Benjamin Shine, the Skoody is minimalist, no fuss, functional clothing that has been adopted by a variety of corporate clients from Arsenal Football

Club to Google Earth. With inclement weather a feature of the football stand and outdoor activities, Skoody offers versatility. It comes with its own convenient carry bag.

   Skoody/Benjamin Shine, UK

polyester micro fleece

lightweight multifunctionality

> OUTERWEAR/TOP

Icebreaker base layers & clothing range

Established in 1994, Icebreaker has forged a reputation for using the best merino sheep wool combined with high-tech, ethical manufacturing and environmentally sound production practices. Selected New Zealand farmers in the Southern Alps produce the fine merino wool fibre. It is soft to the touch with high insulation properties and breathability, plus natural anti-bacterial ingredients, all helping to reduce odour/water build-up. Certified to

Ecotex 1 environmental standards and with ISO14001 certified factories, Icebreaker clothing treads lightly. There are summer and winter ranges in seven different fabrics and funky seasonal colours, catering for tourists as well as hardened explorers in extreme climates. You can build up layers of clothing, from base to insulation and outer windproof layers and multi-layer combinations. Icebreaker BODYFIT 150 Ultralite even looks sexy.

 Icebreaker, New Zealand and worldwide

 merino wool fibre

 certified, environmentally managed, clean production, durable, contemporary modern styles

> TOP
Infiniti

Exhibited at the Well Fashioned exhibition, this conceptual design offers a solution to the age-old problem of the limits of a small travel wardrobe. Infiniti is a cotton jersey garment comprising 14 pieces that may be zipped together in over 100 variations. Combine it with tops of different colours for endless combinations. So the flash, sporty daytime configuration converts into subtle casual or evening wear.

 Benjamin Shine, UK

 cotton jersey fabric

contemporary multifunctionality

> TOP
Patagonia Valley sweatshirt

This women's sweatshirt is a contemporary design that uses 95% brushed organic cotton and 5% Spandex. There are many other garments in the Organic Cotton range, from T-shirts to long-sleeved sweats with round or polo-style necks. Patagonia has long embraced its supply chain to help it source and use lower-impact textile fibres and reveals its transparency throughout the supply chain with its recent Footprint Chronicles™ project.

 Patagonia, USA

 organic cotton, Spandex

low environmental-impact textiles, supply-chain management

> TOP
Patagonia Short-sleeved A/C shirt

Patagonia's new designs for 2008 show its continuing concern to use organic and recycled textile fibres where possible. Patagonia started the Common Threads Garment Recycling Program, which allowed worn-out Capilene® Performance Baselayers, Polartec® fleece and Patagonia organic T-shirts to be returned by customers for recycling. This is a rare example of product take-back that many manufacturers might find obligatory or financially prudent in the future.

 Patagonia, USA

 organic cotton

low environmental-impact textiles

> TOP
Tecta

White Sierra, a US outdoor and snowsport clothing company, is now producing a new range of all-climate, urban daytrip shirts, using a blend of 55% bamboo fibre and 45% polyester. The fabric has a silk-like feel, wicks moisture well and, of course, has an improved environmental footprint compared to using conventional cotton fibre. Bamboo could be the new super-plant genus, as its diverse species don't require applications of pesticides and produce large quantities of fibre per hectare.

 White Sierra, USA

 polyester, bamboo fibre

 increased proportion of renewable, low-impact fibre

> TOP
Patagonia Fitzroy Essence T-shirt

This T-shirt is 97% organic cotton with just 3% Spandex to prevent the neck of the shirt from stretching. When it is worn out, and at the end of its useful life, it can be returned to the Common Threads Recycling Program for further recycling.

 Patagonia, USA

 organic cotton, Spandex

 recyclable, low environmental impact textiles, 'cradle-to-cradle' thinking

> TOP
Twice Shy T-shirts

Twice Shy sources organic cotton from a Turkish mill, certified by Social Accountability International and manufactured in Mexico by SC International to high ethical standards. Designs are original and eye-catching, use synthetic but low-impact reactive dyes, no heavy metals or toxic substances.

 Twice Shy, Canada, via Matteria, Spain

 95% organic cotton, 5% Lycra®

 renewable certified organic fibres, safe, non-toxic fabrics

> BOTTOM
Howies canvas trousers

There's something comforting about a pair of trousers that protects you from the hazards and pitfalls of a traveller's life. These heavy-duty canvas trousers fit the bill, being reliable and durable. Eventually they will acquire that 'well-travelled' look that any seasoned wanderer secretly desires. Howies was one of the earlier UK companies to encourage their supply chain to go green and employ a wide range of traceable, certifiable fibres in their clothing range.

 Howies, UK

 heavy-duty cotton canvas

 supply-chain management of textile sources

> UNDERWEAR
Howies Edwyn briefs

These organic cotton poplin briefs will keep you comfortably aired in the most tropical of climes. Being lightweight fabric, they are easy to pack, wash and dry. Other briefs in the Howies range include NBL Stones, superfine merino wool briefs that wick the moisture away, and Grassholm boxer, made from 100% organic cotton jersey. Merino stocks are from the Zque™ merino accreditation programme.

 Howies, UK

 organic cotton or wool

 organic, sustainably produced textiles

Felt slippers

This traditional Finnish design using 100% pure wool felt has a purity of line and purpose. What could be better than slipping these on at the end of a long day sightseeing or scaling the heights? Pack these in your rucksack and they'll be that constant reminder of home waiting for you in any unfamiliar place.

 Huopaliike Lahtinen, Finland, via Matteria, Spain

 wool

 renewable fibre, traditional design

> FOOTWEAR

Dopie sandals

The ubiquitous 'flip-flop' might be cheap but inevitably, after just one summer holiday's heavy use, ends up as landfill. Not so Dopie sandals, which are the result of considerable research, providing the right balance between usability, durability and pleasure. The intra-toe protector, softness of the materials and robust adjustable strap (optional) ensure a balance between a lightweight yet secure sandal. The simple construction does enable materials separation at end-of-life. Suitable for men or women, this footwear is easily squeezed into an already full backpack.

 Terra Plana, UK

 EVA and rubber

 improved ergonomics and durability

> FOOTWEAR

Kalahari Duo sandals

The deal is simple, although only available for women. Send in a pair of your old jeans (and lots of other types of textiles too) and Softwalker will transform them into a new pair of sandals. The Kalahari range is ergonomically designed to encourage good posture when walking. The Duo re-uses denim, whereas the recently introduced Sustain uses hemp textiles.

Soft, easy on the feet and well stitched, these general-purpose sandals tread a little more lightly on the planet.

 Softwalker, UK

 re-used denim and other textiles, hemp textiles, rubber

 re-used and bio-textiles

> FOOTWEAR

Veja Tauá

Combine wild Amazon natural latex with Fair Trade organic cotton from Nordeste into a well-made casual shoe, manufactured in Brazil, and you have the Veja Tauá. The company sees collaboration and cooperation with local producers and paying a fair price for raw materials as essential to their operations. Adopting a responsible business model, Veja prove that you can adorn your feet with something functional and stylish for the pavements of Paris or the beach in Rio.

 Veja, France

 wild latex, organic cotton

 low-impact and renewable materials, ethically produced

> FOOTWEAR

Worn Again

Terra Plana's mission is clear – make contemporary, non-generic shoes with low-impact production techniques sourcing E-leathers (blend of textile and leather fibres), chrome-free leathers, recycled rubbers and foams, latex soles and clean-production synthetic fibres. The Worn Again range utilizes a wide variety of recycled or re-used materials, from old parachutes, T-shirts, leather scraps and jeans to seat belts, motorbike tyres, rubber soles and ex-military jackets. Designs emphasize repairability, lightness, anatomic fit and durability.

Ideal for city cruising or clubbing on holiday, the sneaker range, Worn Again, provides solid wear for any footpad. Oh, and 5% of sales go to Anti-Apathy, a UK organization promoting awareness and action for positive social change.

 Terra Plana and RADDISSHMe Design House, UK

 recycled or re-used materials

 recycling, re-use, percentage of revenue to social enterprise

---

> FOOTWEAR

Greenscapes Mountain Cruiser

It is a sign of the (changing) times that global shoe manufacturers are beginning to consider sustainability issues. Timberland has developed its Green Index footwear, a company index by which impacts of the Greenscapes shoe range can be measured relative to other Timberland products. Scores range from 0 (no impact) to 10 (high impact) for three criteria – climate change, chemicals used and resource consumption. This internal benchmarking system helps the company to improve existing and future designs. The Greenscapes Mountain Cruiser (really a sneaker) is an example,

rating at 4.5, featuring leather tanned without chrome, recycled PET fibre from post-consumer water bottles, reduced VOCs (volatile organic compounds) and 30% recycled outsole adhered to a sewn upper. All this was achieved by applying detailed lifecycle analysis to examine the impacts of materials and shoe assembly techniques.

 Timberland, USA

 chrome-free tanned leather, recycled PET

 renewable, low-impact and recycled materials

> FOOTWEAR

Kickers x Noki

This post-modern hybrid Kicker, in which skinhead meets Goth meets hippy, is a collaboration with the designer Noki, reworking old leather jackets into one-off, ethical, new boots for women. The antithesis of homogenized brand culture, each item pair has a unique appearance. These boots are lightweight, comfy and spot on for city sightseeing.

 Kickers, UK in collaboration with Noki

 recycled leather jackets, various bio-materials and synthetics

 recycled materials

> ACCESSORIES/FOOTWEAR

Teko socks

Teko makes these high-performance socks from materials that minimize their impact on the environment: merino wool from a holistically managed farm in Tasmania, Ingeo™, a bio-fibre made from polylactic acid (PLA) derived from corn plants, recycled polyester and organic cotton (grown without pesticides). Non-toxic dyes exceed European Oekotex 100 standards.

 Teko, USA

 natural fibres including organic wool/cotton; recycled plastic fibres

 clean production and eco-sensitive manufacturing

> ACCESSORIES

Howies belts

Just like those mountains of old car tyres, so too old bicycle tyres tend to end up as landfill waste. So here's an ingenious use for those redundant tyres with the worn-out treads, reincarnated by Howies as tough, durable and individualistic belts for travellers and Goths alike. Each one is handmade, with a choice of slick or semi-slick.

 Howies, UK

 rubber, fibre, steel

 high recycled content

> ACCESSORIES

HeyJute iPod cases

Protecting electronic equipment from the trials and tribulations of your holiday environment – sand, salt, rain, sun – will help you relax. Choosing one from HeyJute (well, it raises a smile), is the next step, as this Canadian collective ensures that 4% of every purchase price goes to Child Rights & You, a not-for-profit NGO that supports underprivileged children in India. There is a range of natural and funky colours for the cases, with a belt strap for hands-free activities.

 HeyJute, Canada

 hemp fibre

 renewable plant fibre material, ethical purchase

> ACCESSORIES

MSR Packtowel Ultralite

Gone is the soggy towel that festers in the bottom of your backpack or suitcase. The fabric of this lightweight towel, 21–102 g (1–4 lb) makes it extremely absorbent but it can also be easily squeezed dry. The wicking and drying ability of the fabric helps ease the discomfort of trekking in humid or wet weather. Sizes range from 69 x 127 cm (27 x 50 in.) to 23 x 51 cm (9 x 20 in.).

 Cascade Designs, USA and Ireland

 microfibre

 lightweight, good functionality, durable

303

specialist

Travel for business, leisure or adventure requires a variety of kit. Here are some classic designs that have stood the test of time and some rather innovative ones too. Just as the apparel manufacturers have gone green, so have those that produce bum-bags, day bags and backpacks. Today a lot of bags use a high percentage of recycled materials in their production.

Products to facilitate drinking, cooking, picnicking and camping need to be lightweight, durable, reliable, easy to use and easily cleaned and maintained. But they also need to give pleasure and meet our contemporary needs. Wind-up, solar and low-energy devices enable us to keep our electronic and lighting accessories working, even in remote locations.

Lastly, there are essential products for specific sports (surfing, sailing, snowboarding), helmets to ensure our safety and gadgets that can save lives. Looking after yourself ensures you don't put others at risk and, in doing so, add to the considerable carbon cost of getting a helicopter to rescue you because you were ill prepared.

> CAMPING

2 Second Tent

Camping seems to be undergoing a renaissance in Europe, encouraged by books, guides, music festivals and people looking for a change. The 2 Second Tent does just what the name implies. Simply throw the circular flat-pack tent in the air and it springs out to form two-person accommodation. Four pegs and you're done. The standard 2 Second is 80 cm (32 in.) in diameter when packed, the 2 Second Light is 65 cm (26 in.), so well suited to leisure camping.

 Quechua/Decathalon, France

 fibreglass, polyurethane-coated polyester, polyethylene, steel

 usability, fun

> CAMPING

Eco THERMO

The Eco THERMO 6 Woman's Sleeping Pad, claimed to be the world's first carbon-neutral sleeping pad, is a technological wonder compared to the pads of yesteryear. Its insulation layer is composed of spun carbonized bamboo fibre and the well-tested 'air-core' design. Extra insulation in the foot provides comfort where it is needed and the 'mummy' outline keeps the weight down to 610 g (1 lb 6 oz).

 Pacific Outdoor Equipment, USA

 carbonized bamboo fibre insulation, undyed bamboo fabric, air valve of recycled aluminium

 bio-materials, ergonomic features

> CAMPING

Big Agnes Battle Mountain

Rated down to −15°C (5°F), this sleeping bag combines traditional goose down filling and an underside insulation layer of a unique bamboo fibre made by burning at 800°C (1,472°F) to create charcoal, which is then spun into fibre. A tough, well-detailed and constructed bag, it has an inbuilt pocket for a sleeping pad and outer and inner layers of rip-stop microfibre nylon.

 Big Agnes, USA

 goose down, bamboo charcoal fibre insulation and nylon

 good combination of bio-materials with durable synthetics to provide long life

> CAMPING

Big Agnes Skinny Fish

An amazing 99% of the materials in this sleeping bag are from recycled sources: the Climashield™ HL Green 100% recycled content insulation has 100% recycled outer / inner liner layers of rip-stop microfibre nylon – even the drawstring cord and stuff sack are derived from recycled content. This bag may be a 'second time around' product, but it feels like new.

 Big Agnes, USA

 insulation, nylon and other recycled materials

an almost 100% recycled product

Solio

Anyone heading for a sunshine holiday and likely to need to charge their mobile and other peripherals might consider slipping a Solio in their bag. Three blades of the fan, each with a thin photovoltaic panel, fold out to gather energy from the sun. One hour of sunlight gives enough charge to run a mobile phone for 25 minutes or an iPod for one hour of playing time. It works with many types of peripherals, from GPS to PDAs. An AC adaptor also allows you to charge it from the mains should rain interrupt your holiday. Weighing just 156 g (6 lb) and measuring about 12 x 3 x 6 cm (5 x 1 x 2 in.), it'll be hardly noticeable in your bag. The manufacturer offsets the carbon dioxide generated in production with Future Forests in new tree-planting schemes.

 Better Energy Systems, USA

 rechargeable lithium-ion battery, photovoltaic panel, various synthetic polymers

 renewable power device

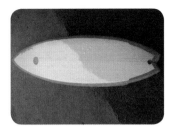

> SPORTS KIT

Greenlight Eco-surfboard

This company's philosophy of minimizing waste and preferring bio-materials avoids using the toxic array of chemicals that is found in most surfboard manufacture. Bamboo is the primary material, used as 'bamboo fibreglass', laminate stringers, fins and deck patches. The manufacturing facility utilizes low-energy equipment, sources some renewable electricity and operates a recycling programme, uses biodegradable packaging and even offsets some of its shipping CO_2 emissions.

 Greenlight Surf Company

 bamboo, bio-plastics, cellulose and recyclable EPS foam

 lower embodied-energy surfboards with low-impact manufacturing and distribution

> SPORTS KIT

Venture Snowboards

Five different types of snowboards are offered by this enlightened company whose factory building utilizes renewable power, passive solar features and waste minimization processes. At the heart of these boards is a poplar/ash 'bookmatched' symmetrical wood core, from sustainable forest resources. Boards are hand-finished and use other durable, high-quality materials including stainless steel, sintered base material and triaxial fibreglass as well as organically produced textiles, such as hemp and cotton.

 Venture Snowboards, USA

 Forest Stewardship Council (FSC)-certified hardwoods, various other materials

 low environmental-impact manufacturing, supply-chain sourcing

> SPORTS KIT

Hobie Mirage Adventure Island

Hobie Cat manufactures a diverse range of kayaks for sports or recreational use, but it is the Mirage Adventure Island that offers an exceptional three-in-one package. It is a 4.8-m (16-ft) trimaran with central kayak body and two outriggers that can be equipped with a 5.34-sq. m (58-sq. ft) sail. The unique Mirage Drive enables the kayak operator to convert pedalling into movement of two flipper-like propellers. The whole outfit weighs just 52 kg (115 lb), so is easily transported by car or camper van. Take the outriggers off and the kayak is suitable for longer-distance touring. Fun with flexibility.

 Hobie Cat, USA

 various materials including rotation-moulded polyethylene

 multifunctional, human/wind-powered, durable water craft

> SPORTS KIT

Roof RO6 Bamboo

You've walked on the flooring, worn the shirt and eaten with the chopsticks. Now you can protect your head with one of nature's wonder materials – bamboo. This unique helmet of laminated bamboo strips is the product of Roof, a company specializing in stylish, original, comfortable and safe helmets for motorcyclists. Roof's range is certified to the European E22/05 regulations. RO6 Bamboo is by special order only.

 Roof via Designer Helmets, Motoretta, UK

 bamboo and durable synthetics

 partly constructed from renewable resources

> SPORTS KIT

Salewa Helium G2 Helmet

This ultra-light helmet, just 260 g (9 oz), set new standards in 2001 for head protection for climbing activities and now, thanks to CE certification, can also be used for cycling and canoeing. It is made of synthetic materials but offers good comfort, ventilation, personal adjustability (there's a rotating knob at the rear of the helmet), durability and ease of cleaning, as internal components, including a fibre net, can be removed for washing.

 Salewa, Germany

 various synthetics

 tough, durable, ergonomic, multi-functional

> SPORTS KIT

Stash helmet

Providing ergonomic, safe and easy-to-use cycling gear is essential if people are to be encouraged back to low-impact methods of travel. The Stash helmet, approved to all relevant CE and safety standards, can be folded to reduce its overall size to a fraction of its original volume, enabling it to be slipped into most day bags, laptop carriers and even your shopping bag. For specialist cyclist commuters there is a pouch to store your helmet or a backpack with a separate Stash compartment. Nice thinking.

 Hatpac, UK

 ABS, EBS synthetic polymers

 lightweight, small volume, easy to use

> SPORTS KIT

Fair Trade Sports balls

Fair Trade coffee, bananas and other food goods may be regular items in our shopping baskets. Sports balls are not, but they could be! Playing ball games is a regular feature of relaxing at home, locally or overseas. So, the next time you want to buy a new ball for soccer, rugby, Australian Rules footie, netball, futsal or volleyball buy a Fair Trade one, approved by the Fair Trade Foundation and Co-op America and guaranteeing a fairer wage and respect all around. Fair Trade Sports supports a number of charities and the

World Day Against Child Labour. Don't travel without one.

 Fair Trade Sports, USA

 Forest Stewardship Council (FSC)-certified natural latex from Indian forests, various synthetics

 environmentally and ethically conscious design, high-quality handmade product, some certified materials

> EQUIPMENT/CAMPING

Ting Sling

Sometimes it is just too much effort to go anywhere. It is times like this when one needs a good book and somewhere to read it. Inghua Ting provides just that with her luxury, super-strong, comfy hammock. The tension bars either end provide for a more commodious design than those string-vest hammocks that truss you like a prime vegetable. The Ting Sling cossets you in slinky re-used car seatbelt fabric that is end-of-line or

didn't meet the original specifications. As each strap has a breaking strain of up to 2.5 metric tonnes, this product embodies a long second life for the material.

 Inghua Ting, Ting, UK

 textile fibres, stainless steel

 re-used car seatbelt

> SPORTS KIT

Reelight S120

Studies in Denmark have shown that cyclists with daytime bicycle lights had 32–40% fewer accidents than the control group. While motorcyclists seem to have adopted the practice of using lights during the day, cyclists have not. Here's a robust, simple solution to ensure you too can have this added safety feature. Two curved magnets are fitted opposite each other on the spokes of each wheel, while the light unit is attached to the axle. When the wheels turn, the magnets pass by the side of the light

unit, generating a small voltage through electro-magnetic induction, enough to make the twin LED bulbs continuously blink as you pedal and continue for three minutes even after you've stopped thanks to a built-in capacitor.

 Reelight, Denmark

 various, including polymers, metal, neodymium magnets

 human-powered, improved cyclist safety

> EQUIPMENT/SPORTS KIT

Sigg water bottles

These seamless bottles, extruded from pure aluminium, are a homage to high-quality industrial manufacturing. They are a pleasure to use and will last years. Today, the range of bottles suits diverse needs and tastes, but the classic lines of the Traveller, round or oval, are hard to beat. The only thing you might need to replace over the years is the O-ring seal for the tops.

 Sigg, Switzerland

 aluminium, polymer top with rubber seal

 light, durable, recyclable product

> EQUIPMENT

Katadyn Mini Filter

This compact filter, weighing just 210 g (7 oz), is fitted with a silver-impregnated ceramic filter capable of removing bacteria and protozoa from a 'found' water supply. A little hand pump sucks up water from the supply. Exceptionally dirty water can be pre-filtered using the storage bag, thereby extending the life of the ceramic filter. Equipped with this filter and a Sigg bottle (see above), the trekker, adventure sportsperson or tourist can maintain a safe supply of drinking water, a crucial resource in any survival situation.

 Katadyn, Switzerland

 plastics, ceramic filter, silver

 obviates the need to carry expensive and ecologically unsustainable commercial 'bottled' water

> ELECTRICAL GOODS

Greenheat

Greenheat is a non-explosive, non-toxic, 100% organic, fuel cell for use with dedicated camping stoves, Trangia®. The fuel is produced from sugar cane derivatives and is an ideal replacement for stoves burning meths. The standard size of 200 g (7 oz) has a long burn time of 100–120 minutes per 'fuel cell', but larger and smaller cells are available for 'base camp' and 'picnic' requirements.

 Burton McCall, UK

 sugar cane fuel, steel, plastic lid

 renewable fuel source

> EQUIPMENT/CAMPING

Magic Flame

This is an updated version of the tried and tested steel can with holes, used by itinerant travellers worldwide. Weighing in at just 550 g (1 lb 3 oz) and folding in to a tiny package of 15 x 11 x 1 cm (6 x 4 x ½ in.), this might just be the world's smallest cooking stove. Unfolded and in position it can utilize any locally found wood and even damp material.

 Künzi Creative Concepts, Switzerland

 chromium-nickel stainless steel

 durable, lightweight, uses naturally available fuel

Kelly Kettle

Long in use by generations of fishermen in the windy, wet Emerald Isle, the Kelly Kettle is a robust yet versatile travelling kitchen appliance. All you need is a few dry twigs, some driftwood or a sprig or two of heather set to burn in the fire pan. Place your double-skinned kettle on top and the flames boil 1.4 L (0.37 gallons) of water through the central vent in next to no time. An accessories package includes a pot support to enable you to heat food in a saucepan while you boil, and a grill and frying pan to use over the fire pan when you're enjoying your fresh cup of tea. There's a mini 0.5-L (0.13-gallon) version too for the lone traveller.

 Kelly Kettle Company, Ireland

 aluminium, brass, cork, wood

 durable, lightweight, eco-efficient, natural renewable fuel

> EQUIPMENT/SPORTS KIT

Field 7

For anyone venturing into unknown territory a compass is a prerequisite bit of kit. The Field 7 is a bestseller because of its simplicity, reliability and usability. A waterproof housing of Dryflex, good graphics and map measuring scales at 1:25,000 and 1:50,000 make this an indispensable direction-finder, ensuring the safety of yourself and others.

 Silva, Sweden

 Dryflex, perspex

 durable, 'classic' design

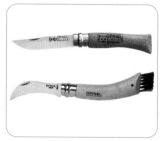

> EQUIPMENT/SPORTS KIT

Opinel knives

Established in 1890 in the Savoie region of France, Opinel have sold an estimated 260 million knives in over 70 countries. This is testament to the durable, functional design of these folding knives. The Traditional range offers a sharp, dependable carbon steel blade folding out of a wooden handle. Blades over 7 cm (3 in.) are secured in position by twisting the Virobloc double safety ring to prevent the blade folding back on itself. Giving a good edge when sharpened and years of service, Opinel knives are a classic design. New variants have been offered in recent years including Slim Line. Handles are usually beech wood or other European hardwoods including hornbeam, oak and olive. There's even a special knife for gathering mushrooms.

 Opinel, France

 carbon steel, stainless steel, wood/plastic

 durable, functional, lasts a lifetime

> EQUIPMENT/CAMPING

Snow Peak cutlery

This will last you a lifetime because it is made of astonishingly tough, durable but lightweight titanium. Although many people will not consider this an essential item for the traveller, those who have spent some time on the road will know it is the little luxuries, especially the rituals surrounding eating, that turn tiredness and discomfort into pleasure. Having your own dependable cutlery is important, so choose well. At just 52 g (2 oz), you'll hardly notice it in your backpack. If you are just a weekend rambler or picnicker it will do nicely too.

 Snow Peak, Japan

 titanium

 lightweight, durable, dependable, lasts a lifetime

Flat Salad

Whether you are a Sunday afternoon beach lounger or a serious trekker, packing your kit demands attention to weight and 'packability'. Designer J. C. Karish thought about both these issues as he developed prototypes for his flat-pack cutlery. With his salad servers, dessert spoons and other cutlery, Karish reminds us of the innate beauty of plastic and creates a design that we simply can't throw away, but lovingly keep for another day.

 Pandora Pandemonia, Italy, and J. C. Karish Industrial Design Studio, France

 plastic or wood

 lightweight, flat pack

> ELECTRICAL GOODS
Jonta

Three beam settings, full power and energy saving or flashing LED give this wind-up torch flexibility. The 1-watt super-bright LED gives a beam of 15 m (49 ft) or more and has a lifetime of over 100,000 hours. A 30-second wind gives 10 minutes on 'energy-saving' mode; the fully charged NiMH battery guarantees two and a half hours on full power. Weighing in at 445 g (1 lb), this is more suited to leisure camping or travelling, rather than serious trekking. Nonetheless, it is a robust, dependable source of light.

 Freeplay Energy, South Africa

 various materials including NiMH battery, glass-reinforced nylon and acetyl gearing

 human-powered charger, rechargeable battery

> ELECTRICAL GOODS
Indigo LED Lantern

You know the scenario – the torch batteries run out just at the crucial stage in erecting the tent, cooking your only meal of the day or reading the last chapter of the latest Harry Potter adventure. With this ultra-efficient wind-up lantern/torch, such scenarios are consigned to the primitive past. Giving one hour of brilliant white light from the LED bulbs for just 60 seconds of winding, the bulb is designed to provide 100,000 hours during its lifetime. The tough crank has a light to indicate optimum wind-up speed, the 3.6v nickel metal hydride battery lasts for over 10,000 crank cycles, there's a dimmer switch and the light

is multifunctional. An AC/DC lead permits indoor use too, although that seems a strange addition. Robust, functional, indispensable.

 Freeplay Energy, UK

 LEDs, NiMH battery, nylon, acetyl

 renewable energy power source, low-hazard battery, durable

> ELECTRICAL GOODS
Cyba-lite Eco Wind-up Torch

Just one minute of winding keeps the three 5 mm (¼ in.) ultra-bright LEDs lit for five minutes in this basic wind-up torch. This is ideal for everyone from the casual walker to the car driver (there's even an optional 12v car charger for boosting the rechargeable battery). The manufacturer donates 0.5% of the purchase price to the Woodland Trust.

 Wind-up Products, UK

 plastics, LEDs, various metals

 human-powered accessory

> ELECTRICAL GOODS

Cyba-lite AURA

This adjustable, strap-mounted headlight offers a range of lighting intensities by enabling the user to switch on one, two or three LEDs. Where extra light is required, the four-bulb, an ultra-bright Xenon lamp, can be switched on, giving an intensity equivalent to 200% more than a standard bulb. An adjustable, multi-surface reflector helps direct light. It is battery-powered but using high-quality rechargeable AA batteries is an option.

 TTI UK

 various plastics, webbing, LEDs, batteries

 very low-energy bulbs, option to use rechargeable AA batteries

> ELECTRICAL GOODS

M4

This is a lightweight, bright LED headlamp, with a fully waterproofed housing and fitted with an easily adjustable strap. There are four light modes, including a blinking mode, useful in emergencies. Three AAA batteries give up to 90 hours' maximum illumination time and a beam of up to 10 m (33 ft).

 Silva, Sweden

 LEDs, AAA batteries, polymers

 durable, functional, reliable

> ELECTRICAL GOODS

Freecharge portable energy source

This is a heavy-duty, 8-kg (18-lb) charger system capable of operating at 110–240v AC or 13–21v DC, so the 7Ah lead-acid gel battery can be charged from a mains electricity supply or any 12v renewable system (solar, wind, water). In remote locations you can charge it by operating the swinging handle by foot. The 12v cigarette lighter socket permits mobile phone/GPS/VHF equipment charging too.

 Freeplay Energy, South Africa

 various including lead-acid gel battery

 human-powered generator/charger

> ELECTRICAL GOODS

Freecharge mobile phone charger

This robust, wind-up phone charger, weighing only 310 g (11 oz), comes with its own adaptor into which you can plug your Nokia or Motorola phones to be charged (other phones require special adaptors). Just 45 seconds of winding give 2–3 minutes of talk time. A fully charged Freecharge can recharge 60% of the capacity of a mobile phone battery.

 Freeplay Energy, South Africa

 Various materials including nickel metal hydride battery pack

 human-powered charger

> BAG
Voltaic solar backpack

These days travellers seem to carry a veritable array of battery-hungry gizmos, from digital cameras to mobile phones, PDAs, GPS devices and MP3 players. Carrying a mains battery charger is not stylish or practical. Voltaic spotted this gap in the market and were one of the early manufacturers of a dedicated backpack with in-built solar panels. The photovoltaic panels generate up to 4 W stored in a 2,200mAh lithium-ion rechargeable and recyclable battery that you can set at 3.5, 6 or 7.2 volts. Simply plug your device into a USB or standard car charger socket using one of the 10 standard adaptors supplied. There are four bag options – courier and three backpacks for day excursions or serious hiking. The backpack weighs 1.59 kg (3 lb 8 oz) and has a capacity of 30 L (8 gallons).

 Voltaic Systems, USA

 photovoltaic array, recycled PET fabric, UV-resistant polyurethane, nylon mesh

 renewable energy, recycled materials content

> BAG
Mountainsmith Backpacks

Over 35 bags in Mountainsmith's production now utilize 100% recycled PET fabric in their construction. Of the Backpack range, the men's Phoenix, Cross Country, Circuit 3.0, Boundary, Maverick and Approach and the women's Trillium, Scarlet, Laurel, Lily and Ivy all use recycled PET. The Circuit 3.0, with a capacity of 88 L (23 gallons), weighing 2.35 kg (5 lb 3 oz), is made from 60 recycled water/ soda bottles. Stacked with an array of functional features, this rucksack is ideal for long backpacking trips where ease of use, flexibility, adjustment and comfort are de rigueur.

 Mountainsmith, USA

 recycled PET fabric, other materials

 recycled content

> BAG
Osprey ReSource series

Osprey makes a various range of packs for everyone from urban cyclists to professional mountaineers. The difference with the ReSource series is that these backpacks and courier/day bags are made of 70% recycled materials by content, giving real credibility to the concept of 'cradle-to-cradle' thinking and product reincarnation. The main body fabric, mesh pockets, binding tape, webbing and zipper pulls are from 100% recycled materials sources; other components contain 55–60% recyclate. It even comes packaged in a biodegradable polymer bag. The backpacks have a capacity between 22 L (6 gallons) and 32 L (9 gallons) and weigh from 0.71 to 1.13 kg (1 lb 10 oz–2 lb 8 oz) respectively. Day/ courier bags are 18 L (5 gallons) to 25 L (7 gallons) in capacity and weigh 0.99 to 1.13 kg (2 lb 3 oz–2 lb 8 oz). Both come in a range of contemporary colours.

 Osprey, USA

 recycled PET, mesh, zipper pulls, webbing

 high recycled materials content, contemporary designs

> BAG
Osprey Circuit rucksack

This daypack from Osprey's ReSource range is a voluminous 32 L (9 gallons) capacity, weighs just 1.08 kg (2 lb 6 oz) and is made from 70% recycled content. There's a 43-cm (17-in.) padded laptop pocket and a 'port' for an MP3 player, so this can double as a work/pleasure rucksack. Other packs in the range include day rucksacks and shoulder or courier bags in contemporary colours.

 Osprey Europe, UK, and Osprey, USA

 main component is recycled PET fabric woven from post-consumer water and soda bottles

 high recycled content, durable

> BAG
Mountainsmith Classic Lumbars

The Swift II is one of a range of seven different lumbar bags suitable for short exercise walks/jogs, day trips or day hikes. The range utilizes 100% recycled PET fabric sourced from Asia with 420-denier nylon and nylon reinforcements. All of the Classic Lumbars feature a headphone cord exit port. The Swift II is a mid-size model, having a capacity of 4.5 L (1 gallon) and weighing 0.45 kg (1 lb).

 Mountainsmith, USA

 recycled PET fabric, nylon

 recycled content

> BAG
Mountainsmith Cyber camera bags

The Cyber range of camera bags comes in XL, L, M, S and XS sizes, suitable for everything from point-and-shoot to compact digital/analogue or small SLR cameras. The fabric is recycled PET and even the zippers are from recycled sources. All versions have removable shoulder straps and belt fitting option.

 Mountainsmith, USA

 recycled PET fabric, recycled zippers, Velcro

 recycled content

PART FOUR

Resources

Here you'll find advice on how to find things to do 'on your doorstep', how to lower your carbon footprint and more. There is a comprehensive list of web resources, a glossary and suggestions for further reading. And there are listing and contact details enabling you to find the best eco-destination and to locate the manufacturer or supplier for an eco-travel product.

Tips for the eco-traveller

On your doorstep

Before thinking about travelling anywhere distant for a weekend or holiday break, it pays to look more locally for an experience that can be just as satisfying. Here are a few ways to reconsider what's on your doorstep in the UK, although many tips work just as well overseas, where you will find similar types of organizations.

> Contact your local/regional tourism information centre staffed by those who really do know 'what's on'.
> Take the human-powered option. Strap on your walking boots, mount your bicycle or, if possible, jump aboard your canoe, boat or yacht. Get grounded and see familiar landscapes anew.
> Take a leaf out of the sideways guide to local or distant places, *A Mis-Guide to Anywhere*, by Wrights & Sites,[1] which offers curious and fun-filled suggestions for seeing where you are in a different light.
> Camping is undoubtedly more exotic when in faraway places, but there are often unexpected sites near by, even in towns: see Cool Camping guides.[2]
> Enlist on a wilderness skills course (Ray Mears's Bushcraft courses[3] are well-known), to learn everything from building your own shelter to foraging for food and cooking it too. Enrol in a local craft or countryside skills course on hedge-laying, stone- or cobb-wall construction, basket making or other skills.
> Volunteer on a local conservation or wildlife project. See the British Trust for Conservation Volunteers (BTCV)[4] for the latest projects.
> Forget leaving home and work on creating new plantings to encourage wildlife into your garden. See how at the BBC Gardening website.[5]

Enjoying being an eco-traveller

Becoming an eco-traveller starts well before you contemplate packing your bags. It begins with reflection, research and planning.

> Where do you want to go and why? How do you balance personal motives with personal responsibilities for the local and global impacts of your decision? Can the destination afford your visit?
> Can you consider destinations closer to home or even find relaxation 'on your doorstep'?
> What's the most eco-efficient (low-carbon, low-pollution) and financially affordable way to travel? If you have to travel by air, can you stay longer and contribute more to the places you visit?
> How much time can you afford for your holiday? Is *slow travel* an option?
> Do you self-organize or do you use a travel organization or tour operator? If the latter, do you know how ethical and

responsible the company is? Is the company transparent about its operations, including its policies for the environment and/or *corporate social responsibility* (CSR)?
> What type of destination and accommodation do you require (see Part 2, 'Eco-destinations', pp. 24–275)? Do you choose a destination certified to an existing ecotourism label or standard? Can you go small and local, an effective way of making positive contributions?
> When you pack your bags keep them as light as possible (see Part 3, 'Eco-products' for a few suggestions, pp. 276–317), leaving space for a few locally made goods at your destination.
> When you are there, how do you intend to contribute to the local environment and community/communities? Will you buy local food, use local transport and patronize other local services?
> How are you going to ensure that you are sensitive to local customs, religions and other cultural/ethnic needs?
> What will be the positive legacy of your visit?
> On your return home, can any further benefit(s) accrue to the locality/localities you visited?
> Having experienced something good in one place, how do you spread the message or lessons learnt?

Changing your carbon footprint, changing habits

Whenever we use energy to travel or for living in the home, we are contributing to the exploitation of finite reserves of fossil fuels. These carbon-based fuels (oil, gas, coal) release energy and carbon dioxide, CO_2, and other substances on burning. CO_2 is one of the gases that significantly contribute (53%) to human-produced greenhouse gases, which affect global warming (others include methane, 17%, nitrous oxide, 12%, others, 18%). You can easily calculate how much CO_2 you produce by your activities. This is called your *carbon footprint* (see for example, Lynas,[6] Ghazi and Lewis[7] or any of the carbon calculators of the *carbon offset* companies – see below and Part 4, Resources), and
it's important to measure it so that you can act to reduce it. The worldwide standard units of measurement for carbon are metric tonnes and kilograms (weight).

Air and car travel, heating and food are the areas in which you can get quick results in reducing your carbon footprint. Air travel accounts for 22% and car travel for 15% of the average UK citizen's carbon footprint. Just one return flight from the UK to the southern hemisphere can generate 4–5 metric tonnes of CO_2 emissions. General emissions of CO_2, that is, those beyond the direct control of citizens, push the gross per capita footprint to 12.1 metric tonnes CO_2 per annum. Chris Goodall[8] suggests that the emissions targets set under the UK's commitment to the *Kyoto Protocol* and EU initiatives mean that each UK citizen needs to achieve 3 metric tonnes CO_2 emissions per annum. Clearly, this is a daunting prospect, but everyone can play a part in achieving that goal.

For the average UK citizen[8], the annual carbon footprint is:

UK Carbon Footprint per Capita (Metric tonnes CO2 per Annum)

Transport:	
Air travel	1.8
Car travel	1.2
Public travel (bus, rail)	0.1
Sub-total	**3.1**
Home (energy):	
Heating (space, water)	1.5
Lighting	0.1
Cooking (gas)	0.1
Electrical appliances	0.6
Sub-total	**2.3**
Home (other):	
Food	2.1
Other indirect emissions	0.6
Sub-total	**2.7**

Per Capita Total	**8.1 metric tonnes CO2 per annum**
General emissions from business, government, society (offices, factories, transport, construction, agriculture, etc.)	4.0
Gross per Capita Total	**12.1 metric tonnes CO2 per annum**

The carbon footprint of different transport modes

Comparing the different motorized modes of transport means taking into consideration:
> the carbon emissions of the fuel source (direct use of fossil fuels, electricity generated by fossil fuels, renewable sources of electricity, on-board sources of fuel/electricity)
> the fuel efficiency of the motor at different speeds (e.g. a car burns 30% more fuel at 130 km/h [80 mph] than at 80 km/h [50 mph])
> the number of passengers per 'vehicle' (motorcycle, car, boat or aeroplane).

Here's the CO2 output of a 654-km (406-mile), one-way journey from London to Edinburgh in the UK for one passenger:[9]

Transport mode	CO2 output equivalent (kg)
Electric train (modern type)	13
50 cc moped	16
Coach (bus)	30
Toyota Prius hybrid car	40
1,000 cc motorbike	60
Aeroplane	100

Two people on a moped or four in a Toyota Prius give pretty comparable figures at 8 kg and 10 kg per person CO2 output equivalent, but the figure for an average car (typically double the CO2 output of the Prius's modest 104 g/ CO2 km) would be 20 kg per person for a car with four passengers and 80 kg for a single passenger.

CO2 equivalency data[10] indicate that significant reductions in carbon footprint can be achieved by
> using smaller, lighter cars with good fuel efficiency of 21 km/L (50 mpg)
> taking trains for regional and long-distance travel, and
> taking intercontinental flights, not regional ones.

Transport mode	CO2 equivalent
Car, 8.5 km/L (20 mpg)	0.15/tonne km
Car, 21 km/L (50 mpg)	0.059/tonne km
Train, regional	0.015/person km
Train, long-distance	0.008/person km
Air, passenger, regional	0.44/person km
Air, passenger, intercontinental	0.26/person km

The message is clear. If constraints of time, money and other personal considerations permit, then travel overland, preferably by train, rather than fly.

Driving with care
In 2007 the UK's Driving Standards Agency incorporated questions on 'eco-driving' in tests for learner drivers. Careful driving habits result in savings of 15–20% in fuel. Look after your vehicle with regular servicing and correct tyre pressures and by removing unnecessary weight in the boot. Drive smoothly in the correct gear and avoid high revs and acceleration with excessive braking. Avoid short journeys, as engines and catalytic converters aren't as efficient in the first few kilometres. Reduce the time that you drive at over 80 km/h (50 mph), as fuel consumption increases by up to 30% for speeds over 110 km/h (68 mph). Lastly, try and take passengers with you whenever possible.

Reducing your flying
The *New Internationalist*[11] has suggested ten steps to reduce flying:
> Rule out commuting by air
> Think again about that holiday home
> Find alternatives to flying for work
> Cut out weekend jaunts and 'city breaks'
> Travel by land where possible
> Campaign against airport expansion

> Enjoy travelling slowly
> Holiday closer to home
> Don't 'offset': join the campaign [against climate change and reducing your own footprint]
> Take the pledge ['gold' version – don't travel by air unless it is an emergency; 'silver' – don't take more than two short-haul return or one long-haul return flight in the year to come].

Some of these steps make an ethical (if not moral) judgment, while others are common sense, if challenging to achieve. One notable exception is the 'silver pledge', as it accepts an unrealistic personal CO2 emissions contribution of 2–4 metric tonnes per annum, way above the current average British person's air travel of 1.8 metric tonnes CO2 per annum.

Is carbon-offsetting your travel impacts beneficial?
What is *carbon-offsetting*? It is the concept that individuals can balance their CO2 emissions by giving money to schemes that reduce or neutralize CO2 outputs elsewhere.
Two kinds of schemes predominate:
> those with a focus on restoring the capacity of the environment to absorb CO2. These include the planting of trees or crops or the preservation of existing vegetation, especially forests. Scientific opinion varies considerably on CO2 absorption of different plants and habitats or biomes;
> those that help specific communities to use energy sources with a lower CO2 footprint than 'traditional' more polluting fuel sources, and/or the provision of aid for health and education.

Carbon-offsetting won't head off the effects of climate change, but carefully modelled carbon-offset schemes can produce benefits at a local level.

With any carbon offset scheme, the devil is in the detail. Check the credentials of the offset organization and the schemes it supports; check how much of your cash actually goes to the scheme rather than overhead/admin costs and profit for the organization. The UK government has clarified what constitutes best practice with its 'gold standard', CDM Gold Standard: only Pure, Carbon Offsets, Global Cool and Equiclimate make the grade.

Companies also offset their carbon emissions in what has become a global carbon-trading market. The good news is that CO2 now has a commercial price per tonne; the bad news is that it doesn't reflect the 'true cost' to us and the environment. Some travel companies are only maintaining the CO2, not reducing emission; besides, the growth of business experienced by these companies makes any trading offsets pale into insignificance.

Can alternative fuels maintain current travel habits?
Alternative fuels are those that don't originate from fossil fuels, although some fossil fuel energy expenditure is involved in their manufacturing. Alternative fuels include *bio-fuels*, hydrogen and various renewables (solar- and wind-powered transport). Bio-fuels are made from waste products or from plants. Waste-generated bio-fuels include recycled cooking oil and gas from bio-digestion processes. Bio-fuels from plants include ethanol from grass, wood and agricultural crops like sugar cane and corn, and diesel from soy beans and palm oil.

Bio-fuels are particularly controversial.[12] The European Union has proposed that 10% of fuel by 2020 should originate from bio-fuels. However, the Empa Research Institute in Switzerland studied 26 bio-fuels and found that, although 21 of them reduced greenhouse-gas emissions by 30% when compared to fossil fuels, 12 fuels actually had a higher overall environmental impact than fossil fuels, including loss of farm crops and tropical forests, reductions in biodiversity and loss of hydrological and soil protection. The US government has encouraged farmers to shift from soy production to corn; Brazilian companies have been destroying tropical savannahs to plant soy or sugar cane; palm oil plantations have replaced virgin forest in Malaysia and Indonesia. Balancing global food production with bio-fuel production is another massive conundrum.

Huge land areas would be required for bio-fuels to provide even 10% of current fossil fuel needs, possibly up to 40% of Europe's farmland. Other fuels, such as methane gas from bio-digestion and landfill sites, are fine for domestic or industrial use, but impractical for transport. Another option, liquid hydrogen or on-board hydrogen fuel cells generating electricity, has been exercising car manufacturers for over a decade, yet a viable solution still seems unattainable.

The stark reality is that we need to reduce fossil fuel consumption, because alternative fuel systems offer only limited improvements in overall eco-efficiency and reduction of greenhouse gases.

1 S. Hodge *et al.* (2006) *A Mis-Guide to Anywhere.* Exeter, UK: Wrights & Sites.
2 www.coolcamping.co.uk/
3 www.raymears.com/
4 www.btcv.org/
5 www.bbc.co.uk/gardening/
6 M. Lynas (2007) *Carbon Counter: Calculate your carbon footprint.* Glasgow: HarperCollins.
7 P. Ghazi and R. Lewis (2007) *The Low Carbon Diet: Wise up, chill out and save the world.* London: Short Books.
8 C. Goodall (2007) *How to Live a Low-carbon Life.* London: Earthscan.
9 Adapted from D. Clark (2006) *Rough Guide to Ethical Living.* London: Rough Guides, p. 288.
10 P. White (2007) Corrected Transportation CO2 Equivalency Values, May 2007, International Swaps and Derivatives Association, Inc. http://www.isda.org/whata.
11 'Ethical Travel', *New Internationalist*, 409, March 2008.
12 A. Jha 'Burning biofuels may be worse than coal and oil, say experts', *The Guardian*, 4 January 2008, p. 12.

General Information

SUSTAINABILITY ISSUES

Aviation Environment Federation
W www.aef.org.uk
Since 1975, the not-for-profit AEF has examined the social, environmental and economic impacts and benefits of the aviation industry, with background and detailed reports on key issues from air pollution to climate change and noise.

Bluewater Network
W www.bluewaternetwork.org
Bluewater Network, based in the US, is a division of Friends of the Earth (FoE) that focuses on clean transport on sea and land and the protection of parks, forests and waterways from motorized 'thrillcraft'.

Factor 10 Institute
W www.factor10-institute.org
'Factor 10' is a concept that gained momentum in the early to mid-1990s. It suggests that a tenfold improvement in resource use efficiency is required in the industrialized countries' systems of production and consumption to deliver sustainability to all between 2025 and 2050.

International Institute of Sustainable Development
W www.iisd.org
The IISD, a Canadian-based but worldwide not-for-profit organization, has been contributing to the sustainability debate since 1990. It brings together expertise and commentary, with ways of thinking and ways of doing, to generate innovation to deal with sustainability issues.

International Union for the Conservation of Nature (IUCN) and Red List of endangered species
W cms.iucn.org/index.cfm
   www.iucnredlist.org
Founded 60 years ago, the IUCN is the world's oldest and largest global environmental network, with over 1,000 government and non-governmental organization members in over 160 countries. It supports scientific research and projects about environment and development challenges and the effects these are having on our ecosystems, biodiversity and peoples. It publishes the Red List of endangered species worldwide.

Survival International
W www.survival-international.org
Globalization and current models of tourism are affecting the diversity of the human race just as much as nature's biodiversity and ecosystems. The rights of many tribal peoples are often ignored or lost in the face of 'development'. Survival International gives a voice to these peoples by means of education, advocacy and campaigns.

Worldmapper
W www.worldmapper.org
Worldmapper is an amazing project to visualize the changing shape of our world – from its peoples and their movements to production and consumption of goods, health and wealth, growth and depletion, exploitation, pollution and more. The project comprises 366 land-mass projections of the world, each mapped in the form of a cartogram giving new shapes according to each parameter being measured.

Intergovernmental Panel on Climate Change (IPPC)
W www.ippc.ch
Set up in 1988 by the World Meteorological Organization (WMO) and by the United Nations Environment Programme (UNEP), the IPPC is a worldwide scientific body that monitors climate change and its real and potential effects on the environment and our socio-economic systems.

United Nations Environment Programme (UNEP)
W www.unep.org
The UNEP liaises with a host of scientific organizations including the IPPC (see above) and the Ecosystem Conservation Group (ECG) in order to protect the environment and maintain quality of life.

ECOTOURISM

Eco- and ethical tourism organizations

UN International Ecotourism Year 2002
W www.uneptie.org/pc/tourism/ecotourism/iye.htm

Planeta
W www.planeta.com

Tourism Concern
W www.tourismconcern.org.uk

The International Ecotourism Society
W www.ecotourism.org

The International Centre for Responsible Tourism
W www.icrtourism.org

World Tourism Organization
W www.unwto.org

Association of Independent Tour Operators (AITO)
W www.aito.co.uk

The Travel Foundation
W www.thetravelfoundation.org.uk

Tourism Investigation and Monitoring Team
W www.twnside.org.sg/tour.htm

ECPAT
W www.ecpat.net/eng/index.asp

Ecological Tourism in Europe
W www.oete.de/eng/index.htm

Sustainable Travel International
W sustainabletravelinternational.org

Green Tourism Business Scheme, UK
W www.green-business.co.uk

Blue Flag
W www.blueflag.org

Ecotourism standards, eco-labels and awards

Green Globe, international
W www.greenglobe21.com
www.ec3global.com/products-programs/green-globe/default.aspx

Fair Trade in Tourism, South Africa
W www.fairtourismsa.org.za

Certification for Sustainable Tourism, Costa Rica
W www.turismo-sostenible.co.cr

Ecotourism Australia
W www.ecotourism.org.au

Responsible Tourism Awards, UK
W www.responsibletourismawards.org

Viabono, Germany
W www.viabono.de

Green Key, Europe
W www.green-key.org

La Clef Verte, France
W www.laclefverte.org

Ibex OE-Plus, Switzerland
W www.oe-plus.ch

Audubon Green Leaf, Canada
W www.terrachoice.com

Green Seal, USA
W www.greenseal.org

Voluntary Initiatives for Sustainability in Tourism, VISIT, Europe
W www.visit21.ne

DestiNet, international
W destinet.ew.eea.europa.eu

Brazil Sustainable Tourism Programme
W www.sustainabletourismbrazil.org

Legambiente Turismo, Italy
W www.legambienteturismo.it

The Nordic Swan, Scandinavia and Europe
W www.svanen.nu/Eng/default.asp

Umweltzeichen, Austria
W www.umweltzeichen.at

Responsible and eco-tour companies

Association of Independent Tour Operators (list of 3-star responsible travel operators)
W www.aito.co.uk/corporate_RT_Starclass.asp

Responsible Travel
W www.responsibletravel.com

Ecotravel Center
W www.ecotour.org

Tribes Travel
W www.tribes.co.uk

Discovery Initiatives
W www.discoveryinitiatives.co.uk

Expert Africa
W www.expertafrica.com

Rainbow Tours
W www.rainbowtours.co.uk

North South Travel
W www.northsouthtravel.co.uk

TRAVEL MODES AND OPTIONS

UK Walking

Walk It
W www.walkit.com

Walking Bus
W www.walkingbus.com

European City Cycling

Bicing, Barcelona, Spain
W www.bicing.com

Callabike, Berlin and other German cities
W www.callabike-interaktiv.de/kundenbuchung

City Bike, Copenhagen
W www.visitcopenhagen.com/tourist/plan_and_book/how_to_get_around/bikes/free_city_bikes

OYBike, London and Southampton, UK
W www.oybike.com

Pedicabs, USA and international
W www.pedicab.com/world_operators.html

Vélib, Paris, France
W www.velib.paris.fr

Vélo'v, Lyons, France
W www.velov.grandlyon.com

European cycle schemes

Sustrans, UK
W www.sustrans.org.uk

Véloland, Switzerland
W www.veloland.ch

UK car-on-demand schemes, car clubs and car sharing

Carplus
W www.carplus.org.uk

City Car Club
W www.citycarclub.co.uk

Streetcar
W www.streetcar.co.uk

Whizzgo
W www.whizzgo.co.uk

Zipcar
W www.zipcar.co.uk

Carshare
W www.carshare.com

Car Pool
W www.car-pool.co.uk

Ridesharing
W www.gumtree.com/london/rideshare

European rail travel

Railteam
W www.railteam.eu

The Man in Seat 61
W www.seat61.com

Virtual travel

Google Earth
W earth.google.com

Second Life
W secondlife.com

Skype
W www.skype.com

ALTERNATIVE MODES AND OPTIONS

BBC Gardening
W www.bbc.co.uk/gardening
Go on, get some dirt under your fingernails with inspiration from this excellent, comprehensive gardening portal.

British Trust for Conservation Volunteers (BTCV)
W www2.btcv.org.uk
Cutting back brambles, building stone walls, laying paths and making nesting boxes – there is a conservation activity somewhere near you that meets your needs and helps the environment and its wildlife.

Cool Camping
W www.coolcamping.co.uk
Get there before the rush that is bound to follow the publication of these well-researched guides identifying spectacular and secret places to camp.

Critical Mass
W www.criticalmasslondon.org.uk
Organizes slow cycle rides in many UK conurbations. This one is for London.

Slow Up
W www.slowup.ch
Swiss mass-cycle rides encouraging car drivers to ease off the gas and enjoy the scenery.

Greenmap
W www.greenmap.org
A network of mapmakers in over 50 countries using a standardized icon system and local knowledge to show visitors and locals where green goods and experiences can be found. A brilliant system of participatory design.

A Mis-Guide to Anywhere
W www.mis-guide.com/mg.html
Gets you under the skin of where you really are, parallel worlds right under your nose.

Ray Mears Bushcraft
W www.raymears.com
Offers a range of wilderness bushcraft courses that sharpen your senses, build your indigenous knowledge and enable you to experience a oneness with nature.

Slow Cities
W www.cittaslow.org.uk
Originated in Italy under the title Cittaslow, this now extends to networks in many European countries advocating the renewal of slower rhythms for many aspects of city or town life.

Slow Food
W www.slowfood.com
During the last 20 years Slow Food has grown to over 88,000 international members supporting the philosophy of 'local is beautiful', biodiversity and human-scale food.

Slow travel and low carbon travel
W www.lowcarbontravel.com
This is the blog of Ed Gillespie and family as they (slowly) travel around the world without flying.

Waterscape
W www.waterscape.com
A portal website on everything you want to know about rivers, canals and all things aquatic in Britain.

Carbon offset companies and other organizations

Equiclimate
W www.ebico.co.uk/html/a_climate.php

Global Cool
W www.globalcool.org/myco2

Pure
W www.puretrust.org.uk

The Carbon Trust
W www.thecarbontrust.co.uk

Carbon Calculator
W www.carboncalculator.com

Climate Care
W www.climatecare.org

Gold Standard carbon credits
W www.cdmgoldstandard.org

The Climate Neutral Company
W www.carbonneutral.com

Glossary

Bio-centric – To be bio-centric is to believe that humanity is only one form of life and that all forms of life are of equal value and deserving of their own well-being. Bio-centrism therefore opposes anthropocentrism.

Biodiversity – A term referring to the biological diversity of a place, habitat or other natural community as a statement of fact or a statistic. Alternatively, biodiversity is an aspiration, i.e. 'to maintain biodiversity'. Biodiversity tends to be seen as something applying to non-human living species. However, Survival International is an organization whose aim is to assist tribes from indigenous groups, often living in unique habitats or ecosystems, in upholding their human rights and concurrently maintain human biodiversity. It considers how tourism contributes to solutions and/or generates problems for biodiversity in its broadest sense.

Bio-fuels – Fuels produced from biological matter (plant or animal) that can generate energy on combustion. Bio-fuels have come under intense scrutiny as we see that the supply of fossil fuels (coal, oil, gas) is finite, about half the world's oil reserves having already been consumed. Bio-fuels are produced from agricultural crops or natural vegetation, from bio-digestion of waste to produce bio-gas, from animal bio-products (e.g. wax, oils) and from recycling cooking or other used oils. Controversy rages over the real or potential benefits of bio-fuels, as some seem to produce more adverse effects than fossil fuels if the overall environmental and socio-economic impacts of their production, distribution and use are considered. A major question is how the production of bio-fuels can be balanced with global food production and at the same time minimize natural habitat destruction.

Carbon dioxide (CO2) – This gas absorbs infra-red (long-wave radiation) light, radiating some to space and some back to earth. CO2 is a termed a 'greenhouse gas' because it creates a similar effect to the layer of glass in a greenhouse, trapping heat and causing warming. CO2 comprises 53% of the greenhouse gases (others are nitrous oxide, 12%; methane, 17%; ozone near the surface, 13%; CFCs and HCFCs, 5%). As a consequence of burning carbon-based fossil fuels, human activity has caused the proportion of CO2 in the atmosphere to rise from 300 ppm to over 390 ppm. By fairly recent consensus, the world's scientists believe that CO2 increases have exacerbated the greenhouse effect and caused a temperature increase of 0.8°C, resulting in global warming.

Carbon footprint – Measures how many metric tonnes of carbon dioxide (CO2) each person directly produces each year from daily activities, such as transport, travel, domestic heating, cooking and lighting. The term can also include indirect production from the collective emissions of a society or nation for infrastructure and other common services.

Carbon offset/offsetting – Is the concept that the negative environmental consequences (in terms of global warming) caused by the production of carbon dioxide (CO2) from one activity can be negated by contributing money to organizations or companies that invest in schemes or projects that absorb or reduce CO2 production elsewhere. This balancing out is called offsetting. Investments, or offsets, tend to be made in tree planting and reafforestation, to absorb CO2, and in encouraging the installation of more efficient methods of obtaining energy and/or installing renewable energy technologies (wind, solar, hydro), in order to reduce CO2. Often the latter investments are made in poor communities in developing countries, so the CO2 objective is also tied to humanitarian assistance or poverty relief. Carbon offsetting is perceived by some as a useful mechanism to reduce global CO2 production and by others as an ineffective measure that just assuages the guilt of the dominant CO2 producers. On a global and industrial scale, it is referred to as carbon trading and is the subject of a highly politicized debate negotiated by national and international legislation and regulation.

Climate change – This is the phrase used to describe the belief that human activity is altering the world's climate over and above any natural or geological time variations. Climatologists examine climate change over millennia and in prehistoric times, including former 'Ice Ages'. Advocates of the theory maintain that the production of vast quantities of carbon dioxide by burning fossil fuels (coal, oil, gas) since the beginning of the Industrial Revolution is the cause of rapid, manmade warming, which is resulting in extreme and more frequent incidences of heat, drought, floods, violent storms, ice melting and sea-level rise. An august body of world scientists, the Intergovernmental Panel on Climate Change (IPPC), is predicting a global temperature rise of +3 to +4°C by the end of the 21st century (compared to +0.8°C during the whole of the 20th century). The environmental, socio-economic and political consequences of this change would be enormous.

Corporate social responsibility (CSR) – This refers to an agenda and active management followed by companies that annually audit the reduction of negative environmental impacts and increase in positive social contributions of their business. A company's annual CSR report must be both transparent and honest for it to be seen as a genuine, pro-active business response to the challenge of sustainability.

Deep ecology – Is an ecologically based philosophy that ascribes equal value to humans and non-humans and the systems in which they live. The Norwegian philosopher Arne Naess is credited with coining the phrase 'deep ecology' in 1973 in an effort to focus attention on the impacts of humans because of their integral involvement with the ecosphere (all living things and systems). He saw deep ecology as a means to understand our relationship 'in' and 'with' nature, rather than purely as a branch of science called ecology.

Degrowth – Is an emerging debate, its impetus currently coming from France, that is seeking to find new ways of conceiving and talking about human and economic growth. Décroissance ('degrowth') implies balancing the growth of the economy and personal wealth alongside the growth (and health) of other socio-cultural values, personal development, the restoration of damaged societies, habitats and ecosystems, and other restorative forms of growth. The aspirations of ecotourism are to grow tourism in a different direction, ensuring positive impacts rather than negative ones, but if ecotourism keeps on growing without constraint it too can cause negative impacts.

Ecological footprint – A measure of all the biologically productive land, energy and other resources needed to maintain the products and services for a particular lifestyle. The methodology of ecological footprinting emerged in the early 1990s and is now an established way of highlighting the different consumption habits of nations. An equable ecological footprint for every human on the planet is about 1.9 hectares equivalent (5 acres). The average American's footprint is 10 hectares (25 acres) and a British person's is 6 hectares (15 acres), whereas a Chinese or Indian citizen treads lightly at 1.2 hectares (3 acres) and 1.1 hectares (3 acres) respectively. The total sum ecological footprint of nations is the individual ecological footprint multiplied by the number of people. Thus, the USA's ecological footprint for 250 million people is 2,500 million hectares (6,178 million acres), compared to China's 1,440 million hectares equivalent (3,558 million acres) for 1.2 billion people.

Ecotourism – According to Ron Mader, 'most definitions of ecotourism...meet three criteria: 1) it provides for environmental conservation; 2) it includes meaningful community participation; 3) it is profitable and can sustain itself' (Ron Mader, 'Exploring ecotourism', www.planeta.com, accessed 4 January 2007).

Ecotourism and responsible tourism – This has been defined as 'responsible travel to natural areas that conserves the environment and improves the well-being of local people' (The International Ecotourism Society, quoted by Lorimer, Kerry (2006) in *Code Green*, p. 9). According to this source, responsible tourism takes into consideration the following 'triple bottom line' issues:
> Environment: Travel that minimizes negative environmental impacts and, where possible, makes positive contributions to the conservation of biodiversity, wilderness, natural and human heritage. Travellers and locals learn and share information, leading to better appreciation and understanding.
> Social/Cultural: Travel that respects cultures and traditions and recognizes the rights of all peoples to be involved in decisions that affect their lives and to determine their futures. By involving and engaging local people, there is authentic interaction and greater understanding between travellers and hosts, which builds cultural pride and community confidence.
> Economic: Travel that has financial benefits for the host community and operates on the principles of fair trade. Monies spent by travellers remain in the community through the use of locally owned accommodation, staff and services, funding community initiatives, training or other in-kind support.
Leo Hickman, in *A Good Life* (2005, p. 161), offers the following characteristics of responsible tourism:
> Minimize impact
> Build environmental and cultural awareness and respect
> Provide positive experiences for both visitors and hosts
> Provide direct financial benefits for conservation
> Provide financial benefits and empowerment for local people
> Raise sensitivity to a host country's political, environmental and social climate
> Support international human rights and labour agreements.

Eco-travel – Is defined for the purposes of this book as 'travel to improve one's own flourishing, to contribute to the flourishing of others met on one's travels, to do so with a minimal environmental footprint and, where possible, to help heal and regenerate the communities and places visited'.

Eco-traveller – An eco-traveller has a heightened sense of awareness of the potential and real consequences of his/her actions, but actively seeks ways of travelling better by contributing more to the places visited and by treading with a lighter ecological footprint.

Ethical tourism see Ecotourism

Hypermobility – Is a term coined by Professor Steven Vertovec, Oxford University, UK, to describe the phenomenon induced by low-cost or budget airlines that permits people to travel for leisure, business or new career/lifestyle developments.

The Kyoto Protocol – An international framework brokered by the United Nations at the 1992 Rio Earth Summit, finalized in 1997 in Kyoto, Japan, but not ratified by significant members until 2006, when 163 states signed the treaty. The USA and Australia were notable exceptions from the nations that ratified it, claiming that its science and practice were flawed. The protocol aims at progressively reducing emissions of greenhouse gases that contribute to global warming and (adverse) climate change. However, the protracted process of international negotiation has meant that the well-meaning targets for CO_2 reduction (compared to 1990 levels) set for 2012 will be not be met by most nation signatories. The global situation is delicately balanced, as the world's biggest economy (the USA) produces about 20% of the world's annual CO_2 emissions. In 2007, China, the world's fastest-growing major economy, exceeded total USA CO_2 emissions, although per capita emissions remain a fraction of that of a US citizen. China's emissions increased significantly because of the large number of new coal-fired power stations being constructed to deliver energy for economic growth.

Methane (CH_4) – A gas that exists naturally, but is also created by human activities, and which contributes to the phenomenon of global warming. Methane (1.8 ppm) contributes to 17% of the observed global warming effect, whereas carbon dioxide (380 ppm) contributes to 53%. Manmade sources of methane include decomposition gases from the rubbish in landfill sites, waste treatment and biomass burning natural sources of methane are generated from plant decomposition by soil bacteria. As global warming melts the permafrost soils of northern latitudes, vast quantities of methane are being released. Methane is up to 22 times more powerful in its global warming effect than carbon dioxide, so some climate scientists predict that its increasing generation will cause a rapid rise in global temperature.

Peak oil – Is the concept that during the last hundred years human activities have now consumed half of the world's oil reserves and, at present (increasing) rates of consumption, we may enjoy only another 50 years' supply of this energy source. Peak oil may have been reached in 2000 or 2007 or may yet be reached – there is no consensus because the transnational oil companies, wary of the possible effects on world prices, are reluctant to be transparent about their true exploitable oil reserves.

Peak travel – This expression raises the spectre that, as the world's finite resources of oil are consumed, the ability of people to travel as frequently and widely as they do today will diminish unless alternative energy sources and modes of transport are developed. Arguably, 'peak travel' has a lag time of a decade or two after 'peak oil'. It all depends upon oil prices, the rate of consumption of oil reserves and the geo-political landscape.

Positive slowness – This is a philosophy and set of values to which various contributors to an emerging 'slow movement' of activists, academics and alternative organizations or groups subscribe, and it is gaining attention. 'Slow' has been perceived as a negative since Adam Smith gave a voice to our modern economic model of capitalism in his book *The Wealth of Nations* in 1776. When the assumption that 'faster is better' is contested, our notion of 'progress' is gently interrogated. Positive slowness recognizes that benefits beyond mere wealth accrue from seeking slower rhythms and experiences. The Italian Slow Food and Slow Cities networks led the way from the mid-1980s onwards.

Responsible tourism see Ecotourism

Slow travel – A term that has emerged out of a diverse platform described as the 'slow movement', comprising activists, academics, artists and alternative organizations and groups that espouse the positive benefits of slowing down. Slow travel has existed for centuries in the form of long, often personal journeys overland or at sea, where the speed at which the final destination is reached is less important than the journey itself. Today, slow travel sets itself up against 'fast travel' by aeroplane or car or even by the relatively new high-speed trains. Slow travel really is about the deep experiences found by literally and mentally travelling more slowly.

Sustainability – Is an ageless concept, but the word has a particular socio-cultural meaning today. The question implied by the term 'sustainability' is whether or not natural systems and their associated resources will be able to sustain human activities today and in future. From an anthropocentric viewpoint, the term invokes the relative dynamics of human population size and the biological productivity and ecological capacity of the land area occupied by humans. This defines the carrying capacity of the land in relation to maximum populations. If population grows and consumes at a high level, then the population will exceed the carrying capacity and some of the people will die, until a new balance is restored. Excessive consumption by a population can permanently lower carrying capacity and so can effectively reduce population growth. 'Sustainability' therefore implies that humankind needs to look after the carrying capacity of the Earth for everyone, today and for unborn generations. This notion is embedded in the most-quoted definition, from the Brundtland Commission in 1987: 'Sustainable development is development that meets the needs of the present without compromising the ability of future generations to meet their own needs.'

Tourism – May be defined as 'the practice of travelling for pleasure' or 'the business of providing tours and services for tourists' (Ron Mader, *Exploring Ecotourism*).

Triple bottom line (TBL) – Refers to the business and industry challenge of balancing profits (the bottom line) with environmentally responsible reduction of negative impacts and the generation of social benefits by the activities of the enterprise. TBL is seen as striving to balance the three foci in order to generate a win:win:win for profit, planet and people. Many ecotourism enterprises have engaged with the TBL challenge and see it as a guiding principle for their enterprise. Global eco-label and ecotourism standards also consider various aspects of TBL.

Further reading

Baird, Nicola (ed.) (2005) *Save Cash and Save the Planet*. London: HarperCollins with Friends of the Earth.

Clark, Duncan (2006) *The Rough Guide to Ethical Living*. London: Rough Guides.

Clifford, Sue and Angela King (2006) *England in Particular: A celebration of the commonplace, the local, the vernacular and the distinctive*. London: Hodder & Stoughton.

de Botton, Alain (2002) *The Art of Travel*. London: Penguin Books.

Dorling, Daniel, Mark Newman and Anna Barford (2008) *The Atlas of the Real World: Mapping the way we live*. London: Thames & Hudson.

Faiers, Julia (2005) *Exotic Retreats: Eco resort design from barefoot sophistication to luxury pad*. Hove: RotoVision.

Fuad-Luke, Alastair (rev. ed. 2004) *The eco-design handbook: A complete sourcebook for the home and office*. London: Thames & Hudson.

Ghazi, Polly and Rachel Lewis (2007) *The Low Carbon Diet: Wise up, chill out and save the world*. London: Short Books.

Goodall, Chris (2007) *How to Live a Low-carbon Life*. London: Earthscan.

Henson, Robert (2006) *The Rough Guide to Climate Change*. London: Rough Guides.

Hickman, Leo (2005) *A Good Life*. London: Transworld Publishers.

Hickman, Leo (2007) *The Final Call*. London: Transworld Publishers.

Hodge, Stephen, Simon Persighetti, Phil Smith, Cathy Turner and Tony Weaver (2006) *A Mis-Guide to Anywhere*. Exeter: Wrights & Sites.

Kunz, Martin Nicholas and Patricia Massó (2006) *Best-designed Ecological Hotels*. Ludwigsburg: Avedition.

Lorimer, Kerry (Coordinating author) (2006) *Code Green: Experiences of a lifetime*. London: Lonely Planet.

Lynas, Mark (2007) *Carbon Counter: Calculate your carbon footprint*. Glasgow: HarperCollins.

Mowforth, Martin and Ian Munt (2003) *Tourism and Sustainability: Development and new tourism in the Third World*. Third edition. London and New York: Routledge.

Pattullo, Polly with Orely Minelli for Tourism Concern (2006) *The Ethical Travel Guide: Your passport to exciting alternative holidays*. London: Earthscan.

Sawday, Alastair (Senior ed.) (2006) *Green Places to Stay*. Bristol: Alastair Sawday Publishing Co.

Eco-destinations

Destinations are listed in alphabetical order. Although some destinations only fit into one of the Part 2 categories – Urban, Nature, Culture, Leisure, Adventure – others provide facilities and services that match more than one category.

Key to categories
U – Urban
N – Nature
C – Culture
L – Leisure
A – Adventure

There is a range of guide prices to suit every budget, from basic to luxurious.

Key to pricing:
Budget   ▲
US$0–50 / €0–30 / £0–25
per person per night

Mid-range ▲▲
US$51–150 / €31–94 / £26–75
per person per night

High   ▲▲▲
US$151–400 / €95–250 / £76–200
per person per night

Luxury   ▲▲▲▲
over US$400 / over €250 / over £200
per person per night

Adelaide Hills Wilderness Lodge ▲ NAL
Whitehead Rd,
Mylor, SA 5153,
Australia
T +61 (08) 8388 5588
F +61 (08) 8388 5556
E info@adelaidewilderness.
   com.au
W www.adelaidewilderness.
   com.au

Agriturismo Colle Regnano
▲–▲▲ NCL
C. da Casadicristo, 11,
62029 Tolentino, Italy
T +39 0733 967691
F +39 0733 967691
E agriturismo@colleregnano.it
W www.colleregnano.it

Aislabeck Eco-Lodges ▲▲ NL
Units 1–3,
Aislabeck Plantation,
Hurgill Road, Richmond,
North Yorkshire DL10 4SG,
UK
T +44 (0)7940 379119
F +44 (0)1748 822216
E info@naturalretreats.co.uk
W www.naturalretreats.com

Albergue das Laranjeiras
▲ UCL
Rua da Ordem Terceira,
13 Pelourinho, Salvador,
Bahia, Brazil
T +55 71 33211366
F +55 71 33212816
E hi@laranjeirashostel.com.br
W www.laranjeirashostel.com.br

Alila Manggis ▲▲▲ CL
Desa Buitan, Manggis,
Karangasem, Bali 80871,
Indonesia
T +62 363 41011
F +62 363 41015
E manggis@alilahotels.com
W www.alilahotels.com

Alila Ubud ▲▲▲ CL
Desa Melinggih Kelod,
Payangan, Gianyar,
Bali 80572, Indonesia
T +62 361 975 963
F +62 361 975 968
E ubud@alilahotels.com
W www.alilahotels.com

Alila Villas Uluwatu
▲▲▲–▲▲▲▲ L
T +65 6736 2555 (Singapore)
+44 (0)20 7590 1624 (UK)
E jasmineteow@
   alilavillasuluwatu.com
   Louisa.Barkla@ernalow.co.uk
W www.alilavillas.com/uluwatu

Amazon Yarapa River Lodge
▲▲▲ NCA
124 Av. La Marina,
Iquitos, Peru
T +51 011 5165 993 1172
E reservations@yarapa.com
W www.yarapa.com

Ammende Villa ▲▲–▲▲▲ L
Mere pst 7, Pärnu 80010,
Estonia
T +372 44 73888
F +372 44 73887
E sale@ammende.ee
W www.ammende.ee

Apani Dhani EcoLodge ▲ NC
Jhunjhunu Road,
Nawalgarh, 333042,
Rajasthan, India
T +91 1594 222239
F +91 1594 224061
E apanidhani@gmail.com
W www.apanidhani.com

Apex City Hotel ▲▲ U
No. 1 Seething Lane,
London EC3N 4AX, UK
T +44 (0)845 365 0000
F +44 (0)870 444 0808
E london.reservations@
   apexhotels.co.uk
W www.apexhotels.co.uk

Apex City Quay Hotel & Spa
▲▲ U
1 West Victoria Dock Road,
Dundee DD1 3JP, UK
T +44 (0)845 365 0000
F +44 (0)870 444 0808
E edinburgh.reservations@
   apexhotels.co.uk
W www.apexhotels.co.uk

Apex City Hotels ▲▲ U
61 Grassmarket,
Edinburgh EH1 2JF, UK
T +44 (0)845 365 0000
F +44 (0)870 444 0808
E edinburgh.reservations@
   apexhotels.co.uk
W www.apexhotels.co.uk

Apex European Hotel ▲▲ UC
Jo Harbisher
90 Haymarket Terrace,
Edinburgh EH12 5LQ, UK
T +44 (0)845 365 0000
F +44 (0)870 444 0808
E edinburgh.reservations@
   apexhotels.co.uk
W www.apexhotels.co.uk

Apex International Hotel
▲▲ U
31–35 Grassmarket,
Edinburgh EH1 2HS, UK
T +44 (0)845 365 0000
F +44 (0)870 444 0808
E edinburgh.reservations@
   apexhotels.co.uk
W www.apexhotels.co.uk

Ard Na Breatha ▲▲ NAL
Theresa and Albert Morrow
Drumrooske Middle,
Donegal Town,
Co. Donegal, Ireland
T +353 074 9722288
F +353 074 9740720
E info@ardnabreatha.com
W www.ardnabreatha.com

Ard Nahoo ▲▲▲ NL
Mullagh, Dromahair,
Co. Leitrim, Ireland
T +353 071 9134939
E info@ardnahoo.com
W www.ardnahoo.com

Aruba Bucuti Beach Resort & Tara Beach Suites ▲▲▲▲ L
L.G. Smith Blvd #55-B,
PO Box 1347, Eagle Beach,
Aruba, Dutch West Indies
T +297 5831100
F +297 5825272
E susan@bucuti.com
W www.bucuti.com

Aurum Lodge ▲▲–▲▲▲ NCA
Box 76, Nordegg,
Alberta, ToM 2Ho,
Canada
T +1 403 721 2117
F +1 403 721 2118
E info@aurumlodge.com
W www.aurumlodge.com

Aviemore Youth Hostel
▲ NAL
25 Grampian Road,
Aviemore PH22 1PR,
Scotland, UK
T +44 (0)1479 810 345
F +44 (0)1479 811 013
E reservations@syha.org.uk
W www.syha.org.uk

Baden Youth Hostel ▲ UL
Kanalstrasse 7,
CH5400 Baden (AG),
Switzerland
T +41 (0)56 221 67 36
F +41 (0)56 221 76 60
E baden@youthhostel.ch
W www.youthhostel.ch/baden

Balamku Inn on the Beach
▲▲ NAL
5.7 kms south of Mahahual,
Quintana Roo, Mexico
T +52 983 839 5332
E information@balamku.com
W www.balamku.com

Balenbouche Estate
▲▲–▲▲▲ NC
PO Box VF 707, St Lucia
T +758 4551244
E info@balenbouche.com
W www.balenbouche.com

Banjos Bushland Retreat
▲▲ NAL
Moonabung Mountain
Range,
Vacy (Paterson),
NSW 2421, Australia
T +61 (02)9403 3388
F +61 (02)9449 5873
E bookings@
banjosretreat.com.au
W www.banjosretreat.com.au

Banyan Tree Bintan ▲▲▲▲ L
Jalan Teluk Berembang,
Laguna Bintan, Lagoi 29155,
Bintan Resorts, Indonesia
T +62 770 69100
F +62 770 693200
E bintan@banyantree.com

Banyan Tree Maldives
Vabbinfaru ▲▲▲▲ L
North Malé Atoll, Maldives
T +960 664 31 47
F +960 664 38 43
E Abdul.azeez@banyantree.com
W www.banyantree.com

Banyan Tree Ringha
▲▲▲▲ NCL
Hong Po Village,
Jian Tang Town,
Shangri-la County,
Diqing Tibetan Autonomous
Prefecture, Yunnan Province,
China
T +86 887 828 8822
F +86 887 828 8911
E ringha@banyantree.com
W www.banyantree.com

Bateleur Camp at Kichwa
▲▲▲ NCA
Private Bag X27, Benmore
2010, South Africa

164 Katherine Street,
Pinmill Farm, Sandown,
Johannesburg, South Africa
T +27 11 809 4332
F +27 11 809 4511
E Tarryn.davidson@ccafrica.com
W www.ccafrica.com
www.responsiblesafaris.com

BioHotel am Lunik Park
▲▲ UNCAL
Stolper Straße 8, 16540
Hohen Neuendorf,
Berlin, Germany
T +49 (0)3303 291 0
F +49 (0)3303 291 444
E info@biohotel-berlin.de
W www.biohotel-berlin.de

Bird Island Lodge ▲▲▲ NL
PO Box 1419,
Victoria, Seychelles
T +248 323 322
F +248 323 335
E thelodge@
birdislandseychelles.com
W www.birdislandseychelles.com

Black Sheep Inn ▲–▲▲ NCL
PO Box 05-01-240,
Chugchilán, Cotopaxi,
Ecuador
T +593 3 281 4587
F none
E nfo@blacksheepinn.com
W www.blacksheepinn.com

Blancaneaux Lodge
▲▲▲–▲▲▲▲ L
Mountain Pine Ridge Forest
Reserve, Cayo District, Belize
T +501 824 4912 (Anne)
+468 570 22395 (Neil)
F +501 824 4913
E anne@blancaneaux.com
neilrogers@blancaneaux.com
W www.blancaneaux.com

**Camp Denali and North Face
Lodge** ▲▲▲▲ NCAL
PO Box 67, Denali National
Park, AK 99755, USA
T +1 907 683 2290
F +1 907 683 1568
E simon@campdenali.com
W www.campdenali.com

Can Martil ▲▲ NL
Agroturismo,
07810 San Juan, Ibiza
T +34 971 333 500
F +34 971 333 112
E info@canmarti.com
W www.canmarti.com

Capricorn Caves ▲ NAL
30 Olsens Caves Road,
Rockhampton,
Qld 4702, Australia
T +61 7 4934 2883
F +61 7 4934 2936
E capcaves@cqnet.com.au
W www.capricorncaves.com.au

Cardamom House ▲ NCL
Athoor Village,
Dindigul District,
624701 Tamil Nadu, India
T +91 (0)451 2556 765/66
F +91 (0)936 9691 793
E cardamomhouse@yahoo.com
W www.cardamomhouse.com

Casa Camper ▲▲▲ UCL
Carrer Elisabets 11,
08001 Barcelona, Spain
T +34 93 342 62 80
F +34 93 342 75 53
E Barcelona@casacamper.com
W www.casacamper.com

Casa Melo Alvim ▲▲ UCL
Av. Conde da Carreira n° 28,
4900-343 Viana do Castelo,
Portugal
T +351 258 808 200
F +351 258 808 220
E helenalaranjeira@
meloalvimhouse.com
W www.meloalvimhouse.com

Chalalán Ecolodge
▲–▲▲▲ NC
Calle Sagarnaga n° 189,
Shopping Dorian, Of. 35,
La Paz, Bolivia

Calle Comercio,
Zona Central,
Rurrenabaque, Bolivia
T +591 2 2311451
+591 3 892 2419
F +591 2 2311451
+591 3 892 2309
E info@chalalan.comchalalan_
eco@yahoo.com
W www.chalalan.com

Chan Chich Lodge ▲▲▲ NCAL
1 King St, PO Box 37,
Belize City, Belize
T +501 223 4419
F +501 223 4419
E reservations@chanchich.com
W www.chanchich.com

Key to categories
U – Urban
N – Nature
C – Culture
L – Leisure
A – Adventure

Key to pricing:
Budget ▲
US$0–50 / €0–30 / £0–25
per person per night

Mid-range ▲▲
US$51–150 / €31–94 / £26–75
per person per night

High ▲▲▲
US$151–400 / €95–250 / £76–200
per person per night

Luxury ▲▲▲▲
over US$400 / over €250 / over £200
per person per night

Chiiori ▲▲ NC
770-0206 Tokushima-ken,
Miyoshi-shi,
Higashi-iya Aza-tsurui 209,
Japan
T +81 (0883) 88 5290
F +81 (0883) 88 5290
E einfo@chiiori.org(Eng)
jinfo@chiiori.org (Jap)
W www.chiiori.org

Chumbe Island Coral Park
▲▲▲ N
PO Box 3203,
Zanzibar, Tanzania
T +255 (0)24 2231040
F UK: +44 (0)870 1341284
E enquiry@chumbeisland.com
booking@chumbeisland.com
W www.chumbeisland.com

**Constance Le Prince Maurice
Hotel** ▲▲▲–▲▲▲▲ NCL
Choisy Road, Poste de
Flacq, Mauritius
T +230 402 3636
F +230 413 9129
E resa@princemaurice.com
W www.princemaurice.com

Country Hotel Anna ▲▲ NC
Moldnúpi, 861 Hvolsvöllur,
Iceland
T +354 4878950
F +354 4878955
E hotelanna@hotelanna.is
W www.hotelanna.is

Covert Cabin ▲ NL
Lacaud, 24360,
Busserolles, France
T +33 (0)553 568124
F +33 (0)553 568124
E bobcabin@wanadoo.fr
W www.covertcabin.com

Crescent Moon Cabins
▲▲ NCAL
PO Box 2400, Roseau,
Commonwealth of Dominica
T +767 449 3449
E jeanviv@cwdom.dm
jeanviv@yahoo.com
W www.crescent mooncabins.com

Cristalino Jungle Lodge
▲▲▲ NA
Right margin of Cristalino
River, Alta Floresta, Brazil,
Office: Av. Perimetral Oeste,
2001, 78.580-000, Alta
Floresta, MT, Brazil
T +55 66 3521 7100
+55 66 3521 2221
F +55 66 3521 1396
E Vitoria@cristalinolodge.com.br
W www.cristalinolodge.com.br

Danta Corcovado Lodge
▲–▲▲ NCAL
3 km from La Palma towards
Los Patos, Corcovado
National Park, Peninsula de
Osa, Costa Rica
T +506 735 1111
F +506 735 1212
E info@dantacorcovado.net
W www.dantacorcovado.net

Dantica Lodge ▲▲ NCL
4 km south of the entrance
to San Gerardo de Dota,
Costa Rica
T +506 740 1067/740 1069
F +506 740 1071
E info@dantica.com
W www.dantica.com

Dar Raha ▲ NCL
Hay Amezrou,
45900 Zagora, Morocco
T +212 (0)24 84 69 93
F +212 (0)24 84 61 80
E darraha_zagora@yahoo.fr
W darraha.free.fr

Desert Lodge ▲▲ NCAL
Al Qasr, Dakhla Oasis,
Egypt
T +20 2 690 52 40
F +20 2 690 52 50
E info@desertlodge.net
W www.desertlodge.net

Diamond Beach Hotel
▲▲ NCL
PO Box 348, Lamu,
Kenya 80500
T +254 720915001
E info@diamondbeachvillage.com
W www.diamondbeachvillage.com

Don Enrique Lodge ▲ NCL
Paraje La Bonita,
El Soberbio,
Misiones, Argentina
T +54 11 4723 7020
E info@donenriquelodge.com.ar
W www.donenriquelodge.com.ar

Dunstanburgh Castle Hotel
▲▲ NL
Michael Townsend
Embleton, Alnwick,
Northumberland, UK
T +44 (0)1665 576111
F +44 (0)1665 576203
E stay@
dunstanburghcastlehotel.co.uk
W www.dunstanburghcastlehotel.
co.uk

Eco-cabin ▲▲ NL
Obley, Bucknell,
Shropshire SY7 0BZ, UK
T +44 (0)1547 530183
F +44 (0)1547 530183
E kate@ecocabin.co.uk
W www.ecocabin.co.uk

Ecocamp Patagonia ▲▲▲ NA
Don Carlos 3219,
Las Condes,
Santiago, Chile
T +56 2 2329878
F +56 2 2328954
E Daniel@cascada.travel
W www.ecocamp.travel

EcoHotel L'Aubier ▲▲ NL
Les Murailles 5,
CH2037 Montezillon,
Neuchâtel, Switzerland
T +41 (0)32 732 22 11
F +41 (0)32 732 22 00
E contact@aubier.ch
W www.aubier.ch

Eco Hotel Uxlabil Atitlán ▲ NL
Barrio Xacal,
San Juan la Laguna,
Sololá, Guatemala
T +502 5990 6016
+502 5849 0210
F +502 2366 9555
E atitlan@uxlabil.com
W www.uxlabil.com

**Ecolodge San Luis Research
Station** ▲–▲▲ NCAL
700 m east of Escuela de
Altos de San Luis,
Monteverde, Puntarenas,
Costa Rica
T +506 645 8049
F +506 645 8050
E fabricio@uga.edu
quintn@uga.edu
W www.uga.edu/costarica

**Enigmata Treehouse
Ecolodge** ▲ NCAL
Maubog, Balbagon,
Mambajao, Camiguin Island,
Philippines 9100
T +63 918 2304184
F +63 88 3870273
E enigmatatreehouse@
yahoo.com
W www.enigmata.
mindanaoculture.com

Esquinas Rainforest Lodge
▲▲ NAL
La Gamba, Golfito,
Costa Rica
T +506 741 8001
F +506 741 8001
E esquinas@racsa.co.cr
W www.esquinaslodge.com

Estancia Los Potreros
▲▲▲ NCA
Casilla de correo 4,
La Cumbre X5178 WAA,
Cordoba, Argentina
T +54 11 4878 2692
F +54 35 4845 2121
E bookings@rie-americas.com
W www.estancialospotreros.com

Fazenda Santa Marina
▲▲▲ NCAL
Km 09 road from Cristiano
Otoni to Santana dos
Montes, 36.426-000
Cristiano Otoni, Minas
Gerais, Brazil
T +55 31 9974 4203
F +55 31 3443 1095
E falecom@
fazendasantamarina.com.br
W www.fazendasantamarina.
com.br

Finca Esperanza Verde ▲ NCAL
Apartado 28, Matagalpa,
Nicaragua
T +505 772 5003
F +505 772 5003
E fincaesperanzaverde@
gmail.com
W www.fincaesperanzaverde.org

Finca Rosa Blanca Country Inn
▲▲▲ NCL
Apdo 41-3009,
Santa Barbara de Heredia,
Costa Rica
T +506 269 9392
F +506 269 9555
E info@fincarosablanca.com
W www.fincarosablanca.com

Friday's Place ▲▲ NCL
Poovar Island, Trivandrum,
Kerala, India
T +44 (0)1428 741 510
E amphibious_robinson_
crusoe@hotmail.com
W www.fridaysplace.biz

**Gaia Napa Valley Hotel and
Spa** ▲▲▲ UNL
3600 Broadway (Highway 29),
American Canyon,
CA 94503, USA
T +1 707 674 2100
F +1 707 674 2555
E info@gaiahotel.com
W www.gaianapavalleyhotel.com

Gecko Villa ▲▲ NCL
Baan Um Jaan, A. Prjak,
Sinlaphakom, Udon Thani,
41110 Thailand
T +66 81 9180500
E info@geckovilla.com
W www.geckovilla.com

Guludo Beach Lodge
▲▲▲ NCL
Quirimbas National Park,
Mozambique
T +44 (0)1323 766655
F +44 (0)1323 766655
E contact@bespokeexperience.com
W www.guludo.com
www.bespokeexperience.com

Hapuku Lodge & Tree Houses
▲▲▲ NAL
Station Road, Kaikoura,
New Zealand
T +64 3 319 6559
F +64 3 319 6557
E info@hapukulodge.com
W www.hapukulodge.com

Hog Hollow Country Lodge
▲▲▲ NL
Askop Road, The Crags,
6602, South Africa
T +27 44 534 8879
F +27 44 534 8879
E info@hog-hollow.com
W www.hog-hollow.com

Hoopoe Yurt Hotel ▲▲▲ NL
Apartado de Correos 23,
Cortes de la Frontera,
29380 Málaga, Spain
T +34 951 168 040
+34 696 668 388 (mobile)
+34 660 668 241 (mobile)
E info@yurthotel.com
W www.yurthotel.com

Hotel Adalbert ▲▲ UCL
Markétská 28/1, 169 00,
Prague 6, Czech Republic
T +420 220 406 180
F +420 220 406 190
E recepce@hoteladalbert.cz
W www.hoteladalbert.cz

Hotel Alexandra ▲▲–▲▲▲ UC
H. C. Andersens Blvd. 8,
Copenhagen V, Denmark
T +45 33744444
F +45 33744488
E reservations@
hotel-alexandra.dk
W www.hotel-alexandra.dk

Hotel Balance ▲▲ NL
CH1922 Les Granges,
Switzerland
T +41 (0)27 761 15 22
F +41 (0)27 761 15 88
E info@vegetarisches-hotel.ch
W www.vegetarisches-hotel.ch

Hotel Bourazani
▲–▲▲▲ NCAL
44 100 Konitsa
Greece
T +30 2655 1 61283
+30 2655 1 61320
E bourazani@otenet.gr
W www.bourazani.gr

Hotel Bougainvillea ▲▲ UL
100 m east of Escuela
Pública de Santo Tomás,
Santo Tomas De Santo
Domingo, Heredia,
Costa Rica
T +506 2244 1414
F +506 2244 1313
E info@hb.co.cr
W www.hb.co.cr

Hotel de Lençóis ▲▲ NCAL
R. Altina Alves 747, Centro,
Lençóis, Bahia, Brazil
46. 960-000
T +55 71 3369 5000 Reservations
+55 75 3334 1102 Hotel de
Lençóis
F +55 75 3334 1201
E reservas@hoteldelencois.com
W www.hoteldelencois.com

Hotel Del Rey ▲ UNL
Rua Tarobá 1020, Centro,
Foz do Iguaçu, Paraná,
Brazil
T +55 45 3523 2027
F +55 45 3523 2027
E reservas@hoteldelreyfoz.
com.br
W www.hoteldelreyfoz.com.br

**Hotel Fazenda Baía das
Pedras** ▲▲▲ NC
Rua das Garças, 790,
Ap 1301, Vila Rosa,
Campo Grande, 79010-020,
MS, Brazil
T +55 67 3382 1275
F +55 67 3382 1275
E baiadaspedras@
baiadaspedras.com.br
rita@baiadaspedras.com.br
W www.baiadaspedras.com.br

Hotel Hellnar ▲▲ N
Hellnar, IS-356
Snaefellsbaer,
Iceland
T +354 435 6820
F +354 435 6801
E hotel@hellnar.is
W www.hellnar.is

Key to categories
U – Urban
N – Nature
C – Culture
L – Leisure
A – Adventure

Key to pricing:
Budget ▲
US$0–50 / €0–30 / £0–25
per person per night

Mid-range ▲▲
US$51–150 / €31–94 / £26–75
per person per night

High ▲▲▲
US$151–400 / €95–250 / £76–200
per person per night

Luxury ▲▲▲▲
over US$400 / over €250 / £200
per person per night

Hotel Jardim Atlântico
▲▲ NCAL
Lombo da Rocha, Prazeres,
P-9370-605 Calheta,
Madeira, Portugal
T +351 291 820 220
F +351 291 820 221
E info@jardimatlantico.com
W www.jardimatlantico.com

Hotel Jolie ▲ UCL
Viale Dante 191,
corner of Viale Mascagni,
47838 Riccione, Italy
T +39 (0)541 647800
F +39 (0)541 648184
E info@hoteljolie.it
W www.hoteljolie.it

Hotel Kubija ▲▲▲ NCL
Männiku 43a,
65 603 Võru, Estonia
T +372 78 66 000
F +372 78 66 001
E info@pintmann.ee
W www.pintmann.ee

Hotel Kürschner ▲▲ NCAL
Schlanke Gasse 74,
A-9640 Kötschach-Mauthen,
Austria
T +43 (0)4715 259
F +43 (0)4715 349
E info@hotel-kuerschner.at
W www.hotel-kuerschner.at

Hotel Mocking Bird Hill
▲▲▲ NAL
PO Box 254, Port Antonio,
Jamaica
T +1 876 993 7267
   +1 876 993 7134
E info@hotelmockingbirdhill.com
W www.hotelmockingbirdhill.com

Hotel Pension Hubertus
▲–▲▲ UNCAL
Gartenstraße 4,
A-5700 Zell am See, Austria
T +43 (0)6542 72427
F +43 (0)6542 72427
E 3sterne@hubertus-pension.at
W www.hubertus-pension.at

Hotel Posada Del Valle
▲–▲▲▲ NL
33549 Collia, Arriondas,
Asturias, Spain
T +34 985 84 11 57
F +34 985 84 15 59
E hotel@posadadelvalle.com
W www.posadadelvalle.com

Hotel Vila Naia ▲▲▲ NL
Praia do Corumbau,
Corumbau, Bahia, Brazil
T + 55 11 3061 1872
F + 55 11 3061 1872
E nadia@vilanaia.com.br
W www.vilanaia.com.br

Hôtel Villas Les Goëlands
▲▲ UNL
4 and 6 avenue Etcheverry,
64500 Saint Jean de Luz,
France
T +33 (0)5 59 26 10 05
F +33 (0)5 59 51 04 02
E reception@
   hotel-lesgoelands.com
W www.hotel-lesgoelands.com

Hunas Falls Hotel ▲▲ NL
Hunas Falls Hotel,
Elkaduwa, Kandy, Sri Lanka
T +94 81 2470041/2470042/
   2470045/2476402/2476403
F +94 71 2735134
E hunasfalls@sltnet.lk
W www.jetwing.net

Il Duchesco ▲–▲▲ NCL
Strada Provinciale 59, n° 29,
58010 Alberese,
Natural Park of Maremma
Toscana, Grosseto, Italy
T +39 (0)564 407323
F +39 (0)564 407323
E info@ilduchesco.it
W www.ilduchesco.it

Inn at Coyote Mountain
▲▲–▲▲▲ NA
Calle La Table de La Guaria
de Piededades Sur,
San Ramon,
Alajuela, Costa Rica
T +506 383 05 44
F +1 800 980 0713
E info@cerrocoyote.com
W www.cerrocoyote.com

Inverness Youth Hostel ▲ UNL
Victoria Drive, Inverness,
Iverness-shire IV2 3QB
Scotland, UK
T +44 (0)1463 231 805
E info@syha.org.uk
W www.syha.org.uk

Iona Hostel ▲ NAL
Iona, Argyll PA76 6SW,
Scotland, UK
T +44 (0)1681 700 781
E john@ionahostel.co.uk
W www.ionahostel.co.uk

Jake's ▲▲–▲▲▲ L
Calabash Bay,
Treasure Beach,
St Elizabeth's, Jamaica
T +876 965 3000
F +876 965 0552
E jakes@cwjamaica.com
   reservations@islandoutpost.com
W www.islandoutpost.com

Jean-Michel Cousteau Fiji
Resort ▲▲▲–▲▲▲▲ CL
921 Front Street, Suite 200,
San Francisco, CA
94111, USA

Level 1, 714 Glenferrie Rd,
Hawthorn, Melbourne,
Vic 3122, Australia
T +1 800 246 3454
   +415 788 5794
   +61 (0)3 9815 0379
   1300 306171 Australia (local)
F +415 788 0150 USA
   +61 (0)3 9819 1263 Australia
E info@fijiresort.com
W www.fijiresort.com

Juma Lodge ▲▲▲ NCAL
Margem Esquerda do Rio
Juma, Autazes, Amazonas,
Brazil
T +55 92 3232 2707
F +55 92 3232 2707
E juma@jumalodge.com
W www.jumalodge.com

Jungle Bay Resort & Spa
▲▲▲ NAL
PO Box 2352, Roseau,
Commonwealth of Dominica
T +767 446 1789
F +767 446 1090
E info@junglebaydominica.com
W www.junglebaydominica.com

Kalmatia Sangam Himalaya
Resort ▲▲▲ NCAL
Kalimat Estate, Almora,
263601 Uttaranchal, India
T +91 5962 233625
F +91 5962 231572
E manager@
   kalmatia-sangam.com
W www.kalmatia-sangam.com

Kapawi Ecolodge & Reserve
▲▲ NCAL
Urbanizacion Santa Leonor,
Manzana 5, Solar 10,
Guayaquil, Ecuador
T +593 4 228 5711
F +593 4 228 7651
E lmontalvo@canodros.com
W www.canodros.com

Kasbah du Toubkal
▲–▲▲ NCAL
BP31 IMLIL,
Asni Par Marrakech,
Morocco
T +212 (0)24 48 56 11
F +212 (0)24 48 56 36
E kasbah@discover.ltd.uk
W www.kasbahdutoubkal.com

Koidulapark Hotell ▲▲ U
Kuninga 38, Pärnu, Estonia
T +372 447 7032
F +372 447 7033
E info@koidulaparkhotell.ee
W www.koidulaparkhotell.ee

Korubo Safari Camp Jalapão
▲▲ NA
110 Sul, Alameda 19,
MF 12 Casa 05,
77020-154 Palmas, TO,
Brazil
T +55 63 3213 2662
E Korubo@korubo.com.br
W www.korubo.com.br

La Cusinga Eco-Lodge ▲▲ NL
Apdo 41-8000, Pérez
Zeledón, San José, Costa Rica
T +506 770 2549
F +506 770 4611
E info@lacusingalodge.com
W www.lacusingalodge.com

La Laguna del Lagarto Lodge
▲ NA
7 km north of Boca Tapada,
Pital, San Carlos, Alajuela,
PO Box 995-1007,
San José, Costa Rica
T +506 289 8163
F +506 289 5295
E lagarto@racsa.co.cr
W www.lagarto-lodge-costa-rica.
com

La Lancha Resort ▲▲▲ L
Lake Petén Itzá, Tikal,
Guatemala
T +501 824 4912
F +501 824 4913
E info@blancaneaux.com
W www.blancaneaux.com

Landhotel Urstromtal ▲▲ NCL
Kemnitzer Hauptstr. 18,
14947 Kemnitz, Germany
T +49 33734 50742
F +49 33734 50017
E info@bb-urstromtal.de
W www.bb-urstromtal.de

Lane Cove River Tourist Park
▲–▲▲ UNL
Plassey Rd, Macquarie Park,
NSW 2113, Australia
T +61 (0)2 9888 9133
F +61 (0)2 9888 9322
E Andrew.daff@environment.
nsw.gov.au
W www.lcrtp.com.au

Larsbo Gård ▲▲ NCL
Larsbogård s-82596,
Enånger, Sweden
T +46 (0)650 553010
F +46 (0)650 553010
E info@larsbogard.nu
W www.larsbogard.nu

L'Ayalga Posada Ecológica
▲ NCAL
Luis Alberto Díaz y Conchi
de la Iglesia,
La Pandiella s/n 33537,
Piloña- Asturias, Spain
T +34 616 897 638
F +34 985 710 431
E layalga@terrae.net
W www.terrae.net/layalga

**Le Hameau du Sentier des
Sources** ▲ NCL
Le Cambord,
24200 Sarlat, France
T +33 (0)553 28 12 96
E contact@
gites-du-perigord.com
W gites-du-perigord.com

Le Parc aux Orchidées
▲–▲▲ NL
723 route de Trou Caverne,
97116 Pointe-Noire, France
T +33 (0)590 38 56 77
F +33 (0)590 38 56 77
E contact@
parcauxorchidees.com
W www.parcauxorchidees.com

Le Relais du Bastidou ▲▲ NL
32160 Beaumarches, France
T +33 (0)562 69 19 94
F +33 (0)562 69 19 94
E info@bastidou.com
W www.le-relais-du-bastidou.com

Levendi's Cottages & Estate
▲ NCL
Aphales Bay, Ithaca, Greece
T +30 6944 169 770
F +30 2674 031 648
E levendis@otenet.gr
W www.levendisestate.com

Locanda della Valle Nuova
▲–▲▲ NCL
La Cappella 14,
61033 Sagrata di Fermignano,
Pesaro e Urbino, Le Marche,
Italy
T +39 (0)722 330303
F +39 (0)722 330303
E info@vallenuova.it
W www.vallenuova.it

Lochmara Lodge ▲–▲▲ NL
Lochmara Bay,
Queen Charlotte Sound,
PO Box 172, Picton,
New Zealand
T +64 3 573 4554
F +64 3 573 4554
E enquiries@lochmaralodge.
co.nz
W www.lochmaralodge.co.nz

Loch Ossian Youth Hostel
▲ NA
Courrour By Fort William,
Inverness-shire
PH30 4AA, Scotland, UK
T +44 (0)1397 732 207
F +44 (0)1397 732 342
E reservations@syha.org.uk
W www.syha.org.uk

Lyola Pavilions in the Forest
▲▲ NAL
198 Policeman Spur Rd,
PO Box 418, Maleny 4552,
Qld, Australia
T +61 (0)7 54296900
E stay@lyola.com.au
W www.lyola.com.au

Malealea Lodge ▲–▲▲ NCAL
Malealea, Mafeteng,
Lesotho
T +266 (082) 552 4215
F +266 (0866) 481 815
E malealea@mweb.co.za
W www.malealea.com

Matuka Lodge ▲▲▲ NL
Old Station Road, 395 Glen
Lyon Road, Twizel,
New Zealand
T +64 3 435 0144
F +64 3 435 0149
E info@matukalodge.co.nz
W www.matukalodge.co.nz

**Meliá Bali Villas & Spa
Resort** ▲▲–▲▲▲▲ NL
PO Box 88, Nusa Dua,
80363 Bali, Indonesia
T +62 361 771 510
F +62 361 776 880
E pr@meliabali.com
W www.meliabali.com
www.solmelia.com

Milia Mountain Retreat
▲–▲▲ NCL
73012, Vlatos, Kissamos,
Chania, Crete, Greece
T +30 28210 46774
+30 28220 51569
M +30 6945 753 743
F +30 28220 51569
+30 28210 46774
E info@milia.gr
W www.milia.gr

Moinhos da Tia Antoninha
▲–▲▲ NCL
Lugar do Cabeço de Lebrais,
Leomil 3620-198 MBR,
Portugal
T +351 254 588 095
F +351 254 588 099
E tiantoninha@sapo.pt
W www.moinhostiaantoninha.
com

Key to categories
U – Urban
N – Nature
C – Culture
L – Leisure
A – Adventure

Key to pricing:
Budget ▲
US$0–50 / €0–30 / £0–25
per person per night

Mid-range ▲▲
US$51–150 / €31–94 / £26–75
per person per night

High ▲▲▲
US$151–400 / €95–250 / £76–200
per person per night

Luxury ▲▲▲▲
over US$400 / over €250 / over £200
per person per night

Mombo Camp ▲▲▲▲ NL
Mombo Island
within the Moremi Game
Reserve in the Okavango
Delta, Botswana
T +44 (0)20 7471 8780
E info@botswanaodyssey.com
W www.mombo.co.uk

**Momopeho Rainforest
Home Hacienda** ▲ NCAL
Km. 19, Via Los Bancos,
Valle Hermoso, San Pedro,
Ecuador
T +593 9 8309202
F +593 2 2439460
E momopeho@yahoo.com
W www.momopeho.com

Mowani Mountain Camp
▲▲▲ NL
Twyfelfontein, Damaraland,
PO Box 40788, Windhoek,
Namibia
T +264 61 232 009
F +264 61 222 574
E mowani@visionsofafrica.
com.na
W www.mowani.com

Natural Lodge Caño Negro
▲–▲▲ NCA
Los Chiles, Alajuela,
Costa Rica
T +506 265 3302
F +506 265 4310
E info@canonegrolodge.com
W www.canonegrolodge.com

Nipika Mountain Resort
▲▲–▲▲▲ NCAL
9200 Settlers Road
(14 km off Hwy 93 between
Radium Hot Springs, BC – 32 km
– and Banff, Alberta – 114 km),
Canada
T +1 250 342 6516
F +1 250 342 6516
E info@nipika.com
W www.nipika.com

**Nomadic Expeditions and
Three Camel Lodge**
▲▲▲ NCAL
Bulgan County, South Gobi
Province, Mongolia
T +800 998 6634
+609 860 9008
F +609 860 9608
E info@nomadicexpeditions.com
W www.nomadicexpeditions.com
www.threecamellodge.com

Ocotal Beach Resort
▲▲–▲▲▲ NAL
3 Km from Coco Beach,
Guanacaste, Costa Rica
T +506 2280 4976
+506 670 0321
F +506 2234 8432
E sales1@ocotalresort.com
W www.ocotalresort.com

Onguma Safari Camps
▲–▲▲▲ NL
Etosha National Park,
left of Namutoni gate,
PO Box 6784, Namibia
T +264 61 232 009
F +264 61 222 574
E onguma@visionsofafrica.
com.na
W www.onguma.com
www.ongumanamibia.com

Orchard Garden Hotel
▲▲▲ U
466 Bush Street,
San Francisco, CA 94108,
USA
T +1 415 399 9807
F +1 415 393 9917
E mhaney@theorchardgarden
hotel.com
W www.theorchardgardenhotel.
com

Orri de Planès ▲ NL
Cases del Mitg,
66210 Planès, France
T +33 (0)468 042947
F +33 (0)468 042947
E contact@orrideplanes.com
W www.orrideplanes.com

Palace Farm Hostel ▲ Nl
Down Court Road,
Doddington, Sittingbourne,
Kent ME9 0AU, UK
T +44 (0)1795 886200
F +44 (0)1795 886365
E info@palacefarm.com
W www.palacefarm.com

Paperbark Camp ▲▲–▲▲▲ NL
571 Woollamia Road,
PO Box 39, Huskisson,
NSW 2540, Australia
T +61 (0)2 4441 6066
F +61 (0)2 4441 6066
E info@paperbarkcamp.com.au
W www.paperbarkcamp.com.au

Papillote Wilderness Retreat
▲▲ NL
PO Box 2287, Roseau,
Commonwealth of
Dominica
T +767 448 2287
F +767 448 2285
E papillote@cwdom.dm
W www.papillote.dm

Paradise Mountain Lodge
▲–▲▲ NAL
200 M north of Fortuna
Waterfall, La Fortuna,
San Carlos, Arenal Volcano
Region, Northern Zone,
Costa Rica
T +506 858 384 3653
F +506 239 540 2338
E info@americasparadise.net
W www.arenalwaterfall.com

Pension Jelen ▲–▲▲ NCAL
Zamecka 250,
671 03 Vranov nad Dyji,
Czech Republic
T +420 724 774 774
E jelen@vranov.com
W www.vranov.com

Ponta dos Ganchos
▲▲▲▲ NL
Rua Eupídio Alves do
Nascimento,
104 Ganchos de Fora,
Governador Celso Ramos,
SC, 88190-000, Brazil
T +55 48 3262 5000
F +55 48 3262 5046
E contato@pontadosganchos.
com.br
W www.pontadosganchos.com.br

Posada Amazonas ▲▲ NC
Tambopata, Peru
T +51 1 421 8347
F +51 1 421 8183
E mschmidt@rainforest.com.pe
W www.perunature.com

Pousada dos Monteiros
▲▲▲ NCA
Rua Chaad Scaff, 345,
Campo Grande, MS, Brazil
T +55 67 3324 8237
F +55 67 3324 8237 or
+55 67 3383 1813
E lemosmonteiro@uol.com.br
W www.pousadadosmonteiros.
com.br

Pousada Picinguaba ▲▲▲ NL
Rua G, 130,
Vila Picinguaba,
11680 000, Ubatuba,
SP, Brazil
T +55 12 3838 9105
F +55 12 3838 9103
E info@picinguaba.com
W www.picinguaba.com

Pousada Pouso da Marujo
▲ NL
Rod. João Gualberto Soares,
17421, Barra da Lagoa,
Florianópolis, SC,
88061-500, Brazil
T +55 (0)48 3232 3357
F +55 (0)48 3232 3357
E pousadamarujo@uol.com.br
W www.guesthousemarujo.net

Pousada Vale das Araras
▲ NCA
Estrada Cavalente,
Colinas do Sul, Km 3,
Cavalcante, Goiás, Brazil
73790-000
T +55 62 3459 0007
E contato@valedasararas.com.br
W www.valedasararas.com.br

Pousada Vila Serrano ▲ NCA
Rua Alto do Bonfim, 08,
Centro, 46960-00,
Lençóis, Bahia, Brazil
T +55 75 3334 1486
F +55 75 3334 1486
E vilaserrano@uol.com.br
W www.vilaserrano.com.br

**Pousada Vila Tamarindo
Eco-lodge** ▲▲ NL
Av. Campeche, 1836,
Praia do Campeche,
88063-000,Florianópolis,
SC, Brazil
T +55 48 3237 3464
F +55 48 3338 2185
E reservas@tamarindo.com.br
W www.tamarindo.com.br

Primrose Valley Hotel ▲▲ L
Primrose Valley,
Porthminster Beach, St Ives,
Cornwall TR26 2ED, UK
T +44 (0)1736 794939
E info@primroseonline.co.uk
W www.primroseonline.co.uk

Quilálea Private Island
▲▲▲▲ NAL
PO Box 323, Pemba,
Mozambique
T +258 272 21808
F +258 272 21808
E enquiries@quilalea.com
W www.quilalea.com

Quinta do Barrieiro ▲▲▲ NCL
Quinta do Barrieiro,
Reveladas cx 10, 7330 336,
Marvão, Portugal
T +351 96 404 3733 /
96 405 4935 / 24 596 4308
E quintadobarrieiro@netc.pt
W www.quintadobarrieiro.com

Quinta do Rio Touro ▲▲ NCL
Azoia, 2705 001 Colares,
Sintra, Portugal
T +351 21 929 2862
F +351 21 929 2360
E info@quinta-riotouro.com
W www.quinta-riotouro.com

Radisson SAS ▲▲▲ UL
80 High Street, The Royal
Mile, Edinburgh EH1 1TH,
UK
T +44 (0)131 473 6551
F +44 (0)131 473 6503
E Alexandra.hammond@
radissonsas.com

Ratagan Youth Hostel ▲ NL
Glenshiel, Kyle, Ross-shire
IV40 8HP, Scotland, UK
T +44(0)1599 511 243
E reservations@syha.org.uk
W www.syha.org.uk

Rawnsley Park ▲▲ N
Rawnsley Park Station,
Eco-villas Wilpena Road,
via Hawker, SA 5434,
Australia
T +61 (0)8 8648 0030
F +61 (0)8 8648 0013
E info@rawnsleypark.com.au
W www.rawnsleypark.com.au

Refúgio Ecológico Caiman
▲▲▲ NCAL
Av. Brigadeiro Faria Lima
3015, cj. 161, Itaim Bibi,
01452 000, São Paulo, SP
Hotel: Estância Caiman S/N,
79380 000, Zona Rural,
Miranda, MS, Brazil
T +55 11 3706 1800
F +55 11 3706 1808
E marketing@caiman.com.br
W www.caiman.com.br

**Rose Gums Wilderness
Retreat** ▲▲ NL
Land Road,
via Lake Eacham,
Atherton Tablelands,
PO Box 776, Malanda,
Qld 4885, Australia
T +61 (0)7 4096 8360
F +61 (0)7 4096 8312
E info@rosegums.com.au
W www.rosegums.com.au

Ruboni Community Camp
▲ NCAL
PO Box 320, Kasese,
Uganda
T +256 41 4501866
E ruboni.communitytourism@
gmail.com
W www.ucota.or.ug

Rufflets Country House Hotel
▲▲▲ L
Strathkinness Low Road,
St Andrews,
Fife KY16 9TX, Scotland, UK
T +44(0)1334 472 594
F +44(0)1334 478 703
E reservations@rufflets.co.uk
W www.rufflets.co.uk

Sadie Cove Wilderness Lodge
▲▲▲–▲▲▲▲ NAL
Inside Kachemak Bay State
Park, Box 2265, Homer,
Alaska 99603, USA
T +1 907 235 2350
E email@sadiecove.com
W www.sadiecove.com

Salamander Hideaway
▲▲–▲▲▲ L
18 Km north of San Pedro,
PO Box 120,
Ambergris Caye, Belize
T +501 209 5005
E info@salamanderbelize.com
W www.salamanderbelize.com

Sankt Helene ▲–▲▲ NL
Danhostel Tisvildeleje,
Vandreerhjem Bygmarken 30,
Denmark
T +45 4870 9850
F +45 4870 9897
E booking@helene.dk

SarapiquíS Rainforest Lodge
▲–▲▲ NCAL
La Virgen de Sarapiquís,
PO Box 86-3069, Sarapiquís,
Heredia, Costa Rica
T +506 (2)761-1004
F +506 (2)761-1415
E sarapiquis@ice.co.cr
W www.sarapiquis.org

Saunders Gorge Sanctuary
▲▲ N
RSD 72 Palmer,
SA 5237, Australia
T +61 8 8569 3032
E nature@saundersgorge.com.au
W www.saundersgorge.com.au

Key to categories
U – Urban
N – Nature
C – Culture
L – Leisure
A – Adventure

Key to pricing:
Budget ▲
US$0–50 / €0–30 / £0–25
per person per night

Mid-range ▲▲
US$51–150 / €31–94 / £26–75
per person per night

High ▲▲▲
US$151–400 / €95–250 / £76–200
per person per night

Luxury ▲▲▲▲
over US$400 / over €250 / over £200
per person per night

Scandic Hotels ▲▲ UL
Scandic Hotels AB
130 hotels in 9 countries:
Sweden, Finland, Denmark,
Norway, Estonia, Lithuania,
Germany, Netherlands,
Belgium
Please go to this link for a
complete list of all hotels:
www.hiltonfamily-ebrochures.
com/cgi-bin/ebrochure
T +46 8 517 350 19
F +46 8 517 350 11
E Inger.mattsson@scandic-
   hotels.com
W www.scandic-hotels.com
   www.scandic-hotels.com/
   betterworld

**Shenandoah National Park
Lodgings ▲–▲▲ NCAL**
Mile 41.7 on Skyline Drive in
Shenandoah National Park,
PO Box 727, Luray,
VA 22835, USA
T +1 540 843 2100
F +1 540 743 7883
E shenandoah@aramark.com
W www.visitshenandoah.com

**Six Senses Hideaway at
Samui ▲▲▲ L**
9/10 Moo 5,
Baan Plai Laem,
Bophut, Koh Samui,
Surat Thani 84320, Thailand
T +66 (0)77 245678
F +66 (0)77 245671
E reservations-samui@
   evasonhideaways.com
W www.sixsenses.com

**Sofitel Amsterdam
▲▲–▲▲▲ UL**
Nieuwezijds Voorburgwal,
671012 RE, Amsterdam,
Netherlands
T +31 20 6275900
F +31 20 6238932
E Francis.windt@accor.com
W www.sofitel.com
   www.accorhotels.com

**Sonaisali Island Resort
▲▲▲ NCL**
PO Box 2544, Nadi,
Fiji Islands
T +679 670 6011
F +679 670 6092
W www.sonaisali.com

**Soneva Fushi & Six Senses
Spa ▲▲▲▲ L**
Kunfundahoo Island,
Baa Atoll,
Republic of Maldives
T +960 660 0304
F +960 660 0374
E rochelle@sixsenses.com
W www.sixsenses.com

Stayokay ▲ UNCL
Main office, Timorplein 21a,
1094 CC Amsterdam,
Netherlands
T +31 (0)20 5513155
F +31 (0)20 6230199
E info@stayokay.com
W www.stayokay.com

Tahuayo Lodge ▲▲▲ NCA
c/o Amazonia Expeditions,
Av. La Marina 100,
Iquitos, Peru
T +1 813 907 8475
F +1 813 907 8475
E Amazonia.expeditions@
   verizon.net
W www.perujungle.com/lodge.
   html

**Tamarind Tree Hotel &
Restaurant ▲▲ NCAL**
PO Box 754, Roseau,
Commonwealth of Dominica
T +1 767 449 7395
F +1 767 449 7395
E hotel@tamarindtreedominica.
   com
W www.tamarindtreedominica.
   com

The Green Hotel ▲▲ UCL
Chittaranjan Palace,
2270 Vinoba Road,
Jayalakshmipuram,
Mysore, 570 012, India
T +91 821 425 5000
F +91 821 251 6139
E thegreenhotel@
   airtelbroadband.in
W www.cardaid.co.uk/greenhotel

**The Lodge at Big Falls
▲▲ NCA**
PO Box 103, Punta Gorda,
Toledo district, Belize
T +501 671 7172
E info@thelodgeatbigfalls.com
W www.thelodgeatbigfalls.com

**The Lodge at Chaa Creek
▲▲▲ NCAL**
77 Burns Avenue,
San Ignacio, Cayo, Belize
T +501 824 2037
F +501 824 2501
E reservations@chaacreek.com
W www.chaacreek.com

**The Lighthouse Hotel & Spa
▲▲▲ NCL**
Dadella, Galle, Sri Lanka
T +94 91 22 23 744
F +94 91 22 24 021
E lighthouse@lighthouse.lk
W www.lighthousehotelandspa.
   com

**The Second Paradise Retreat
▲▲▲ NCL**
RR3, Lunenburg,
Nova Scotia, B0J 2C0,
Canada
T +1 902 634 4099
F +1 425 930 4722
E stay@secondparadise.ns.ca
W www.secondparadise.com

The Summer House ▲▲ NL
424 Kerikeri Road, Kerikeri,
Bay of Islands, New Zealand
T +64 9 4074294
F +64 9 4074297
E summerhouse@xtra.co.nz
W www.thesummerhouse.co.nz

**Three Rivers Eco Lodge &
Sustainable Living Centre
▲–▲▲ NC**
Newfoundland Estate,
Rosalie, Commonwealth
of Dominica
T +1 767 446 1886
F +1 510 578 6578
E jem@3riversdominica.com
W www.3riversdominica.com

**Tiger Mountain Pokhara
Lodge ▲▲▲ NCAL**
GPO Box 242, Kathmandu,
Nepal
T +977 (0)1 436 1500
   +977 (0)61 691887
F +977 (0)1 436 1600
E tmpkr@tigermountain.com
W www.tigermountain.com/
   pokhara

Tobermory Youth Hostel
▲ NCL
Main Street, Tobermory,
Isle of Mull PA75 6NJ,
Scotland, UK
T +44 (0)1688 302 481
F +44 (0)1688 301 210
E reservations@syha.org.uk
W www.syha.org.uk

Tongabezi Lodge ▲▲▲▲ NL
Private Bag 31, Livingstone,
Zambia
T +260 33 27 468
F +260 33 24 282
E honour@tongabezi.com
W www.tongabezi.com

Tree Tops Jungle Lodge
▲▲ NCA
Buttala, Sri Lanka
T +94 (0)777 036 554
E treetopsjunglelodge@gmail.com
W www.treetopsjunglelodge.com

Tui Nature Reserve
Wilderness Park ▲–▲▲ N
Wilderness Park,
Waitata Reach,
Outer Pelorus, Marlborough
Sounds, New Zealand
T +64 27 448 3447
(0800 107077 free phone in
New Zealand)
E tuireserve@xtra.co.nz
W www.tuinaturereserve.co.nz

Udayana Eco-lodge ▲–▲▲ CL
PO Box 3704,
Denpasar 80001,
Bali, Indonesia
T +62 (0)361 7474204
F +62 (0)361 701098
E lodge@ecolodgesindonesia.com
W www.ecolodgesindonesia.com

Uig Youth Hostel ▲ N
Uig, Isle of Skye IV51 9YD,
Scotland, UK
T +44 (0)1470 542 746
F +44 (0)1470 542 736
E reservations@syha.or.uk
W www.syha.org.uk

Ullapool Youth Hostel ▲ NC
Shore Street,
Ullapool, Ross and
Cromarty, IV26 2UJ,
Scotland, UK
T +44 (0)1854 612 254
F +44 (0)1854 613 254
E reservations@syha.or.uk
W www.syha.org.uk

Ulu Ai Project ▲▲ NCAL
Borneo Adventure
55 Main Bazaar, 93000
Kuching, Sarawak, Malaysia
T +60 82 245175
F +60 82 422626
E emomg@borneoadventure.com
W www.borneoadventure.com

Verana ▲▲▲ NL
Verana Yelapa SA,
1461 Brookings Trail,
Topanga, CA 90290, USA
T +1 310 360 0155
F +1 310 360 0158
E pr@verana.com
W www.verana.com

Villas Ecotucan ▲ NL
#88 Calle 3 x 36,
Colonia Mario Villanueva,
Bacalar, Quintana Roo,
Mexico
T +52 983 120 5743
+52 983 834 2516
E ecotucan@yahoo.com
W www.villasecotucan.info
www.activenaturebacalar.com

Villa Sebali ▲▲▲ NCL
Griya Puser Sari,
Jl Gunung Sari, Peliatan,
Ubud 30571, Gianyar, Bali,
Indonesia
T +62 (0)81 2383 6227
F +62 (0)361 975759
E ritadewi@gmail.com
W www.villasebali-bali.com

Wenhai Ecolodge ▲ NCAL
Wenhai village, Baisha
Township, Yulong County,
Lijiang, Yunnan, China
T +86 13908881817(English)
+86 13908888976(Chinese)
F +86 08885162768
E wenhaieco@yahoo.com.cn
wenhaieco@sina.com
W www.northwestyunnan.com

Whare Kea Lodge & Chalet
▲▲▲▲ NAL
Rapid #494,
Mt Aspiring Road,
Lake Wanaka, New Zealand
T +64 3 443 1400
F +64 3 443 9200
E admin@wharekealodge.com
W www.wharekealodge.com

Whitepod ▲▲▲–▲▲▲▲ NCAL
Les Cerniers,
CH1871 Les Giettes,
Switzerland
T +41 24 471 38 38
E sofia@whitepod.com
W www.whitepod.com

Wilderness Lodge Arthur's
Pass ▲▲▲ NAL
Highway 73, Arthur's Pass,
PO Box 33,
Arthur's Pass 8091,
New Zealand

Highway 6, Lake Moeraki,
South Westland,
New Zealand
Postal address: Private Bag 772,
Hokitika but note this is 256 km
north of Wilderness Lodge
T +64 3 318 9246 (AP)
+64 3 7500 881 (LM)
F +64 3 318 9245 (AP)
+64 3 7500 882 (LM)
E arthurspass@wildernesslodge.
co.nz
lakemoeraki@wildernesslodge.
co.nz
W www.wildernesslodge.co.nz

Xandari Resort & Spa
▲▲–▲▲▲ NL
Apdo 1485-4050,
Alajuela, Costa Rica
T +506 443 2020
F +506 442 4847
E info@xandari.com
W www.xandari.com

Yelverton Brook Eco Spa
Retreat & Conservation
Sanctuary ▲▲ NL
118 Roy Road, Metricup,
Margaret River Region,
WA 6280, Australia
T +61 (0)8 9755 7579
F +61 (0)8 9755 7579
E retreat@yelvertonbrook.com.
au
W www.yelvertonbrook.com.au

YHA Alfriston ▲ L
Frog Firle, Alfriston,
Polegate, East Sussex
BN26 5TT, UK
T +44 (0)1323 870423
F +44 (0)1323 870615
E wendynicholls@yha.org.uk
W www.yha.org.uk

YHA Ninebanks ▲ NL
Orchard House, Mohope,
Hexham, Northumberland
NE47 8DQ, UK
T +44 (0)1434 345288
F +44 (0)1434 345414
E Ninebanks@yha.org.uk
W yha.org.uk

Yogamagic Canvas EcoTel
▲▲–▲▲▲ NCL
1586/1 Grand Chinvar,
Anjuna, Bardez 403509,
Goa, India
T +91 (0)9370 565717
+91 (0)8325 652 3796
E info@yogamagic.net
W www.yogamagic.net

Eco-products

MOBILITY

A. Winther A/S
Rygesmindevej 2,
DK-8653 Them, Denmark
T +45 (0)86 84 85 28
W www.winther-bikes.com

Airnimal Europe Ltd
37 High Street, Longstanton,
Cambridge, CB24 3BP, UK
T +44 (0)1954 782 020
W www.airnimalfoldingbikes.com

Aixam-Mega Group
France
W www.aixam.com

Baroni Electric Vehicles Ltd
UK
T +44 (0)20 8123 4698
W www.baroni-EVs.com

Biomega
Skoubogade 1, 1. MF
1158 Copenhagen K,
Denmark
T +45 (0)70 22 49 19
W www.biomega.dk

Brammo Motorsports
USA
W www.brammo.com

Brompton Bicycle Ltd
Kew Bridge DC,
Lionel Road South,
Brentford, Middlesex,
TW8 9QR, UK
T +44 (0)20 8232 8484
W www.bromptonbicycle.co.uk

Cadek, Ing. Josef
Koulova 1597,
Prague 6 – 160 00,
Czech Republic
W www.cadekdesign.com

Cycloc
Space 1, Fitzroy House,
Abbot Street,
London E8 3DP, UK
T +44 (0)20 7249 8858
W www.cycloc.com

Ellsworth Ride
W www.ellsworthride.com

Finisterre
Wheal Kitty Workshops
St Agnes,
Cornwall TR5 0RD, UK
T + 44 (0) 1872 554481
W www.finisterreuk.com

FuelVapor Technologies, Inc.
USA
W www.fuelvapour.com

Go-one LLC
44 East Central Avenue,
Maywood,
New Jersey 07607, USA
T +1 201 206 1768
W www.go-one.us

Mayhem Ltd
140 Wales Farm Road,
London W3 6UG, UK
T +44(0)20 8752 1499
W www.a-bike.co.uk

Microcab Industries Ltd
Bugatti Building,
Coventry University,
Coventry, Warwickshire,
CV1 5FB, UK
T +44 (0)24 7688 7842
W www.microcab.co.uk

MIT Media Lab & Smart Cities
USA
W cities.media.mit.edu

MW-Line SA
Ch. des Cerisiers 27,
CH1462 Yvonand,
Switzerland
W www.mwline.ch

Nice Car Company Ltd
332 Ladbroke Grove,
London W10 5AH, UK
W www.nicecarcompany.co.uk

Piaggio Ape
UK and Italy
W www.piaggio.com
W www.piaggioape.co.uk

Piaggio & C SpA & Vespa
Italy
W www.piaggio.com

Renault
France

Renault UK Ltd
The Rivers Office Park,
Denham Way,
Maple Cross,
Rickmansworth,
Hertfordshire WD3 9YF,
UK
W www.renault.fr
www.renault.com
www.renault.co.uk

Sakura Battery Company Ltd
Unit 1, 10–24 Standard Road
London NW10 6EU, UK
T +44 (0)20 8965 4567
W www.sbsb.co.uk

Seat
Spain and UK
T +44 (0)0500 222 222
W www.seat.com
www.seat.co.uk

Segway, Inc.
14 Technology Drive,
Bedford, NH 03110,
USA
T +1 877 889 9020
W www.segway.com

Sinclair Research Ltd
1A Spring Gardens,
Trafalgar Square,
London SW1A 2BB, UK
T +44 (0)20 7839 6868
W www.sinclair-research.co.uk

Solar Sailor Holdings Ltd
The Bentleigh, Suite 206,
1 Katherine Street,
Chatswood, NSW 2067,
Australia

PO Box 640, Lane Cove,
Sydney, NSW 2066,
Australia
T +61 (0)2 9418 6011
W www.solarsailor.com

Tata Motors
India
W www.tatanano.com

Tesla Motors
USA
W www.teslamotors.com

Toyota Motor Company
UK, USA, Japan
W www.toyota.com
www.toyota.co.uk
www.toyota.co.jp

Transatlantic 21
Switzerland
W www.transatlantic21.org

Trek Bicycle Corporation
Maidstone Road, Kingston,
Milton Keynes MK10 0BE,
UK
T +44 (0)1792 522 060
W www.trekbikes.co.uk

801 W Madison St,
Waterloo, WI 53594, USA
W www.trekbikes.com

University of Bath
UK
W www.bath.ac.uk

Vectrix Corporation
11 Touro Street, Suite 201,
Newport, RI 02840, USA
T +1 401 848 9993
W www.vectrix.com

Elm Farm
Suite 1,
Hensting Lane, Eastleigh,
Hampshire SO50 7HH, UK
T +44 (0)1962 777600
W www.vectrix.co.uk

Volkswagen
Germany
W www.volkswagen.de
www.volkswagen.co.uk

Waldmeister
Industriestr. 11,
D-79194 Freiburg, Germany
T +49 (0)761 585 390 87
W www.waldmeister-bikes.de

ZiPee
UK
T +44 (0)20 7691 1830
W www.zipeebikes.com

Zytek Group Ltd
Lancaster Road,
Fradley Business Park,
Fradley, Lichfield,
Staffordshire WS13 8NE,
UK
T +44 (0)1543 412 789
W www.zytekgroup.co.uk

PERSONAL

Alice Kaiserswerth
Belziger Str. 29,
D-10823 Berlin,
Germany
W www.a-kaiserswerth.com

Benjamin Shine, UK
602 Naylor Building,
Alder Street, Aldgate East,
London E1 1HD, UK
T +44 (0)870 112 0897
W www.skoody.co.uk

**Cascade Designs and
Mountain Safety Research**
4000 1st Ave S,
Seattle, WA 98134, USA
T +1 206 505 9500
+1 800 531 9531
W www.cascadedesigns.com
www.msrgear.com

Heyjute
Megalith Management Ltd,
24 Manor Ridge Trail,
Mt Albert, Ontario L0G 1M0,
Canada
T +1 905 473 4090
W www.heyjute.com

Howies
Bath House Road,
Cardigan,
Cardiganshire SA43 1JY, UK
T +44 (0)1239 61 41 22
W www.howies.co.uk

Huopaliike Lahtinen
Partalantie 267,
42100 Jämsä, Finland
T +358 14 768 017
W www.huopaliikelahtinen.fi

Icebreaker New Zealand Ltd
Level 2,
Hope Gibbons Building,
7–11 Dixon Street,
Wellington 6011, PO Box 959,
New Zealand
T +64 4 385 9113
W www.icebreaker.com

Kickers
Airborne Footwear Ltd,
The Pentland Centre,
Lakeside, Squires Lane,
London N3 2QL, UK
T +44 (0)845 603 7151
W www.kickers.co.uk

Matteria Ltd
Zamora 46-48 atico 3,
08005 Barcelona, Spain
W www.matteriashop.com

Patagonia
Patagonia Mail Order,
8550 White Fir Street,
PO Box 32050, Reno,
NV 89523-2050, USA
T +1 800 0000 0041
W www.patagonia.com

Softwalker
Factory Shop, Duddon Road,
Askam in Furness,
Cumbria LA16 7AN, UK
T +44 (0)800 093 2460
W www.softwalker.co.uk

Sympatex Technology GmbH
Feringastrasse 7A,
D-85774 Unterföhring,
Germany
T +49 89 940058 0
F +49 89 940058 297
W www.sympatex.com

Teko
1435 Yarmouth Avenue,
Suite 102, Boulder,
CO 80304, USA
T +1 303 449 7681
T +1 800 450 5784
W www.tekosocks.com

**Terra Plana & RADDISSHMe
Design House**
124 Bermondsey Street,
London Bridge,
London SE1 3TX, UK
T +44 (0)20 7407 3758
W www.terraplana.com
www.wornagain.co.uk
www.raddisshme.com

Timberland
USA, UK and worldwide
T +1 888 802 9947 USA
T +44 (0)800 023 2478 UK
W www.timberland.com

Twice Shy
2018 Manitoba Street,
Vancouver BC
V5Y 3V3, Canada
T +604 707 1073
W www.twice-shy.com

Veja
France
W www.veja.fr

White Sierra
USA
T +1 800 980 8688
W www.whitesierra.com

SPECIALIST

Better Energy Systems
Better Energy Systems LLC,
1508–1510 6th Street,
Berkeley, CA 94710, USA
T +1 510 868 8714
W www.solio.com

Better Energy Systems Ltd
85–87 Bayham Street,
London NW1 0AG, UK
T +44 (0)20 7424 7999
W www.betterenergy.co.uk

Big Agnes
PO Box 773072,
Steamboat Springs,
CO 80477, USA
T +1 877 554 8975
T +1 970 871 1480
W www.bigagnes.com

Burton McCall
163 Parker Drive,
Leicester,
Leicestershire LE4 0JP, UK
T +44 (0)116 235 8031
W www.burton-mccall.co.uk

Fair Trade Sports
USA
T +1 800 716 4674
W www.fairtradesports.com

Freeplay Energy
Unit 12, M5 Business Park,
Black River Parkway,
Capetown, South Africa
T +27 (0)21 514 3864
W www.freeplayenergy.com

Greenlight Surf Company
Philadelphia, PA, USA
T +1 215 805 1506
W www.greenlightsurfsupply.com

Hatpac
Unit 8d,
Gosport Business Centre,
Aerodrome Road, Gosport,
Hampshire PO13 0FQ, UK
T +44 (0)1329 848 105
W www.stashkit.com

Hobie Cat
4925 Oceanside Blvd,
Oceanside, CA 92056, USA
W www.hobiecat.com

J.C. Karish Industrial Design Studio
France
W www.karishdesign.com

Katadyn Products, Inc.
Birkenweg 4,
CH8304 Wallisellen,
Switzerland
T +41 (0)44 839 21 16
W www.katadyn.ch

Kelly Kettle Company
Newtown Cloghans,
Knockmore PO, Belina,
Co. Mayo, Ireland
T +353 96 76643
W www.kellykettle.com

Künzi Creative Concepts
Reinerstr. 6,
CH4515 Overdorf,
Switzerland
T +41 (0)32 621 48 65
W www.kuenzi.com

Mountainsmith
8301 West Colfax Ave,
Building P, Golden,
CO 80401, USA
T +1 800 551 5889
W www.mountainsmith.com

Opinel, France
508 Boulevard Henry,
Bordeaux, 73000 Chambéry,
Savoie, France
T +33 (0)4 79 69 46 18
W www.opinel.com

Osprey & Osprey Europe
115 Progress Circle,
Cortez, CO 81321, USA
T +1 970 564 5900
W www.ospreypacks.com
Unit 3
Brackley Close,
Bournemouth International
Airport, Dorset
BH23 6SE, UK
T +44 (0)1202 572 775

Pacific Outdoor Equipment
521 East Peach, Unit 4,
Bozeman, MT 59715, USA
T +1 406 586 5258
W www.pacoutdoor.com

Pandora Pandemonia & J. C. Karish Industrial Design Studio
Pandora Pandemonia,
Via Canonica 40,
Milan 20154, Italy
T +39 (0)2 316157
W www.pandoradesign.it

Quechua/Decathlon
France
W www.quechua.com

Reelight
Hasselager Centervej 11,1,
8260 Viby J, Denmark
T +45 8674 2490
W www.reelight.com

Roof via Designer Helmets, Motoretta
Motoretta Limited,
2 Halifax Road,
Hipperholme,
Halifax,
West Yorkshire HX3 8ER,
UK
T +44 (0)870 125 3932
W www.designerhelmets.com

Salewa Sportgeräte GmbH
Saturnstr. 63,
D-85606 Aschheim,
Germany
T +49 89 909930
W www.salewa.com

SIGG Switzerland AG
Walzmühlestrasse 62,
CH8501 Frauenfeld,
Switzerland
T +41 (0)52 728 63 30
W www.sigg.ch

Carousel Outdoor Ltd
Rear of 28,
Oakleigh Road South,
London N11 1NH, UK
W www.sigg-aluminium.co.uk

Silva
Sweden
UK supplier:
Unit 7, Elphinstone Square,
Deens Industrial Estate,
Livingstone,
West Lothian EH54 8RG, UK
T +44 (0)1506 419 555
W www.silva.se

Snow Peak
Overseas Sales Division,
Snow Peak, Inc.,
958 Sanganji,
Sanjo-City, Niigata, Japan
T +81 (0)25 638 1110
W www.snowpeak.co.jp

Ting, Inghua
16 Chelsea
Farmers Market,
Sydney Street,
London SW3 6NP, UK
T +44 (0)20 7751 4424
W www.tinglondon.com

TTI & Wind-up Products
Unit 58,
Joseph Wilson Industrial
Estate, Whitstable,
Kent CT5 3PS, UK
T +44 (0)845 226 41 8
W www.tti.uk.com
W www.windup-products.com

2Pure
Unit 8,
Pentland Industrial Estate,
Loanhead, Edinburgh,
EH20 9QH, UK
W www.2pure.co.uk

Venture Snowboards
951 Green Street,
PO Box 547, Silverton,
CO 81433, USA
T +1 970 387 5078
W www.venturesnowboards.com

Voltaic Systems
252 W. 14th Street #3,
New York, NY 10011, USA
T +1 646 257 4071
W www.voltaicsystems.com

Key: Top – t; middle – m; bottom – b; right – r; left – l

Eco-travel
p2 Courtesy of Dick Sweeny, Paperbark Camp.

PART I The idea of travel
Courtesy of the eco-destinations and the photographers: p6 Conservation Corporation Africa, CCAfrica.com, Bateleur Camp; p10 Discover Ltd and Kasbah du Toubkal, Trekking Lodge; pp. 12, 13 The Atlas of the Real World, pub: Thames & Hudson, 2008; p18 tl John Grimshaw, Sustrans; br Alastair Fuad-Luke; p19 © Scania CV AB (publ); SkySails GmbH & Co. KG.

PART II Eco-destinations
Courtesy of the eco-destinations and the photographers: p24 Akira Taeichi, Kunfunadhoo Island, Soneva Fushi & Six Senses Spa; p26 lt Senderos; lb Camp Denali & North Face Lodge; mt Scandic Hotels AB; mb Ponta dos Ganchos Resort; rt, rb Stayokay; p27 Senderos; p28 from left to right, Stayokay, Apex Hotels, Apex Hotels, t Stayokay; p29 from left to right, Apex Hotels, t Palace Farm Hostel, b Stayokay, Apex Hotels, Apex Hotels; p30–31 Apex Hotels; p32 Hotel Bougainvillea; p33 Gaia Napa Valley Hotel & Spa; p34 Hotel Adalbert; p35 Lane Cove River Tourist Park; p36–37 The Orchard Garden Hotel; p38 Scandic Hotels; p39 Radisson SAS; p40–41 Sofitel Amsterdam; p42 Hotel Jolie; p43 Kodulapark Hotell; p44–45 Hotel Alexandra; p46 Hotel del Rey;

p47 Stayokay; p48 tl, b Alastair Fuad-Luke; tr Casa Camper; p49 Casa Camper; p50 from left to right, Senderos, Senderos, Visions of Africa, t Hapuku Lodge, b Senderos; p51 from left to right, Hotel Bourazani, t Senderos, b Hoopoe Yurt Hotel, Senderos, Kalmatia Sangam Himalaya Resort; p52–53 Tongabezi Lodge; p54 Amazon Yarapa River Lodge; p55 Don Enrique Lodge; p56 Dantica Lodge & Gallery; p57 Danta Corcovado Lodge; p58 Paperbark Camp, tbr Dick Sweeney, bl Mike Gebicki; p59 Paperbark Camp, Dick Sweeney; p60–61 Hapuku Lodge & Tree Houses; p62 Rosegums Wilderness Retreat; p63 Inn at Coyote Mountain; p64 Tree Tops Jungle Lodge; p65 Borneo Adventure; p66 Three Rivers Eco-Lodge; p67 Quilálea Private Island/Classic Representation; p68 Cristalino Jungle Lodge, l Gill Carter, m, r Katia Kuwabara; p69 Cristalino Jungle Lodge, Edson Endrigo; p70 La Laguna del Lagarto Lodge; p71 Saunders Gorge Sanctuary; p72–73 Finca Rosa Blanca Country Inn; p74 Le Parc aux Orchidées; p75 The Lodge at Big Falls; p76 Sarapiquí S Rainforest Lodge; p77 Xandari Resort & Spa; p78–79 Visions of Africa, Mowani Mountain Camp; p80–81 Visions of Africa, Onguma Safari Camps; p82 Jeff Greenberg and ARAMARK Parks and Resorts; p83 Ecolodge San Luis & Research Station (University of Georgia, UGA, Costa Rica Campus); p84 EcoHotel L'Aubier; p85 Hotel Fazenda Baia das Pedras; p86–87 Jungle Bay Resort &

Spa; p88 Tui Nature Reserve Wilderness Park; p89 Wilderness Lodges NZ; p90 Scottish Youth Hostels Association; p91 Moinhos da Tia Antoninha; p92 Lochmara Lodge; p93 t Wilderness Safaris, b Michael Poliza; p94 Chumbe Island Coral Park, t, bl © Craig Zendel, br, t ©Guido Cozzi, br, b ©Joonas Sandholm; p96 Adelaide Hills Wilderness Lodge; p97 Eco Hotel Uxlabil Atitlán; p98 Ard Nahoo Health Farm; p99 Scottish Youth Hostels Association; p100–101 Refúgio Ecológico Caiman; p102 Hog Hollow Farm; p103 Catlins, Eco-cottages at Mohua Park; p104 Sadie Cove Wilderness Lodge; p105 Camp Denali & North Face Lodge; p106–107 Posada Amazonas; p108 Natural Lodge Caño Negro; p109 Yelverton Brook Eco Spa Retreat & Conservation Sanctuary; p110 Papillote Wilderness Retreat; p111 Pousada Vale das Araras; p112 Iona Hostel; p113 Country Anna Hotel; p114 Hoopoe Yurt Hotel; p115 Hotel Bourazani; p116–117 Finca Esperanza Verde; p118 Esquinas Rainforest Lodge; p119 La Cusinga Eco-Lodge; p120 Rawnsley Park; p121 Hotel Hellnar; p122–123 from left to right, Senderos, Senderos, t Visions of Africa, Mowani Mountain Camp, b Refúgio Ecológico Caiman, Nipika Mountain Resort, Senderos, t Senderos, b Posada Amazonas, Monica Oliveira, Korubo Safari Camp Jalapão, Senderos; p124–125 Ecocamp Patagonia; p126 ©Tiger Mountain (P) Ltd 2007; p127 Whitepod; p128–129 Aurum Lodge; p130–131 Pousada dos Monteiros; p132 l

Monica Oliveira, Korubo Safari Camp Jalapão, r Korubo Safari Camp Jalapão; p133 Juma Lodge; p134–135 Conservation Corporation Africa, CCAfrica.com; p136 l Scottish Youth Hostels Association, r ©Nick Priest; p137 Capricorn Caves; p138–139 Kalmatia Sangam Himalaya Resort; p140–141 Estancia los Potreros; p142–143 Nipika Mountain Resort; p144–145 from left to right, Ponda dos Ganchos, Desert Lodge, Hotel Posada del Valle, t James Walsche, Jean-Michel Cousteau Fiji Island Resort, b Senderos, Hotel Posada del Valle, The Lodge at Chaa Creek; t, b Desert Lodge, Ponta dos Ganchos; p146 Bird Island, photographs copyright of: Joop Kroh, Grant Neal, Georges, Laurence & Phil Norah, Chris Feare; p147 Hotel Posada del Valle; p148 Jean-Michel Cousteau Fiji Resort, l Galen Rowell, t James Walsche, b Rick Wallis; p149 Jean-Michel Cousteau Fiji Resort, t Rick Wallis, bl Greg Taylor, br James Walsche; p150 Blancaneaux Resorts; p151 Levendi's Cottages & Estate; p152 Jake's; p153 Ponta dos Ganchos; p154 Locanda della Valle Nuova; p155 L'Ayalga Posada Ecológica; p156 Can Marti; p157 l Quinta do Barrieiro, tr, br João Frazão, Quinta do Barrieiro; p158 Constance Le Prince Maurice Hotel; p159 Aruba Bucuti Beach Resort & Tara Beach Suite; p160 Hotel Villas Les Goëlands; p161 Hotel Pension Hubertus; p162–163 The Lighthouse Hotel & Spa; p164 Udayana Eco-lodge; p165 Palace Farm Hostel; p166 Cardamom House;